Protestant Christianity

INTERPRETED THROUGH ITS DEVELOPMENT

John Dillenberger

Claude Welch

CHARLES SCRIBNER'S SONS, NEW YORK

Library of Congress Catalogue Card Number 54-10367
ISBN 0-684-14719-X

TO ELOISE AND HILDA

Contents

Preface

This book is an essay in the interpretation of Protestant Christianity. It has grown out of the conviction that the nature and meaning of Protestantism can be seen only in the light of its historical development. We have, therefore, deliberately abandoned many of the usual patterns for interpreting Protestant life and thought. Survey descriptions of the various Protestant denominations almost invariably lack unity and historical depth and fail to disclose the spiritual dynamics which both cut across and give rise to denominational patterns. Interpretations which focus exclusively on the Reformation cannot give due weight either to the new impulses which have appeared in Protestant history or to the varying development of the Reformation principles. Efforts to develop independent statements of Protestant "principles" or "beliefs" tend to be so general and filled with all manner of qualifications as to be often meaningless, or they are sufficiently partisan as to exclude important motifs.

In view of these difficulties and of our conviction that Protestantism must be seen as an historical community of faith, by far the larger part of this book is devoted to historical development. The concluding chapter, "What is Protestantism?", is intended as a summary in retrospect. It is not a separate statement of principles, but an attempt to bring into focus the understanding of Protestantism which arises from the entirety of the historical analysis.

We do not suppose, of course, that history simply speaks for itself apart from the human beings who interpret it. We are quite aware that this book is throughout an interpretative study. It is intended as such. At the same time, we have sought to shape and test our interpretation by the historical materials which need to be interpreted. We hope that we have entered sufficiently into the perspectives of the men and movements studied as to communicate something of their spirit and self-understanding. We have also offered certain critical reactions which spring from our own perspectives as twentieth-century Protestant Christians. These are expressed in the conviction that Protestantism requires constant self-criticism, and that our views are in turn subject to criticism.

The content of the discussion is weighted on the side of Protestant thought. This is deliberate, for one of our prime concerns is to delineate the self-understanding of Protestant Christians. But we have tried always to set the development of theology in the context of the whole life of the religious community. Theology is only one way in which the vitality of faith is expressed, and we have sought to relate thought directly to the crucial events in church history. Moreover, we have tried to see the development of thought and institutions alike in their social and cultural settings. We reject the thesis that the life of the religious community is simply determined by social and cultural factors. But the notion that Protestantism can be understood apart from these is rejected with equal vigor. Of course, our concern is primarily with the Protestant story. We have, therefore, not attempted independent treatments of other modern currents of life and thought, even when these may have been more dominant in the Western world as a whole. Such movements are dealt with only as they have influenced the internal development of Protestantism.

In the organization of this book, certain further principles have guided us. First, we have emphasized those movements and men which seem to be of most significance for the understanding of the development as a whole, either in the expression of dominant themes and patterns or in the appearance of new life and thought. Needless to say, no attempt has been made to apportion space in relation to the number of adherents of a particular denomination. But we hope that in each case we have been true to the spiritual dynamic and the religious convictions of the various groups.

Second, we have followed the early movements in Protestantism only to the point where they achieved more or less classic expression, or where they became the occasion for reaction to themselves. There is, for example, no attempt to bring orthodox

Lutheranism or Calvinism, or Anglican or Methodist patterns, up to the present, except through an occasional reference. Third, and this principle is related to the second, denominational lines and groupings have been followed only as, especially in their emergence, they developed distinctive religious ideas and new forms of church life. Where denominational distinctions became secondary to movements which cut through them—and this has been generally true since the beginning of the nineteenth century—we have largely omitted them from consideration.

This project was undertaken at the request of the Committee on Projects and Research of the National Council on Religion in Higher Education. It was felt that there is a very serious need for a single book on Protestantism which could be used in college and university courses in religion, and which would in general make available to intelligent laymen a deepened understanding of Protestant Christianity. It is this need that we have tried to meet.

In a venture as extensive as this, we have naturally drawn from a great many sources. Primarily, we have depended upon the major original writings which are a part of Protestant history. We have been guided also by numerous recent works on various aspects of Protestantism. The number and excellence of these works suggest a renaissance of Protestant studies. In the "Suggestions for Further Reading" we have listed both some of the most important original documents and some of the major recent interpretations in English.

This book also requires a rather special note of appreciation to those who have helped by their criticism of the early drafts of the manuscript. Professors William Christian and Seymour Smith of Yale University, E. Harris Harbison and Paul Ramsey of Princeton University, and Albert C. Outler of Perkins School of Theology have served as a subcommittee of the National Council on Religion in Higher Education to assist in our work. They have helped in the planning of the project and have rigorously scrutinized the initial drafts. Their comments have been immensely valuable. We also owe much to our fellow members of the Society for Theological Discussion, who, in two series of week-end meetings, used our drafts of the manuscript as the basis for their discussions. To Professor H. Richard Niebuhr of Yale University, we are grateful for suggestions which resulted in a more radical recasting of parts of the manuscript than he knows.

We are grateful for the assistance of all of these persons. By their suggestions for refocusing, clarification and outright correction in fact and interpretation, they have made this a far better book than it would otherwise have been. We are aware of many limitations, for Protestantism is a vast and intricate subject. But in conception and execution, this has been a common venture of the authors. While we divided the work of writing the initial drafts, the final text has been formulated by both of us, and for the whole we assume joint responsibility.

JOHN DILLENBERGER
CLAUDE WELCH

May 1954

I

A New Era Begins

1. PRELIMINARY NOTES ON THE NATURE OF PROTESTANTISM

The fact of diversity in belief and practice is a striking part of the Protestant heritage. Men think different thoughts even when they seek to witness to the same gospel. This may be due to human creativity and human finitude; even more it may be due to prideful men who think too highly of their own outlook upon life. Protestantism accepts this ambiguity as a part of its heritage. It accepts its diversity as a sign of health and of sickness. Even in the ecumenical movement, where men are keenly conscious of the broken and divided nature of the churches as the body of Christ, the fact of necessary difference is accepted. The hoped-for re-union of many of the churches of Christ will not and ought not bring men to one opinion, but it may provide a framework within which different nuances of life and thought may in effect be considered to strengthen rather than weaken the Christian cause. It may provide a place where differences are considered a sign of health and vitality as well as of pride and sin. Revitalization in the churches may conceivably be possible without the breaks in community which were once inevitable.

Moreover, diversity is peculiarly inevitable where a movement consciously assumes the burden of relating its message directly to the concerns and problems of men in particular historical periods. There may be a certain constancy in the problems which

I

men face, but the particular questions which they ask are forged by the cultural outlook, expressed and unexpressed, of the period. Protestantism is, on principle, concerned to relate the gospel to such particular questions. The strength of such an approach lies in the bold attempt to relate the biblical message directly to the needs of men. At its best, this means that certain aspects of the gospel are featured because of the particular needs of the time. Luther emancipated men from the fear of God by stressing God's merciful acceptance of man apart from every concern of self; Wesley showed men the warmth of the new life in Christ in a time when men verbally believed in the gospel but did not feel its power. Luther and Wesley do not essentially contradict each other, but the major emphases are different. To this day, these men disclose something about the respective character of Lutheranism and Methodism (though it must be recognized that today the differences between major Protestant denominations are far less clear-cut than at the time of their appearance).

The dangers in a movement which relates itself directly to the concerns of every period is that its message may be distorted and weakened because its problems and answers are forged too exclusively out of the historical context. It may lose its vitality in the very attempt to gain it. The great concern in nineteenth-century Liberal theology for human dignity was a noble attempt to save man in a period when many thought of him as no more than animal, but the partial deification of man by some theologians was a serious departure from the gospel which informs Christendom (see Chs. IX, X). Here liberalism's genius turned out to be its liability. But in spite of such problems, Protestants have generally felt that such difficulties were to be preferred to any imposition of uniformity upon culture.

In Protestantism we have to do not so much with a Church as with a movement made up of churches. Protestantism is a story to be told. One cannot define it by a single religious concept or by a combination of religious concepts. This, together with its diversity, accounts for the recurring false impression that Protestantism is synonymous with the right to think what one wishes in religious matters. Protestants do generally maintain that each individual must think his own thoughts and himself stand directly under God, but they have always maintained also that one's life and thinking take their cue from the message of the biblical tradition, however differently that message is understood. In fact, the striking thing about Protestantism is not its diversity, but its unity. Protestants claim that the vitality of their faith is nowhere more evident than in the stress upon each man's own experience of the biblical faith which produces so many authentically similar expressions of faith. From this perspective, the differences which do exist are not as important as is usually assumed.[1]

Nevertheless, Protestantism is the story of individuals and groups who have taken their understanding of the gospel so seriously that they have been willing to create new forms of the church. In so doing they have not been unaware of tradition or of church history, but have insisted that they were reforming or changing the form of the church in the light of the demands of the gospel. Historically, of course, Protestantism begins with the Reformation in the sixteenth century. Although the reformers reluctantly broke with the medieval church, they did not think that they were starting a new church. On the contrary, they maintained that they were calling the church back to its genuine basis. Spurred to action originally because of the abuses in the medieval period, they soon became conscious that their understanding of the gospel was fundamentally different from that of the existing church. Since they were frustrated in every attempt to renew the church from within, their only recourse was to bring Christians together in new forms of church life.

The Protestant story must begin with an understanding of this attempt to recover the life and vitality of the church in the light of the gospel. Hence, it is necessary to give a picture of many currents within the medieval period and of the life of the medieval church as the background from which the work of the reformers is to be understood. We must begin by understanding Martin Luther in the context of his time.

[1] Although Protestantism has proliferated into more than two hundred fifty separate bodies in America, approximately 85 percent of the individuals who comprise these groups belong to twelve major denominations.

2. FACTORS IN THE DISSOLUTION OF
THE MEDIEVAL SYNTHESIS

The period of the Middle Ages was far from uniform in thought or in life. But in contrast to other periods of history it is unsurpassed in the uniformity of its religious ethos. It was marked by a "religious culture" in which the life of the church was not separate from other activities, but rather pervaded all of them. Politics, economics, art and philosophy were the direct concerns of the church. The papacy was a political as well as a spiritual power. Much of the economic life was organized around and controlled by the parish churches. Art was religious by definition. Painting and architecture alike reflect the concern with the transcendent. There is no clearer evidence of this than the vertical thrust of the cathedrals. Even the rediscovery and acceptance of Aristotle did not disturb the total pattern, for the more earthbound character of Aristotle's philosophy only served, when slightly reinterpreted, to provide a picture of nature which longed for its completion by a more significant aspect of reality, the grace of God itself. It is no wonder that the culture was characterized as the *Corpus Christianum,* the body of Christendom.

In many areas of life and experience the Middle Ages were indeed creative. They stood for a way of life which, after the collapse of the Roman Empire, had slowly conquered an alien and pagan world and fashioned it after its own designs. It had literally created a Christian culture in which many remnants of Graeco-Roman culture were baptized and reworked into a grand Christian scheme. This was indeed a tremendous and important achievement and upon its stability men felt able to depend.

But in this very culture forces were forming and discoveries were made which threatened its foundation and supplied the Reformation with the possibility of success which might otherwise have been denied to it. The Reformation cannot be explained as simply an aspect of the dissolution of the Middle Ages; but it certainly cannot be understood apart from this. For example, one can ponder what might have happened had the printing press not appeared on the human stage in time to carry Luther's prophetic protest and provide wings for his positive gospel message.

Within the citadel of the church, three movements contributed to the church's losing its hold on the life of the time.

1) The first was mysticism. Mysticism had a long and glorious history ranging from the dubious Christian orientation of Dionysius the Areopagite (a fifth-century writer later confused with one of St. Paul's converts at Athens) through the classical figures of the medieval mystical tradition—Bernard, Eckhart, Tauler, Ruysbroek. *comparable to effect of charismatic*

Common to the Christian mystics was the conviction that God *move-* could be directly experienced, though in essence he remained *ment* incomprehensible. Most of the mystic's time and energy were *Replaces* spent in preparation and discipline, with the aim that God might *church* enter his soul and lift him to ecstatic heights. Such experiences *life* made life livable since they introduced one into the very presence of God himself. Sometimes the experience was that of the presence of Christ, at other times of God himself apart from Christ. On the one hand, St. Bernard spoke with great warmth of the presence of the exalted Christ, nearer to himself than anything else, because Christ permeated and filled his being. On the other hand, Tauler's sermons describe God's direct presence almost without reference to the mediation of Christ.

Although the church insisted that God was known and mediated through the sacramental system, mysticism was not initially considered a serious threat. Mystics were incorporated into the fold and they comprised one component, though a subordinate one, of the medieval synthesis. Even Dionysius the Areopagite, influenced more by Greek than by Christian ideas, had been incorporated into the Christian framework because of his supposed connection with St. Paul. He was extensively quoted by Aquinas, the foremost theologian of the classical Middle Ages. In any case, mystics were not sufficiently numerous to become a major problem. Only when the individual mystics were supplemented by communities of a mystical orientation, did the difficulty appear. Eckhart and Tauler in Strasbourg, Ruysbroek and à Kempis in the Netherlands, and Rolle and Julian of Norwich in England were powerful figures. But without mass support the effectiveness even of powerful individuals is limited. This does not mean that the movements were direct products of the individual mystics. In fact, this was usually not the case. But groups of a mystical bent who emphasized the directness of man's access to God did arise, such as the Brethren of the Common Life in Holland and the Friends of God in the Rhine Valley. To many of them the *Theologia Germanica,* an anonymous mystical work which Luther initially praised, was a source of great inspiration.

Neither the individual mystic nor the mystical group wanted to undermine the witness of the church. Communities developed in part as a reaction to formalization of life in the church and directed their energies to revitalizing church life. But in point of fact, they helped to undermine the church whose life they intended to restore. Without wanting to do so, the new associations and communities did compete with the church. This was inevitable, for the emphasis upon the direct personal experience of God contradicted the notion that God was known and mediated exclusively or primarily through the church as the sacramental agent.

Individuals and groups which stressed the direct experience of God helped prepare the soil upon which the Reformation grew. Although Protestantism is not to be equated with the mystical groups or merely with an emphasis upon direct accessibility to God, recruits to Protestantism did come from people of mystical and similar persuasions. Luther was quick to see that the gospel which he proclaimed spoke to these people, in contrast to those who accepted the increasing authority of the church in life and in thought.

2) The second force leading to dissolution within the society of the church was nominalism. According to the classical medieval view, reality was characterized by structure and order. Patterns of rational thought were understood to be inherent in reality itself. Hence, language as a medium of discourse expressed and reflected reality. Concepts expressed universal realities. Nominalists, on the other hand, maintained that names, concepts, and generalizations were but tags which men used to talk about individual things. Moreover, only individual things were real.

One consequence of the nominalist outlook was that even God could not be described in terms of rational structure. In the traditional view, God's will was always understood as an expression *stress on individualism — thing is more important than its name.*

of his being. God willed in conformity with his nature and the created order itself reflected the structure of this willing. But in the nominalist view, God was understood as sheer will, wholly free from humanly conceivable structure or consistency. As a result, his declared intent to save sinners could not be taken as seriously as men would like, since God might act in ways different from his disclosed purpose. This called revelation into question as a trustworthy medium of the disclosure of God.

The new philosophy had implications, too, for the understanding of man, church and society. Man now felt unique. The concept "man" no longer referred to an experience of belonging to something universal and quite real, humanity itself. "Man" was a generalized name applied to discreet individual men considered in the aggregate. In his self-understanding, man no longer felt that more than anything else he belonged to a whole. His self-consciousness was as significant, if not more so, as his feeling for community. *one result — quest for individual salvation*

The understanding of the church and society was also challenged by this new outlook. On the basis of nominalism, one could not speak of the church and of society as corporate, organic bodies, or of the body of Christendom, or of the church as the body of Christ. One no longer belonged to a social body which sustained and carried; the body now referred to an aggregate of individuals. The concept of contract between individuals rather than that of organism was the new key to church and society. *God cares for individuals + not just the church*

In this new situation, the church had to assume greater authority in order to take over domains formerly guaranteed through philosophy and a sense of a natural community. In the classical medieval period, reason and revelation, philosophy and theology, fitted together hand-in-glove. Reason could show God's existence and say something about God as a consequence of his existence. Reason was completed by revelation which added that which was essential for a saving knowledge of God. In the new situation, reason was incapable of giving knowledge of God. Even knowledge of God's existence depended completely on revelation. And revelation in itself was not altogether dependable. Only the church as the authority which acted in God's name could guarantee the veracity of revelation.

It was true that the medieval idea of community hardly gave man his due as a unique individual. But in nominalism the sense of belonging together and participating in life on the basis of certain natural bonds had disappeared. Through its stress upon the individual, the discrete, the separate, it helped break the hold of the medieval church. But for a moment it strengthened the church because of the consequent necessity of affirming ecclesiastical authority in order to maintain cohesion in society. Community was no longer felt to be natural; it could only be sustained by authority. But community sustained by authority is explosive and cannot last.

3) The third movement which was to effect a change was the Renaissance, particularly in its humanistic form. The Renaissance, too, was related to the church and not infrequently was sponsored by it. For most of the Middle Ages minimal classical learning had been preserved in the church, primarily in monasteries and in the rising universities. However, the Renaissance version of classical learning marked a new concern with the outlook upon life expressed in Greek and Roman literary and artistic mediums, appearing in the fifteenth century in the city states of Italy. From there it permeated Europe and in the realm of art found its greatest protagonists among the "Renaissance popes." Pope Sixtus IV was interested in the arts and his name is perpetuated in the Sistine Chapel. It was Pope Julius II who discovered the artists Raphael and Michelangelo.

The interest in classical learning demanded new and accurate texts of ancient writings. When the critical acumen acquired in this enterprise was turned toward a number of writings which affected the church, the result was indeed embarrassing. Lorenzo Valla, one of the great humanist scholars, turned his critical eye upon the "Donation of Constantine," reputedly a document in which the Emperor Constantine bequeathed his earthly power to the papacy. By analyzing style and content, he showed that this could not possibly be a fourth-century document and that therefore papal claims to temporal or political authority could not rest upon its contents. He described as legend the claim that the Apostles' Creed comprised twelve statements, one made by each apostle. He further applied his energies to the text of scripture, raising questions at points of the accuracy of the Vulgate as a translation of the Hebrew text of the Old Testament and of the Greek text of the New Testament. But it was Erasmus, the Christian humanist scholar, who pointed out not only more inaccuracies, but also some of the differences a more accurate text made in religious belief.

The impact of Renaissance humanism was greater than the attacks which some of its scholars made upon specific documents and claims of the church. It represented an outlook upon life which was essentially different from that represented by the medieval church. It created a view favorable to the concerns of this life in and for themselves. Renaissance humanists believed in God, and many, like Erasmus, remained faithful members of the church even in the period of the Reformation. But the accent had shifted. The stress of humanists was upon the greatness and nobility of man. They found this nobility particularly in works of Cicero and Plato, rather than in that of scholastic theology. Humanists, in fact, were for reform. They proposed that classical learning be substituted for scholastic theology in the educational curriculum and they attacked superstitions within the church.

Mysticism, nominalism, and humanism thus represent religious and intellectual movements mostly unaware of their threat to the medieval unity and therefore also to the medieval church. Concurrent with the impact of these movements, there were developments in the broad social scene which created a new milieu and tended to undermine the culture which the church had created. In the medieval development the church had become the creator and custodian of social life. In the process, the church acquired half of the land in France and Germany and organized its use along the accepted hierarchical pattern of feudalism. Hence, it is easy to see that social as well as religious life belonged to the orbit of the church.

The breakdown of feudalism and the rise of a middle class preoccupied with trade and commerce created a new segment of society independent of direct influence by the church. Even the crusades, organized with the prompting and blessing of the church to wrest the Holy Land from the Turks, accentuated an economic development which depended upon money and trade rather than directly upon land. Moreover, the contacts made by the crusades facilitated the new interest in trade and commerce.

This development led to a different kind of culture. Small towns and cities now became urban centers in which men were free from direct dependence upon the surrounding land for their livelihood. Although the new members of this class usually felt themselves to be good churchmen, they did feel free from the church in matters which pertained to their vocational interests. They represented a new, independent force, forcefully expressed in the new slogan "City air is free air."

The new middle class was self-conscious of its position and encouraged new loyalties beyond those of church and empire. It fed and frequently supported ethnic groups. It was in part responsible for the waves of national feelings which in many instances eventuated in modern national states. The empire, whether controlled by church or emperor, was transformed and eventually gave way to new social and ethnic forces. This was true in the Germanic lands also, though statehood in the fullest sense came several centuries later.

By the time of the Reformation, the social scene had been so transformed that the effects were evident in a number of ways. There were already unfortunate victims who felt deprived of their dignity and rights under the emerging commercial situation. The new alignment of social forces had also made the peasants conscious of their status, and their discontent finally broke forth in Luther's own day in the Peasants' Revolt.

In many areas new things were happening. The printing press was invented in the latter half of the fifteenth century and in the last decade of the century Columbus discovered a new world. At the very time when Magellan was circumnavigating the globe (1519–1522), Luther wrote three famous treatises and engaged in debates which launched the Reformation. In Luther's own life time the astronomer Copernicus challenged the traditional view of the world by suggesting that the sun, not the earth, was the center around which the planets moved. Although the world was still one in which the church was dominant, many new forces, in addition to the efforts of the reformers, were acting to undermine the church's hold upon the masses of men.

3. THE SITUATION IN THE CHURCH

Since the church was responsible for the political organization as well as the religious life during the early Middle Ages, it was only natural that it was in fact, if not yet in name, a temporal as well as a spiritual power. The church had won its position as a creative, functioning body in a disorganized world and, as new forms arose, its leaders naturally felt that only the continued exercise of the church's power would guarantee a Christian culture. At first this aim seemed guaranteed by the notion that a king or monarch was an arm of God, divinely appointed to serve him. Thus church and state went hand in hand. Although this position was not formally altered, ensuing periods of conflict between church and monarchs brought an elaboration of thought which effectively changed the orientation to the problem of the relation of church and state. The state was an instrument serving only man's temporal life, while the church served to direct his earthly pilgrimage and to deliver him safely to another life. The church naturally felt that the more important function belonged to itself. It felt the responsibility of forming and directing the social life of man, though not of governing it. Even in this realm kings were to act in the church's behalf. On the question of entrance to God's kingdom, kings were impotent, while the ordinary priest, acting on the authority committed to him, was all powerful. Kings might attempt to depose popes, but the real power was the papacy since it dealt with the destiny of every believer. In the thirteenth century, Innocent III was more powerful than any monarch.

The church's claim to control every aspect of life made it almost inevitable that the church would over-extend itself, become secularized in the process, and fall victim of the problems of the world around it. Its very greatness turned into an Achilles' heel. In spite of notable exceptions, this was the case among popes and priests alike. The sojourn of the papacy in Avignon, France, for almost seventy years of the fourteenth century, resulted primarily from the loss of estates in Italy and the consequent dictation by French monarchs that the papacy reside in France in return for financial support. But even in this forced residence, the popes found and perfected ways of raising revenue for main-

taining their extensive empire and for expanding their interests
in many directions, including that of Renaissance art. This,
coupled with the picture of rival claimants to the papacy at the
end of the Avignon period, had the general effect of undermining
the religious, though not the temporal authority of the papacy.
In fact, the effectiveness of the church's formal hold upon its
constituents was temporarily increased by the techniques which
came into prominence to meet the financial needs. On the appointment of a bishop, the first year's income went to the papacy.
To increase the income, bishops were frequently moved and
sometimes vacancies were not immediately filled so that the
papacy could claim the funds in the meantime. Such procedures
made it possible for the papacy to maintain its control and to
secure the necessary financial assistance for doing so.

The techniques developed by the papacy were used by bishops
and priests as well. Frequently they were absorbed in offices of
politics, holding dioceses or cathedrals which they seldom visited,
but from which they collected revenue. In England, Cardinal
Wolsey claimed partial support from the sees of Durham and
Winchester successively, and from sees in France and Spain. Nor
was the situation different in France, Italy and Germany. A
prince might be a political ruler and absentee bishop. He collected funds from his bishopric and not infrequently shared them
with the papacy in payment for the assignment of the bishopric
to him.

Such practices were obviously not conducive to spirituality
among popes or clergy. There were, of course, notable exceptions.
The general development was toward an excessively "worldly"
church, and not infrequently to outright cases of immorality.
There were reform movements within the monasteries; and the
conciliar movement, however ill-fated, was an attempt to reform
the church from the Pope down by a decentralization of its
administrative machinery. Individuals like Wyclife in England
and Hus in Bohemia had vehemently objected to the low state
of affairs in the church. Both religious and secular historians
concede that at the eve of the Reformation, reform of the church
and particularly of the clergy was indeed necessary.

The financial crisis of the church and the general decline in

spirituality had their effects, too, upon the relation of the church
to the average individual. The controversy over "indulgences"
affected the man in the parish more directly than any of the
intellectual or social currents and thereby threatened the church
at a very crucial point. To appreciate the full impact of this, it is
necessary to see the problem of indulgences in the context of the
developing penitential system. The church always claimed that
salvation was grounded in the grace of Christ and quite early
insisted that it was made available primarily through its commis-
sioned agents, the priests. It was taken for granted in the Middle
Ages that upon the confession of sins, the priest, if he considered
the penitent worthy, would declare absolution of sins in the name
of the triune God. This comprised the sacrament of penance and
signified the imparting of grace and the restoration of man to his
full religious position under God. Forgiveness was actual restoration. But the reconstitution of life was not considered complete
until men had made amends, insofar as humanly possible, for the
inescapable consequences of an act of sin. An act of sin offended
God and man. It violated an order of justice. Forgiveness or
absolution saved one from eternal punishment; but punishment
for sin still took its course and was completed in purgatory, prior
to one's final entrance to the kingdom. By making temporal satisfaction, one could already now begin to mitigate and decrease
subsequent punishment. Such temporal satisfaction took the form
of specific acts (frequently prayers) assigned by the priest to the
penitent, and tended to serve two functions. The performance of
assigned acts of penance indicated that a man was indeed con-
trite. But more important, the church declared that such activity
would now begin to pay the penalty of sin, instead of postponing
it all until after death. This claim rested in the notion that God
had entrusted his work of redemption to the church and that
what was "bound" or "loosed" on earth, would be bound or
loosed after man's death.

Initially, "indulgence" was merely a term for the cancellation
under appropriate conditions of a part of this assigned special
activity or work of penance. It was an instrument used by bishops
in cases where assigned acts were a distinct hardship on the
person, or where distinct service to the church, such as a gift of

land or money, merited special consideration. The first extensive use of an indulgence for special meritorious service was Pope Urban II's promise of complete indulgence to all who joined the first crusade. An indulgence, therefore, was usually the substitution of one kind of act or deed for another. It did not alter the fundamental conception that satisfaction must be made or that justice must run its course.

The full development of the idea of a "treasury of merit" considerably changed the initial use of indulgences. Surely Christ and the saints had done such good works that they accumulated merit far beyond their own needs. It was held that this super-abundance constituted a "treasury of merit," from which under appropriate conditions the church could draw to meet the needs of the ordinary man in arrears in completing the assigned penance. Since it was also believed that the average man died before he had completed necessary penance or made satisfaction for his sins, the question arose whether the treasury of merit could be made beneficial to men in purgatory. In purgatory men who were destined eventually for God's kingdom suffered for their sins until final satisfaction was complete. If the merit could be made available to them, both the extent of their suffering and the length of their sojourn might be reduced. On the thesis that the church was the body of Christ, it was decided that the merits of Christ could definitely be made available to those in purgatory. In a healthy body, no part withholds its life and help to the rest.

The church drew from the treasury of merit by authorizing an indulgence. The visible side of an indulgence was a slip of paper upon which was noted its spiritual worth. These could therefore be sold like an article of trade. It was not unusual for the papacy to farm out the sale of indulgences to princes who aspired to ecclesiastical importance. They in turn would send an agreed-upon share of the proceeds to Rome.

The possibility of abuse was great. Any decent person desired that departed friends or relatives might be spared some of the pain and time in purgatory. Since most indulgences were proclaimed for just such relief, a ready market was at hand. Hence, the need for revenue on the part of the papacy became a temptation to issue one indulgence after another.

One of the great preachers of indulgences was a Dominican by the name of Tetzel. He traveled from town to town preaching an indulgence, the proceeds of which were to go to Rome for the completion of the new St. Peter's Church. Albert of Brandenburg had agreed to the sale of this indulgence in his territories in return for an appointment to the archbishopric of Mainz, a link which he needed in the chain he was forging to make himself master of the German lands. Since the stakes in this venture were high for both Albert and the papacy, this indulgence was pushed with all the force and pomp which could be mustered. An eloquent example of the type of preaching which accompanied the promotion of the sale of this particular indulgence is the following from one of Tetzel's sermons:

> Listen now, God and St. Peter call you. Consider the salvation of your souls and those of your loved ones departed. . . . Listen to the voices of your dear dead relatives and friends, beseeching you and saying, 'Pity us, pity us. We are in dire torment from which you can redeem us with a pittance.' Do you not wish to? Open your ears. Hear the father saying to his son, the mother to her daughter, 'We bore you, nourished you, brought you up, left you our fortunes, and you are so cruel and hard that now you are not willing for so little to set us free. Will you let us lie here in flames? Will you delay our promised glory?'

> Remember that you are able to release them, for

> As soon as the coin in the coffer rings,
> The soul from purgatory springs.

> Will you not then for a quarter of a florin receive these letters of indulgences through which you are able to lead a divine and immortal soul into the fatherland of paradise? [2]

Increasingly the careful distinction which had been drawn between forgiveness and temporal satisfaction was obscured. Many of the vendors of indulgences promised forgiveness and redemption on the basis of their purchase and paid scant attention to the fact that officially indulgences had always been confined only to the remission of penalties, whether here or in pur-

---

[2] Roland H. Bainton, *Here I Stand*, 78. Nashville: Abingdon-Cokesbury Press, 1950.

gatory. In the confessional the average man, just as Luther, was
told that the purchase of indulgences were effective also for
salvation. This made them all the more attractive. It more effectively tied man's religious needs to the financial machinations of
the hierarchy. It is apparent that financial interests, coupled with
human foibles and ambitions, played a large part in corrupting
the internal life of the church.

4. FAITH IS REDISCOVERED

Long before Luther men were protesting against the situation within the church. Among the most significant as we have
seen were Wyclife in England and John Hus in Bohemia. As did
the Germans later, Wyclife protested against the importation of
Italian priests and the draining of wealth from the country. He
railed against the corruption of papacy and clergy because of
their fairly exclusive preoccupation with wealth and power. He
emphasized the directness of every man's responsibility under God
without the benefit or hindrance of any intermediate channel.
Further, he protested against the concept of transubstantiation,
the theory that in the consecration of the elements, God performs
the miracle of transforming bread and wine into the actual body
and blood of Christ. He objected that this placed a necessary and
irreplaceable intermediary between God and man. Wyclife's greatest impact upon the popular mind, however, came through his
part in organizing and in sponsoring the translation of the entire
Scripture into the English language. While accused of heresy,
Wyclife died before any official action was taken.

Of no small importance was the influence of Wyclife's writings
on John Hus in Bohemia where there was also a reforming party.
Hus attacked corruption in the church from clergy to papacy.
He was outspoken against indulgences, though more conservative
in his estimate of tradition than Wyclife. A Hussite church was
formed with emphasis upon Christ as its true head. The situation
in Bohemia was complicated by the counter pressures of papacy
and empire, each continually threatening the life of Hus. Actually, Hus was burned at the stake by a council of the church, not
by papacy or empire. This was a shock, though not a fatal one, to

those who placed their hopes upon the deliberations of councils as a means of checking abuses in the church.

When Luther nailed his ninety-five theses to the door of the Castle Church in Wittenberg in 1517, he was only one of a series of individuals and groups which were already in protest against the practices and procedures of the church. Moreover, he was merely following the accepted custom of posting propositions one was prepared to debate. Little did he forsee that his actions would initiate a movement destined to redirect the understanding and visible practice of much of Christendom. Others, too, had repudiated the practice of purchasing and selling indulgences as a way of shortening the time of the departed in purgatory and had rejected the unauthorized claim of some that God's forgiveness could be made available through their purchase. Like them, he must protest. Tetzel's preaching made him particularly indignant. It reduced man's relation to God to the level of barter and trade.

In the ninety-five theses, Luther did not reject indulgences outright. He rejected only the abuses. The papacy, he declared, did not have the power to remit *guilt* in respect to the least of venial sins, nor could indulgences be said to have any effect on purgatory. The Pope could change or cancel only those penalties imposed by his own authority or by the canons of the church. Indulgences were valid only when confined to such human and organizational discipline and had no necessary relation to the final destiny of any individual believer.

Such was the specific religious protest of the ninety-five theses. Behind it lay a new religious understanding, the significance of which became clear to Luther and his contemporaries only under the pressure of subsequent events. The roots of it went back to Luther's days as a young theological instructor who, in his lectures on Psalms in the year 1513 and on Romans in the year 1515–16, discovered a gospel which met the anxiety of his own soul. He had entered the monastery in order to find peace with God, to save his own soul. Having been nearly struck down by a bolt of lightning, he had resolved then and there to follow the noblest and most certain path. But the prescribed path did not

bring the peace he sought. God was a righteous God who demanded the unswerving obedience of man and destined man to
salvation only if he merited it. To be sure, the church existed
in part as a remedy for sins committed, and claimed that it had
been established by God to act in his name. In this way it always
provided man with a new start. Moreover, it was the custodian
of grace and merit which could help make a man righteous.

But the church had a remedy only for sins confessed. If a man
confessed his sins, he could be absolved and undertake to carry
out the prescribed penance. Only so could he become righteous.
It was exactly this which could not satisfy Luther's conscience.
He suspected that there might be sins about which he did not
even know or sins which he committed after leaving the confessional for which he might at any moment be held accountable.
The uncharitable interpretation of his unrest is the suggestion
that such concern is pathological. It is more constructive to understand Luther's unrest as the searching of a sensitive man for
the proper relation to God. The burden of evidence points to the
latter interpretation, for this zeal pervades every move he made
as a monk. He could not put aside the question of certainty under
God; in fact, this quest drove him to confess his sins so frequently
to his fellow monks as to annoy them. The rule of the monastery,
he confessed, was easy to perform, but it did not provide the
peace of soul which a man ought to have under God. The words
of his saintly superior, Staupitz, advising Luther to relax and to
trust in the grace of God, did not help. God's righteous demand
was too serious to permit rest.

The impossibility of finding assurance drove Luther even to
wonder whether God was just at all. Perhaps God was a tyrant
who never gave peace and who was not even trustworthy. According to late medieval nominalism, God could act in opposition to
his declared intention. There were moments when Luther
hated God, when he felt utterly frustrated and among the
damned.

In this state of mind Luther was hardly fit to become a lecturer
in Bible. But out of the necessity of lecturing came his answer. In
the Psalms he discovered two important aspects of the Bible which
shed light on his problem. In the first place, he was struck by the

verse in the twenty-second Psalm, "My God, my God, why hast thou forsaken me?" In line with the prevailing opinion that the Old Testament foreshadowed or anticipated the new, this verse obviously could have reference only to Christ. But that Christ, the son of God, should be forsaken just as he, Luther, had been was incredible until it dawned upon him that this signified how Christ took upon himself the sins of the world. To redeem man, God in Christ took on the lot of man, participating in his despair and lostness. Christ might therefore be not only the righteous Judge, but also the merciful one.

In the second place, the phrase in Psalm 31, "Deliver me in thy righteousness" became a source of insight. The connection of righteousness and deliverance challenged the conception that the former always meant the demanding, judicial, fearful justice of God. If it were such, it could hardly be associated with deliverance.

But the decisive turn did not come until Luther understood the passage in Romans 1:17 which refers to the gospel as the disclosure of the justice or righteousness of God. In fact, this passage had rather kept him from stressing Paul's writings to which he was otherwise attracted. Now it became the basis of a new understanding, including that of Psalm 31. Speaking of this passage in Romans, Luther wrote:

> I greatly longed to understand Paul's Epistle to the Romans and nothing stood in the way but that one expression, 'the justice of God,' because I took it to mean that justice whereby God is just and deals justly in punishing the unjust. My situation was that, although an impeccable monk, I stood before God as a sinner troubled in conscience, and I had no confidence that my merit would assuage him. Therefore I did not love a just and angry God, but rather hated and murmured against him. Yet I clung to the dear Paul and had a great yearning to know what he meant.
> Night and day I pondered until I saw the connection between the justice of God and the statement that 'the just shall live by his faith.' Then I grasped that the justice of God is that righteousness by which through grace and sheer mercy God justifies us through faith. Thereupon I felt myself to be reborn and to have gone through open doors into paradise. The whole of Scripture took on a new meaning,

and whereas before the 'justice of God' had filled me with hate, now it became to me inexpressibly sweet in greater love. This passage of Paul became to me a gate of heaven. . . .[3]

Now Luther had discovered that the gospel spoke about a righteous God who indicated his faithfulness, mercy and love toward men who knew that they were not righteous. Here was disclosed a God who, without rescinding his demand upon men was righteous also in another way. Without asking a sign of worth, he extended his mercy to those who trusted him rather than themselves and their activities. Theologically this was expressed in the term "justification by faith."

To be justified, to be made right and just before God—this was the problem with which Luther started his religious pilgrimage. His life in the church had been geared to that problem, on the basis of the actual and calculable righteousness of man. But that he was really righteous was Luther's doubt, since the calculation of righteousness depended upon whether or not one had confessed all his sins and received absolution. The injunction to disregard as irrelevant and ·not serious sins of which he was not aware might have been good counsel, but it did not help his uneasy feeling.

Now the accent shifted from him who was actually righteous to him "who through faith is righteous." The release was tremendous. Now one might be accepted as he was, since God justified those who came, not on their merit or righteousness, but on their trust in him for their life. Man's status under God was no longer weighed in the scale. Rather, it was a position sustained by God and experienced directly by the believer. In short, the whole base of orientation was transformed. Instead of the question, how can one be righteous? the decisive point now was that God was righteous. He, without easing his demand upon man, had revealed righteousness as mercy and had thereby made it impossible to think of righteousness in respect to one's relation to God. Now the accent was upon the mercy which accepts, which is gracious, which is therefore grace. Where this is experienced, one need no longer be preoccupied with self; he is set free from

[3] *Ibid.*, 65.

himself. But this is only possible if one abandons all calculation and measurability as a false notion in relation to God.

Justification by faith was thus a term for a religious experience whose primary characteristic was faith or trust springing from direct encounter with the redeeming presence of Christ. Redemption centered in the life, death and resurrection of Christ and was said to be experienced by those who found his forgiveness and power in his presence in their lives. This was the logic of righteousness proclaimed in the Bible.

> Now the righteousness of God has been manifested apart from the law, although the law and the prophets bear witness to it, the righteousness of God through faith in Jesus Christ for all who believe. For there is no distinction; since all have sinned and fall short of the glory of God, they are justified by his grace as a gift, through the redemption which is in Christ Jesus, whom God put forward as an expiation by his blood, to be received in faith. This was to show God's righteousness, because in his divine forbearance he had passed over former sins; it was to prove at the present time that he himself is righteous and that he justifies him who has faith in Jesus.[4]

Such was already the central point of Luther's faith at the time he posted the ninety-five theses in protest against the abuses surrounding the sale of indulgences. Only in the controversy which ensued did it become clear to him that indulgences needed to be rejected outright and that his new comprehension of faith demanded a radical reforming of the church.

5. FAITH MAKES ITS PROTEST

The posting of the ninety-five theses did not issue in the debate Luther anticipated. At the request of the Pope, Luther was summoned to a meeting with Cardinal Cajetan. But instead of being invited to discussion, he was ordered to recant. This he refused to do. Even the subsequent discussions and debates, such as the Leipzig debate with Eck and those at the Diet of Worms were aimed only at forcing Luther to retract. In 1520 the Pope issued a bill of excommunication against Luther.

In the meantime, Luther had seen that his protest meant not

[4] Romans 3:21–26 (Revised Standard Version).

only a rejection of abuses, but also a change in the nature of the church itself. Three years after the posting of the theses, Luther rejected indulgences themselves as inconsistent with the gospel and referred to them as the "knavish trick of the Roman Syco-phants." He was now calling for an outright reformation of the church in the light of the biblical faith. Since the church was unwilling to change, Luther called upon the nobles and princes to effect the reformation. (This, too, had been done by Wyclife and Hus in their respective situations.) In *An Open Letter to the Christian nobility of the German nation concerning the Reform of the Christian Faith*, Luther charged these officers with the task of reformation because the church had built around itself three walls which prevented any far-reaching changes. The first wall, he declared, was the claim for supremacy of the spiritual over the temporal order. The church claimed exclusive and absolute authority over the spiritual life of men. Such a unique position under God clearly argued for the church's supremacy over all earthly affairs and for the obedience of the temporal to the spiritual, or even for the spiritual to assume temporal power.

The second and third walls prevented reform which might come from appeal to scripture or to council. One could not utilize the Bible to correct the church since the final right to interpret scripture was in the hands of the papacy. Nor could one instigate proceedings for a council, since the Pope alone was authorized to call a council. Outright attack under the aegis of other constituted authorities remained the only recourse for breaking through the papal walls.

The prescription for the church which Luther had in mind was indeed fairly drastic. It was nothing less than the rejection of an entire sacramental system. Luther rejected the claim that the church was the custodian of God's activity on earth, and that to it had been entrusted the responsibility of doing his work through the treasure of grace which Christ and the saints made and con-tinued to make available to it. In such a system there was an experience of God, but one's status and relation to him was of necessity channeled through the church and assumed a quanti-tative character, becoming a question of the amount of merit. Em-phasis was upon being made right and righteous through the sacraments, which were the agencies for the dispensation of God's grace. For example, baptism was the sacrament through which original sin was erased and grace restored: the moment of baptism was the moment of righteousness, and the sacrament of penance always restored the righteousness of the baptismal state.

Luther's insistence that the gospel of the New Testament was the account of an objective act of mercy to be subjectively appropriated, rather than the establishment of a church which dispenses God's grace, thus challenged the very nature of the constituted church.

In *The Babylonian Captivity of the Church*, Luther appealed to the New Testament for the repudiation of many aspects of the development of the church. He considered the medieval mass as a violation rather than as an expression of the gospel. Just as there were three walls, so were there three captivities in conjunction with the mass. The first was the withholding of the cup from the laity. For this Luther could find no biblical basis and declared further that it served to accentuate the estrangement between clergy and laity. Luther rather cynically remarked that if it was a mortal sin for the priest not to take both elements, then it was also a sin for the laity.

The second captivity, said Luther, was the concept of transubstantiation. Luther's own understanding of the presence of Christ in the bread and wine will concern us in the next chapter. Here it is important to note that the miracle of transforming the bread and wine into the actual blood and body of Christ appeared magical to Luther, and again emphasized the distinction between clergy and laity.

The most basic captivity, however, was the idea that the mass was a good work in which after the consecration of the elements, Christ was offered as a sacrifice to God each time the mass was said. Carried to its logical conclusion, this made the mass a worthy act quite apart from the presence of any believers, except for the priest whose intent, one could reasonably assume, was properly directed. Luther could find in the New Testament no grounds for declaring the sacrament a good work, since it has no efficacy apart from the believers who received it. Nor could he find any basis for the notion of sacrifice since Christ did not offer himself to God but rather was given by God for man. In the theory of mass, of course, Christ is sacrificed to God in order to receive him also. There is both an upward and a downward motion. For Luther there could be no upward motion. He writes:

> as distributing a testament, or acceptance of a promise, differs diametrically from offering a sacrifice, so it is a contradiction in terms to call the mass a sacrifice; for the former is something that we receive, while the latter is something we offer. The same thing cannot be received and offered at the same time, nor can it be both given and taken by the same person. Hence, the only worthy preparation and proper use of the mass is faith in the mass, that is to say, in the divine promise. . . . The safest course, therefore, will be to go to the mass in the same spirit in which you would go to hear any promise of God; that is, not to be ready to perform and bring many works, but to believe and receive all that is there promised, or proclaimed by the priest as having been promised to you.[5]

Not all Protestants agree with Luther's rigid rejection of sacrifice in connection with the mass. Those Anglicans who regard themselves as Protestants prefer to use the word sacrifice, but insist that the sacrificing of Christ to God is an event of the past and is not repeatable by priestly function. While the majority of Protestant bodies reject this also, they often use the term sacrifice in reference to offering the goods of life and themselves to God. Here it is not the word, but its underlying meaning which is important.

While Luther singled out the mass as the pivotal point at which the church's orientation involved a violation of the New Testament, he eventually called all the traditional sacraments into question. Only baptism and the Lord's Supper were instituted in the New Testament as events in which act, word and participation were involved. These three aspects, appearing together in the New Testament, implied that a sacrament had been instituted. Hence, penance, extreme unction, marriage, confirmation and ordination were rejected as sacraments, though all of them may be significant acts in the Christian life.

[5] Martin Luther, *The Babylonian Captivity of the Church,* Holman edition, Vol. II, 202, 212.

The impossibility of achieving a reconstitution of the church in the light of these biblical criteria made an outright break inevitable. Hence, there resulted the constitution of parishes independent of Rome. It should be evident that the basis of the Reformation was ultimately religious in nature. Even Wyclife and Hus, however much they parallel Luther in some of his attacks, did not have the vision of justification by faith as the point around which the life of the Christian and the church must be understood. Here Luther broke through to a clarity of understanding and motivation which distinguished him from all his predecessors.

Protestants affirm that this renewed religious outlook, for all its relation to contemporary social, economic and political forces, can be finally explained only as an act of God in which, for better or worse, the burden of a message was laid upon a human being. Historical and cultural factors, many of them religious in nature, did provide the context in which the beginnings of the Reformation occurred. Without them Luther and his work could not have succeeded. Luther could be threatened, but his work could not be stopped. Thus, in the juncture of a revitalized faith and new historical forces, individuals may discern a genuine providential ordering.

II

A New Theology Develops: Luther and Calvin

The main developments in the life and thought of the various Reformation bodies will be discussed in later chapters. In the present chapter, attention will be focused on the restatement of the faith to which Martin Luther and John Calvin were led by their rediscovery of the biblical perspective. Though Calvin appeared in the Reformation scene some years later than Luther, the two figures are combined in this exposition for not unrelated reasons.[1]

First, Luther and Calvin are the theological giants who stand

[1] John Calvin (1509–1564), father of the Reformed tradition, was born in Piccardy and educated in theology, law, and the humanities at Orleans, Bourges and Paris. Classical studies under leading humanists bore fruit in his first published work, the *Commentary on Seneca's Treatise on Clemency*. His early contacts with the Reform and the time of his conversion to it are matters of dispute, but in 1533 he was among the Protestants forced to leave Paris. He settled finally in Basel. In 1536 he published the first edition of his major work, *Institutes of the Christian Religion*, which was revised and expanded in many editions over the next quarter century. Detained to aid the reform in Geneva in 1536 by William Farel, and banished in 1538, Calvin spent three fruitful years of study, writing and ecumenical activity in Strassburg. He was persuaded to return to Geneva in 1541 where, with the aid of Protestant refugees from all over Europe, he undertook to make the city into a model Christian community. After the expulsion of his opponents from the city in 1555, Calvin was virtually master of the city (although officially only a pastor in the church) until his death.

out in the Reformation above all other individuals and movements. This does not mean, of course, that everything which occurred is to be judged or understood by what these two men thought. Both the more radical groups of the continental Reformation, including the Anabaptists, and the English Reformation, were movements nourished by roots partly independent of the work of Luther and Calvin. And the developments in Lutheranism and the Calvinistic (or Reformed) tradition cannot be measured simply by Luther and Calvin. But few men and movements, either of the Reformation or of later Western religious history, have been able to escape their influence. Their greatness is evident in the opposition to them as well as in attempts to follow them.

Second, the point of departure in religious thinking is for both the same, namely, the concept of justification by faith. Moreover, the implications which they develop from this concept for all other areas of theology are surprisingly similar. There are some fundamental differences between Luther and Calvin and they will be noted, but the basic agreement is striking.

Third, these men together represent the most radical and comprehensive recasting of religious understanding since the beginning of the Christian movement. Their thinking is radical in the sense that they directly challenged traditional developments in the light of a very simple but positive message of God's grace. It is comprehensive in that they rethought the major aspects of Christian faith in the light of the new criterion. This is true whether the theological writing is unsystematic, as in Luther, or systematic in the traditional sense, as in Calvin. Even Luther's unorganized and sometimes hastily conceived theological statements are informed by and frequently revised under the criterion of faith. Calvin's *Institutes* begins with the concept of God and only in Book Three does he deal directly with justification; nevertheless, the notion of faith is presupposed in the entire first part. Both Luther and Calvin knew that Christian thinking is a totality, that each affirmation is related to every other one. Faith was the burning problem of their time and from this base, they rethought the other problems.

1. GOD AND MAN

a. Man as Sinner

"True and substantial wisdom principally consists of two parts, the knowledge of God and the knowledge of ourselves. But, while these two branches of knowledge are so intimately connected, which of them precedes and produces the other, is not easy to discover." [2] So writes Calvin in the opening sentence of the *Institutes*. Here he reflects the temper of a time in which men believe that knowledge of self and God are inseparable, but are no longer sure exactly how the two are to be understood or from which vantage point. Man is a problem to himself, but he is not himself and does not truly know himself apart from God. In a sense, Calvin's theological enterprise is nothing else than an exposition of this polar relation in the light of his faith. Luther, too, knew the duality of this single problem. Only as he was able to comprehend both God and himself in a new light did he find the peace of a religious wisdom.

Both the medieval church and the reformers assumed that the problem of God and man was one with which man could not adequately cope. However different the understanding of both God and man in the medieval church and the reformers, they assumed that man could not finally understand himself apart from God's redemptive work. It went without saying that apart from God, man was lost.

But for the reformers, in contrast to the medieval church, this "lostness" was illumined only by justification as conceived in the biblical tradition. Only in the light of the answer to man's problem, declared Luther, could one have the courage to see himself as he is, a creature separated from God and disrupted from his fellow men. For the reformers, this state of man is depicted in the Genesis story of the Fall—a story which they interpreted as historical—and can be characterized as "total depravity." Depravity, however, does not mean terrible acts which some men commit. Depravity concerns man's *acts* only as they reflect the broken character of man's relation to God and his fellowmen. It refers to the inability of man to institute a relation with God on

[2] John Calvin, *Institutes of the Christian Religion*, I, i, 1.

the basis of human activity. Depravity is considered "total" because no aspect of life or activity is exempt from the corruptions of self.

When Luther and Calvin consider man as sinner, they thus have in mind a state, a position, and every act of sin is but a reflection of this state. Sin is not to be equated with specific acts of sin. It can be described as the tendency of man to build the world around himself, to corrupt even his best achievements by being conscious that they are *his* achievements. It is the pride and self concern which manifests itself even in men's noblest deeds. It is the activity of men which is done apart from faith and which therefore is not done only for God and neighbor but also for self. This is why Luther spoke of sin as separation from God, or unbelief, and why Augustine declared the glorious virtues of the good pagans to be splendid vices. It was not that the activity of the good pagans was bad. Their acts might even have been better than those of many Christians. The question is one of relation to God and of fundamental motivation. What is not of faith is sin. That is why Luther almost shockingly declares that "if a man were not first a believer and a Christian, all his work would amount to nothing at all and would be freely wicked and damnable sins." Or as Luther also declares, the heart of natural man is curved within itself. As long as this is the case, sin is inevitable.

The reformers contended also that man continually attempts to cover up his true state. Part of his sin is his unwillingness to accept himself as sinner, as one who needs to be rescued by some reality other than himself.

For both Luther and Calvin the "law," particularly in its Old Testament form, revealed the situation of man. It was a preparation for the gospel, exactly because it made God's demand so crystal clear that one ought to see himself as sinner and therefore turn to the mercies of Christ. It shows the demands of God's righteousness in a concreteness which leaves no doubt as to where one stands. For Luther and Calvin, the law is a problem, not because it destroys the spirit, but because it shows how far one is from the genuine spirituality which belongs to an adequate relation to God. The law convicts of sin.

For Luther and Calvin, the teachings of Jesus also belong to the level of law. They are the most concrete and graphic presentation of the kind of life required under God. Instead of joyfully accepting the teachings of Jesus as the new disclosure of God, Luther saw in them the last barrier which stood between God and man. Even when the spirit and intent of the teachings were stressed, he found them no more tolerable, since that only focused the issue more clearly. Precisely because the crucial problem is not what is done, but how and why it is done, the teachings of Jesus were so depressing, apart from justifying faith, that they became a new source of despair. They exhibited a life in full relation to God and therefore one which fully expressed and lived out the teachings. Since the teachings represented the life, the last door to self-redemption was closed. Where sin is act, there is some hope of an act or acts which will turn the tide; but where sin is a state, a position, a disease, there a cure, not a new act, is essential.

That is why no one could speak of contributing to his justification. The reformers believed that the relationship out of which came a life resembling Christ's was established only by God's initiative. This was exactly the message of the New Testament. Any insistence on the righteousness of one's activity, declared Calvin, itself furnishes grounds for inordinate pride and takes from God the glory which is his. To believe even partly in the merit of one's works or righteousness is pride, i.e., sin. To insist upon contributing anything to one's justification is to invert and reject the gospel. It is itself an expression of sin. Justification is the declaration of God that the sinner is accepted, not that he is no longer sinner. For Luther and Calvin, man is inevitably sinner. His refusal of faith, his attempt to rely on some activity of his own, is itself the final expression of his revolt against God. It is corruption at the point of his noblest ambition, his desire to be related to God.

b. Faith and Decision

This understanding of sin means that there is no final hope for man apart from God's redemptive activity. The goodness of the gospel is the acceptance of the sinner—the possibility, as Luther put it, of trusting God rather than oneself. It is the power

in which the reformers saw an answer both to man's obvious sin
and to his more deceptive attempts to escape his plight in a round
of activity. Certainly, neither Luther nor Calvin counseled that
a man should sit by, with folded hands, waiting for something
to happen. They merely asserted that activity in the world would
not guarantee the reconstitution of a satisfactory relation to God,
and that every activity which was predicated upon that could
only spin the web around man more tightly than ever. They knew
that probably only those who seek God would find his presence
(and primarily as they sought it through the Bible). They knew
also that every finding was a gift, an actual experience of God's
merciful, justifying presence.

Luther and Calvin affirmed that faith is both a gift and a
decision. Without the gift, the decision is not related to the experience of God's forgiving love. Yet the experience of God's
mercy, and the affirmation that God has led one to this experience, do not vitiate decision. Those who insist upon decision
without ascribing the credit to God distort the meaning of faith
by making it a work. On the other hand, those who stress the
activity of God without reference to human decision, make
automatons and objects out of men.

The reformers followed St. Paul and St. Augustine in respect
to this problem. St. Paul's eloquent declaration, "I, yet not I, but
Christ who dwells within me" bears witness to individuality and
decision which are based, supported, and understood from the
standpoint of Christ's work. St. Augustine expressed the same
conviction when he declared "I would not have found Thee,
hadst Thou not first found me." Calvin, discussing the familiar
medieval view that repentance came before faith (repentance was
the medieval description of a decision), inverted the order, explaining that "When we speak of faith as the origin of repentance,
we dream not of any space of time which it employs in producing
it; but we intend to signify that a man cannot truly devote himself to repentance, unless he knows himself to be of God. Now, no
man is truly persuaded that he is of God except he has previously
received his grace." [3]

The question at issue was not chronological or psychological

[3] *Ibid.,* III, iii, 2.

precedence, but that of foundation in a specific reality, either God or man. Obviously, faith is only experienced by the self and there is a decision of faith; nevertheless, the reformers insisted, it cannot be manufactured by the self. It is based in the gracious activity of God. Faith is born; it is not made. When faith occurs, men confess that not their own doing but God's work was responsible, regardless of how much they sought. The person who insists that faith is an individual decision to accept God's offer of mercy has not yet experienced its transforming presence. Those who have, know that faith's source is truly in God. God's offer of mercy is not like an object which man takes or leaves; God both confronts and is himself at work in the decision. Yet this does not exclude human responsibility and decision.

It is on this level that the debate on the "freedom of the will" can be understood. When Luther and Calvin denied freedom of the will, they were emphatically not interested in reducing the human will to a sub-personal object of mechanical determination. This is most clear in Luther's *Bondage of the Will*. Speaking of the scholastic problem of freedom, he wrote:

> I could wish, indeed, that we were furnished with some better term for this discussion, than this commonly used term, *necessity*, which cannot rightly be used, either with reference to the human will or the divine. It is of a signification too harsh and ill-suited for this subject, forcing upon the mind an idea of compulsion, and that which is altogether contrary to *will*; whereas, the subject which we are discussing, does not require such an idea: for Will, whether divine or human, does what it does, be it good or evil, not by any compulsion, but by mere willingness or desire, as it were, totally free. The will of God, nevertheless, which rules over our mutable will, is immutable and infallible; as Boethius says, 'Immovable Thyself, Thou movement giv'st to all.' And our own will, especially our corrupt will, cannot of itself do good; therefore, where the term fails to express the idea required, the understanding of the reader must make up the deficiency, knowing what is wished to be expressed—the immutable will of God, and the impotency of our depraved will; or, as some have expressed it, the *necessity of immutability*, though neither is that sufficiently grammatical, or sufficiently theological.[4]

[4] Martin Luther, *The Bondage of the Will*, 40–41.

The denial of freedom of the will (as well as the concept of total depravity) refers only to the inability of the sinner to will himself to faith. Man can will and decide many things; but he cannot give himself faith. Even if this were possible, said Luther, he would gladly give up that "freedom" to take the burden of his salvation from the shaky reed, namely, himself, and rest it in God.

The decision of faith is rooted in the experience of the merciful presence of Christ. Faith as a decision has a plus side which ordinary decisions do not have. God lays hold of a man, and he experiences this in faith. The inward experience refers to a ground outside itself. In the Reformation sense, faith can be said to be the subjective side of the objective reality of God in Christ which has grasped one. It is experienced as real and its reality is experienced.

The reformers, Luther in particular, also knew that this experience is not an enduring possession which man can claim as perpetually present. If it were, the mercy of God would be a possession rather than a promise. God's mercy may be consistently offered, and faith is sustained by the gracious activity of God. But sustaining does not mean that God will always be experienced or present, not even when man most desires this. In fact, Luther's darkest days were not those *before* he experienced God's righteousness as also his mercy; they occurred when the mercy which he had experienced was no longer present, and came only in moments which could not be controlled as to time or place. Luther found peace only after he recognized that the merciful God whom he *had* experienced was also the God whom he might experience *again*.

If faith is experience of God's mercy, it must therefore also be trust. In this sense, it is an attitude or a decision, based on the promise and hope of God's trustworthiness. The mistake of many in the sixteenth century was to assume that the experience brought and kept them so in the presence of God that they were above the necessity of trust. Against this, Luther contended vigorously. But he also insisted that trust must be anchored in a prior experience of God's mercy. The total dimension of faith includes both the mercy of God, rooted in God's activity, and trust in God when he is not experienced. The second is genuine only on the basis of the first, though it may occupy the moments of man's life more often than not. The man who has experienced God's gracious presence and who, frequently or infrequently, continues to do so, will at least know whom he is trusting.

For Luther particularly, predestination must be understood in exactly this context. Predestination is a confession about the trustworthy character of God at two crucial points. First, one would not have become a believer unless in the mystery of God's activity he had been led to faith. Second, since one has been led to this destiny under God, he can trust God even when his faith is at a low ebb. Predestination therefore has meaning only for believers and is not a concept for general speculation. And just because of this, Luther finally rejected the notion of "double" predestination (namely, that God wills the damnation of some as well as salvation of the elect) in favor of the concept of "single" predestination. God is to be held accountable only for salvation. Luther rejected double predestination because he could not make a statement about God's activity apart from faith, and faith can speak only of God's merciful choice. The most that Luther could say was that apart from faith, men naturally excluded themselves from God's kingdom. (This did not solve the problem, of course, for it must be recalled that there is nothing man can do to change his lot but to seek God with no guarantee of finding him.)

Calvin, who accepted the concept of double predestination, was equally certain about his starting point. The doctrine was meaningful for God's elect, those who found themselves as believers. Calvin moved from faith to an elaboration of predestination as a way of showing that God is wholly the author of our faith and that every notion of work or merit must be rejected. His motivating principle is most clearly expressed in a comment on St. Paul: "By saying that they were elected before the creation of the world, he [St. Paul] precludes every consideration of merit." [5] The notion of double predestination is a last drastic guarantee against any concept of merit and a final affirmation that our destiny is entirely in the hands of God. In the passages in which Calvin most vigorously defends double predestination,

[5] John Calvin, *op. cit.*, III, xxii, 2.

the exclusion of merit is central. God's gratuitous mercy operates in election irrespective of human merit, and in damnation by a just but incomprehensible judgment. In either case, human calculation is excluded.

On the basis of the opposition between faith and merit or work, Calvin elaborates a deterministic view of God's entire operation in the world. It may be necessary to reject his determinism, but it should also be remembered that he developed it in contrast to the concepts of fate and chance. Like the early church Fathers, he found determination by God a liberating and meaningful destiny in contrast to the darkness of fate or the undependableness of fortune. So also, it is important to remember that Calvin moved from faith to predestination, not predestination to faith. The latter, as we shall see in Chapter IV, was the pattern of most of his successors.

c. The Life of the Christian as Saint and Sinner

The experience of the forgiving, accepting mercy of God, for both Luther and Calvin, is in reality the presence of the living Christ in the believer. The Christian, therefore, lives in the presence of Christ. Although this experience, as we noted in the previous section, may vary in intensity from time to time in any individual, it is of the essence of the Christian that he has the strength and motivation of his life in the encounter with the living, transforming presence of God. He lives by a power not his own, because he lives by the power of Christ. Christ is experienced as both forgiveness and power. In movements of ecstatic utterance about the presence of Christ, Luther can even speak of being "one cake" with Christ. It is Christ who dwells within.

But neither Luther nor Calvin dwells on this experience as an end in itself. Christ drives one from self to neighbor. All activity is in fact the result of this relation to Christ. Therefore the reformers speak not against works, but against a false understanding of the place of works. "Our faith in Christ does not free us from works, but from false opinions concerning works, that is, from the foolish presumption that justification is acquired through works," wrote Luther in the *Treatise on Christian Lib-*

erty.[6] Calvin makes the same point many times in the *Institutes*. The following sentence is typical: "For we reject the notion of justification by works, not that no good works may be done, or that those which are performed may be denied to be good, but that we may neither confide in them, nor glory in them, nor ascribe salvation to them."[7]

He who experiences Christ may be said to be free from all works which enslave him, but bound by the encounter to serve the neighbor. Luther eloquently expressed this in the paradox: "A Christian man is a perfectly free lord of all, subject to none. A Christian man is a perfectly dutiful servant of all, subject to all."[8] The first axiom is the expression of a faith set free from every demand, and gives joy and zest in living. Man is no longer bound by rule or command. But his freedom is not license. He is the servant of all and his freedom is above, not beneath, the law. More often than not Luther assumes that the Christian is so directed by Christ as to do freely and naturally even more than the law required. A statement such as the following is not uncommon:

> From faith flows love and joy in the Lord, and from love a joyful, willing and free mind that serves one's neighbor willingly and takes no account of gratitude or ingratitude, of praise or blame, of gain or loss. For a man does not serve that he may put men under obligations, he does not distinguish between friends and enemies, nor does he anticipate their thankfulness or unthankfulness, but most freely and willingly he spends himself and all that he has, whether he wastes all on the thankless or whether he gains a reward. . . . As our heavenly father has in Christ freely come to our help, we also ought freely to help our neighbor through our body and its works, and each should become as it were a Christ to the other, that we may be Christs to one another and Christ may be the same in all; that is, that we may be truly Christians.[9]

This is a picture of the grateful Christian whom Christ has made into a new man. Luther went so far as to say that Chris-

[6] Martin Luther, *A Treatise on Christian Liberty*, Holman edition, Volume II, 344.
[7] John Calvin, *op. cit.*, III, xvii, 1.
[8] Martin Luther, *op. cit.*, 312.
[9] *Ibid.*, 338.

tians would not need the restraints of the state, since they would
naturally live together in love and unity, but that they were
obliged to obey the state out of love for the unchristian neighbor who did need it. If this was an unwarranted assumption on
the part of Luther, it nevertheless shows his confidence that the
presence of God's mercy in Christ transforms the life of man.

In his better moments, Luther knew that the Christian was
not so Christian as to do naturally what was required and that
more often he fell quite short of the mark. Where gratitude for
redemption in Christ did not suffice, Luther was quick to point
to the claim of God upon men. The Redeemer makes demands
of those who belong to him and in this respect law necessarily
enters the Christian life. Luther did not mean primarily the
biblical law, but the law of the conscience captive to God and
the law of society for justice and order. Law takes over whenever
faith is weak, and its necessity is a reminder that the Christian
remains a sinner who constantly stands in the need of forgiveness.

While Calvin's position on the transforming power of Christ
is essentially the same, there are important nuances of difference
which it is important to note. Luther speaks with great exuber-
ance about the presence of Christ and almost regrets the necessity
of law within the Christian life. Calvin, too, stresses the new life
in Christ, but he is sober rather than ecstatic in his account.

Whereas Luther spoke of the qualitatively new and decisive
redirection of the Christian life, Calvin preferred usually to speak
of the path in which the Christian walks, and in which, with
diligence, he can make some progress.

> Let us every one proceed accordingly to our small ability,
> and prosecute the journey we have begun. No man will be
> so unhappy, but that he may every day make some progress,
> however small. Therefore, let us not cease to strive, that we
> may be incessantly advancing in the way of the Lord; nor
> let us despair on account of the smallness of our success; for
> however our successes may not correspond to our wishes, yet
> our labor is not lost, when this day surpasses the preceding
> one; provided that with sincere simplicity we keep our end
> in view, and press forward to the goal, not practicing self-
> adulation, nor indulging our own evil propensities, but per-
> petually exerting our endeavors after increasing degrees of

38 A NEW THEOLOGY DEVELOPS: LUTHER AND CALVIN

amelioration, till we have arrived at a perfection of goodness, which indeed we seek and pursue as long as we live,
and shall then attain, when divested of all corporeal in-
firmity, we shall be admitted into complete communion in
him.[10]

In one passage Calvin even dares hope that the Christian will
have nothing left but the most venial of sins if he keeps on the
path toward righteousness.

On this path, Calvin sees a very positive role for biblical law,
(i.e., the moral law, including both the moral demand of the Old
Testament and the teaching of Jesus). Not only does this law
convict of sin and lead to Christ and preserve order in a world
of sin; its most significant place is that it supplies the Christian
with a better and more certain understanding of the divine will,
and by his meditation upon it, exhorts him to obedience and
keeps him "untainted from the slippery path of transgression."
Thus Calvin urged the preparation of a compendium of biblical
texts which might serve as a guide for the Christian.

While Luther was concerned with the qualitative transformation of the Christian life and while Calvin emphasized the possibility of progress within it, both seriously affirmed that the
Christian remains a sinner who needs God's justifying mercy at
all times. "Even we who have the first fruits of the spirit, groan
and travail within us," writes St. Paul in the eighth chapter of
Romans. The Christian stands at every moment under a mercy
which is more infinite than anything which man can accomplish
in faith. That is why, in the estimation of Luther, man is both
sinner and not a sinner at the same time. Similarly, Calvin
declares:

I assert that the best of their [believers] performances are
tarnished and corrupted by some carnal impurity and de-
based by a mixture of some alloy. Let any holy servant of
God select from his whole life that which he shall conceive
to have been the best of all his actions, and let him examine
it with attention on every side; he will undoubtedly discover
in it some taint of the corruption of the flesh; since our
alacrity to good actions is never what it ought to be, but
our course is retarded by great debility. . . . There is not

[10] John Calvin, *op. cit.*, III, vi, 5.

a single action performed by the saints, which, if judged according to its intrinsic merit, does not justly deserve to be rewarded with shame.[11]

Calvin was clear that no works or activity could survive the scrutiny of the Almighty except in forgiveness, but he did believe that they could be a confirmation of faith. They could be a sign for the believer of his faith and therefore of his election. "When we exclude the confidence of works," writes Calvin, "we only mean that the mind of the Christian should not be directed to any merit of works as a means of salvation; but should altogether rely on the gratuitous promise of righteousness. We do not forbid him to support and confirm this faith by marks of the Divine benevolence in him."[12] Or again, "They who are justified by true faith, prove their justification, not by a barren and imaginary resemblance of faith, but by obedience and good works."[13]

It is natural to expect that being a Christian makes a difference. It was Luther's genius which saw what the presence of Christ automatically does without reference to signs of any type. It was a liability that some of his successors interpreted this unconcern in the direction of license and freedom from all restraint. It was Calvin's greatness which saw that guidance and results both belong to the Christian life. But this could become a liability when individuals began to look at their works to discover whether or not they were truly of Christ's company. Such self-consciousness leads easily to self-righteousness. It is spiritually dangerous to look for signs of election.

In spite of the differences of emphasis, Luther and Calvin were in fundamental agreement on the place of works in the Christian life. These are not trustworthy in respect to salvation. Nevertheless, they belong to the life of faith. Granting this, however, there is no way of calculating to what extent works are essential. Any rigid definition could destroy the vitality of the Christian life in one of three directions—license, complacency, or self-righteousness produced by despair.

Luther's and Calvin's basic approach can perhaps best be ex-

[11] *Ibid.*, III, xiv, 9.
[12] *Ibid.*, III, xiv, 18.
[13] *Ibid.*, III, xxvii, 12.

pressed by speaking of "faith not without works." By way of contrast, this phrase may take a sharper meaning. It excludes both works plus faith, and faith plus works. The first is essential to the Roman Catholic position, in which the emphasis is upon worthiness, to which is added grace (the equivalent of what Protestants mean by faith). The second represents a late nineteenth-century motif which still informs much of Protestantism. Sensing the essential priority of faith, exponents of this position stress that works are derivative, that one trusts God and does the best he can. The contrast to the reformers is in the "both and" character of the expressions. Both faith and works are included, but not as a matter of addition, from one side or the other. Such alternatives destroy the vitality which the reformers saw in the proper relation between faith and action.

In defining the proper relation, the reformers begin always with justification, which stands over every human endeavor and over man in every moment. A man is always related to God finally on the basis of faith, for without this he could not even begin. He can also trust that this faith is more trustworthy than his actions or his own nature. Forgiveness stands and needs to stand over the best of human hopes, aspirations, and activities. It is a continual necessity and a continual possibility. All works and all human activities are grounded in this. That is why the Christian makes no claims for his works. The reformers would never say that God is easy in his demands as long as one's heart is in the right place (as some more recent generations have said); they emphasized that it is serious to fall into the hands of the living God even though his mercy over-rides every demand.

Where there are no works, there is no faith. But the place of works is relative. The biblical passages sometimes cited in support of a stress upon works actually places these in the context of faith. The injunction to "work out your own salvation with fear and trembling" needs to be quoted in its entirety, "for it is God who works in you both to will and to do." It is possible for Luther and Calvin to speak of working out one's own salvation when this is predicated upon the initiating and directing activity of God. Likewise, the biblical statement that "not every one who says unto me, Lord, Lord, shall enter into the kingdom of heaven,

but he that does the will of my father who is in heaven," does
not preclude but rather affirms the necessity of saying "Lord,
Lord"—the equivalent of trusting the mercy of God—as the
first word.

The phrase, faith not without works, expresses Luther's and
Calvin's insistence upon the priority of the mercy of God at
every point, and the necessity of works as a result. It carefully
avoids making works the basis of redemption and takes away
every quantitative calculation. The infinite patience and mercy
of God, far surpassing that of man, is expressed in the biblical
affirmation that God will forgive not seven, but seventy times
seven. This is not arithmetic, but the assertion that God's mercy
is continuous and inexhaustible. At the same time, where forgiveness does not in some sense issue in new life, it is doubtful that
it is actually forgiveness. Forgiveness itself directs and demands
man's responsibilities. But no one can simply add forgiveness and
the results of forgiveness, and expect to have the gospel. Man is
both in greater certainty and greater uncertainty. He is more
certain because everything hinges on God's mercy. He is more
uncertain because he does not have the possibility of resting
assured that he has done all, or done it correctly. The gospel sus-
pends man in the world, but gives him a point of security—God's
abiding mercy and his ultimate victory over the forces of evil.
The Christian wrestles, seemingly at times in vain; but he who
waits upon the Lord will renew his strength for the battle of life.
He need not fear, because God's mercy is ample for every con-
tingency.

It was from such a perspective that Luther asserted "sin
bravely, yet more bravely still believe." This is not a counsel to
sin; it is the recognition that life involves sin, that at no point
can man completely escape it. It is a counsel against those who are
so afraid of sin that they refuse to act or participate freely in the
events of life. Man can venture confidently, because his resource
is not a state of sinlessness but the mercy of God. This faith is
the emancipating power of the reformers' rediscovery of the Bible.
Through God's unqualified acceptance of man, man is freed from
calculation, terror, and self, and set free to love his neighbor and
to work responsibly in the world. He is the continually forgiven

man who trusts nothing else and whose earthly life is that of
being simultaneously saint and sinner.

2. GOD AND CHRIST

Luther and Calvin assumed the existence of God. This was
not seriously challenged in their own time. Even Luther, who
made very pointed remarks against reason as an avenue to knowledge of God, did not deny the possibility of such knowledge. He
only denied its usefulness in respect to decisive issues. Calvin
stated that all men are naturally endowed with the knowledge of
God. They distort this knowledge, but only reality can be distorted. Calvin further spoke of natural impulses toward justice
and goodness in men generally. But he understood these from the
perspective of a believer analyzing the life of the unbeliever. He
assumed that all men lived by the gifts of God even though they
did not recognize them as such.

Genuine knowledge of God, in Luther and Calvin, is related
to the meaning of life. To use a modern word, such knowledge is
existential, i.e., related to one's very existence. The two opening
chapters of Calvin's *Institutes* make the relation crystal clear.
"True and substantial wisdom principally consists of two parts,
the knowledge of God, and knowledge of ourselves. . . . The
knowledge of ourselves is not only an excitement to seek after
God, but likewise a considerable assistance towards finding him.
On the other hand, it is plain that no man can arrive at the true
character of himself without having first contemplated the divine
character, and then descended to the consideration of his own." [14]
From this perspective, the question of God really matters only as
his existence has consequences for human existence.

Thus, while the two reformers accepted a natural knowledge
of God, they immediately judged it from the standpoint of their
faith and pushed beyond it to a genuine knowledge of God in
Christ. They found much about God in the Bible apart from
Christ, but when they spoke of God it was always with the revelation in Christ at least in the background. Calvin, who is known
for stressing the majesty and honor of God, emphasized particularly the grace of God in Christ, as did Luther. (The stress

[14] *Ibid.*, I, i, 1 and 2.

on the honor of God is not as central in Calvin's writings as it is in later Calvinism and in the Westminster Confession of Faith.) Luther, who had so much to say of the gracious presence of God in Christ, had startling things to say of God's majesty apart from Christ. He reiterated how terrifying it is to confront his terrible, naked majesty. But even this was considered a form of disclosure not unrelated to God's merciful presence. Luther and Calvin completely agreed that God is known adequately only in Christ.

The precise relation of Christ to the Godhead was not a problem of direct concern, as it had been in the early church. The issues of the sixteenth century concerned justification, and such doctrines as the Incarnation and the Trinity were largely taken as part of the received faith which needed no reformation. Luther expressed some distaste for the formulations which emerged from the early controversies, but he accepted and expounded them. His battle was not on that level. Calvin wrote with greater detail than did Luther but also followed the lead of the earlier centuries.

Far more important for the reformers was the claim that God assumed the sins of mankind in the life, death and resurrection of Christ. This was the question of Christ's "work" rather than his "person." "For our sake he made him to be sin who knew no sin," writes St. Paul. For Luther, Christ is the true sinner who never committed sin, and for Calvin, "the Son of God, though perfectly free from all sin, nevertheless assumed the disgrace and ignominy of our iniquities, and, on the other hand, arrayed us in his purity." [15] Calvin further declared that Christ is the "sacrifice" for our sins and that he has enough merit for us all. In one way or another the reformers claimed that God took sin upon himself, that it cost God something to overcome sin but not in such a way as to threaten or frustrate his being. The glory of God's righteousness is that he did not ask man to assume the responsibility for unbelief and offenses, but took it upon himself.

On the *way* in which God assumed the sin of man, Luther and Calvin differed. Stressing the titles *prophet, priest,* and *king,* Calvin described how Christ fits these categories more adequately than all predecessors. Taken together they point to the exalted majesty of Christ in roles which took him through suffering to

[15] *Ibid.,* II, xvi, 6

glory. For Luther, however, the recurring theme is the majesty of God descending to the lowliness of a human form in which no titles of honor are implied. God's strength is hidden in his weakness, and this marvel never ceased to fascinate Luther. In this form God outwitted even the devil. Luther declared Christ to be the bait with which God caught the devil, for the latter expected a display of power, not a power of weakness which was stronger than the strength of all other power. Luther did not mean that the weakness of Christ was weakness as usually understood, nor that weakness as such has particular strength. He was more interested in the form of apparent weakness through which God's power was manifest. Such power, whatever its form, was to be given its full weight as power.

Christ's redemptive power is particularly evident as power in view of the forces over and against which it is exercised. Luther, as St. Paul before him, said that we wrestle not only with flesh and blood (human beings), but also with principalities and powers (that is, structures of evil and sin which are more powerful than individuals and the sum of their evil activities. Feeling for such structures has been lost in the modern world generally, but recurs in relation to the political constellations of evil.) The words *sin, death, the devil, powers of darkness,* include the sins of individual men, but they represent forces which are a part of the structure of things. The sins of individuals belong to situations of evil which have a reality greater than the individuals involved. That is why they represent powers to be opposed and overcome by a strength not one's own. Christ is the sure conqueror of these forces. His reign means that although the powers of evil are not yet subdued, their final subjugation is already assured. The clearest expression of this outlook is in Luther's hymn, "A Mighty Fortress is Our God."

The stark contrast between the forces of evil and the lowliness of Christ is one of the reasons for Luther's conviction that God's presence in Christ is not self-evident. God hides himself in Christ in order to make himself known. Faith must pierce the veil; it must be given to one to see the power and love of God in his lowliness. God for Luther is not self-evidently love. God's love is the miracle which human eyes are not able to see, unless it

has been given to them to see through the providential activity
of God. God is never apprehended directly. He makes himself
known through a veil. He is to be found only as he is in Christ,
but even in Christ he cannot be possessed. He confronts man from
out of the mystery of his being as genuine love. There is sufficient
knowledge of God to exclude the plea that he is sheer mystery,
attractive or unattractive; there is sufficient mystery so that man
can never claim he has understood or fathomed the miracle of
God's love and concern.

It is such faith also which lies behind the affirmations of creation and God's providential governance of the world. Both Luther
and Calvin were convinced that the concept of God as the creator
distinguishes the biblical idea of God from all other gods in the
history of religion. Such a positive affirmation of the world is to
be found nowhere else. As men of their time, the reformers accepted the Genesis story in its cosmological detail as well as in its
meaning for faith. But they were not concerned with "scientific"
proofs or disproofs. God as creator was an item of faith.

It was also affirmed that the God who made the world was
still at work in it and exceedingly active in its history. This attes-
tation, too, rested upon faith, not upon proof. Calvin was willing
to offer some evidence of God's activity. But Luther, more often
than not, could find no reason for believing in God on the basis
of ordinary observation of the world. The world appeared to
him as a spectacle of disorder rather than of order, or unreason
rather than reason, of injustice rather than of justice. His faith
triumphed over his inclinations, as in the famous assertion that
the essence of faith is to believe God just though he looks so
terribly unjust.

3. BIBLE, CHURCH AND TRADITION

a. Word within the Bible   *Shades of neo-orthodoxy*

For Luther and Calvin, God can be known adequately only
through the Bible. It was, after all, on the basis of the Bible that
the Reformation was launched. But when the reformers referred
to the Bible as the Word of God they did not in the first instance

mean that the book and the revelation were the same. Calvin, more than Luther, insisted also upon the text of the Bible as itself the Word of God, but he did so on the basis of the word which spoke to man from the Bible. The Bible's authority as the Word rested upon its *content,* its central message. There was no acceptance of the Bible simply as "sacred book."

Even the content of the Bible must be *experienced* as the judging, forgiving presence of God in Christ for it to be the Word of God. The Word is discovered through the Bible, but it is Word because confirmed in the hearts of believers through the Holy Spirit. At the same time, that which the Spirit confirms corresponds to the Christ portrayed in the Bible. Calvin declared that

> the word has not much certainty with us, unless confirmed by the testimony of the Spirit, for the Lord hath established a kind of mutual connection between the certainty of reverence for the word, when by the light of the Spirit, we are enabled therein to behold the Divine countenance; and, on the other hand, without the least fear of mistake, we gladly receive the Spirit, when we recognize him in his image, that is, in the word . . . God did not publish his word to mankind for the sake of momentary ostentation, with a design to destroy or annul it immediately on the advent of the Spirit; but he afterwards sent the same Spirit by whose agency he had dispensed his word, to complete his work by an efficacious confirmation of that word.[16]

This equally excludes all appeals either to the scripture apart from the Spirit or to the Spirit apart from the scripture. The Word must live through the Spirit, and the life in the Spirit must be checked by its correspondence to the content of scripture. On this point, Luther and Calvin were in total agreement.

They differed in the understanding of the scope of the content. For Luther there is a Bible within the Bible. This inner Bible is Christ, and the whole Bible is characterized as the cradle in which Christ is laid. Only Christ is finally important; everything else in the Bible is important only as the matrix in which Christ is found. This implies that not everything in the Bible is of the same value. For instance, Luther called the epistle of James a "right strawy epistle," since it did not conform to what

[16] *Ibid.,* I, ix, 3.

he believed to be the central norm of the Bible, that is, Christ
and his redeeming activity. Instead of anchoring works in faith,
it made works a clue to faith. Though a lofty document, he felt
it missed the central point in an important problem. He further
affirmed that anybody with sufficient inspiration could write biblical books, though he believed that inspiration had disappeared
and therefore we are safe only if we confine ourselves to the
present canon.

In the eyes of Luther, the emphasis upon the Bible within the
Bible resulted neither in subjectivism (that is, taking what one
wants and leaving the rest) nor in inability to determine what
is the core of the Bible. He was certain that there was a sufficiently clear and central body of material concerning Christ
which would be common property to those who searched the
Bible and had been grasped by God's redeeming work. He was
convinced that a clear reading of the Bible would result in the
emergence of God's justifying work as the central point.[17]

Although Calvin, like Luther, emphasized that faith in Christ
is the central part of the gospel and therefore of the Bible, his
interpretation was distinctly different. Calvin insisted on the
fundamental unity of the Bible and therefore on the validity of
most everything within it. For example, in considering the relation of law and gospel, Calvin distinguished between the two but
also insisted upon their unity. Word and Spirit are conjoined on
every page of the Bible and, although Christ is the center of the
gospel, God speaks through every page of the Bible. At times,
this principle made it necessary for Calvin to devote pages to
reconciling contradictory passages of scripture. It should be made
clear, however, that Calvin identified the Bible with the word of
God only in the sense that faith in Christ attested to its authen-

[17] This has always been the contention of Protestants and there is ample
evidence of its validity. Protestants, as the following chapters will show,
have not always seen this as the central point nor understood it in the
same way. But they have frequently been driven back to it. Even the many
denominations and sects do not destroy this principle. This diversity is not
considered too great a price for the freedom which each individual has of
direct access through the Bible to God's disclosure of himself. As a matter
of fact, the stress on individual interpretation arose partly out of this Reformation emphasis, but partly also as a reaction to the fact that the original churches of the Reformation themselves did not permit the freedom
which their principle of interpretation demanded.

ticity. He was not a literalist or fundamentalist in the twentieth-century sense (see Ch. X). He did not move from a conviction of verbal inspiration to faith, but from faith in Christ, grounded in the Bible, to a concept of total inspiration. In this sense, he was less free in dealing with the Bible than Luther was.

Both agreed that God can use any vehicle in addressing man. Luther declared that if God once spoke through Balaam's ass, he can speak through anything, whether stone, stick, thunder or what not. Nevertheless, both agreed that men should look for God in the Bible, and primarily in the witness which the Bible makes to Christ. Every other disclosure of the divine ought to be checked by its correspondence with what is known of God through Christ, and that is mediated through the Bible.

b. Church and Sacraments

Since faith is born and based in a gospel indissolubly connected with the Bible, the Bible must stand over the church as the continual norm for its faith. Luther and Calvin were, of course, aware that the Bible was originally the product of the church, but they insisted that the gospel is nevertheless based in the inspired character of books which in a unique way become the means of faith. The church therefore is nourished by the Word of God, particularly as found in the Bible. The church is not the guardian of the Bible; rather the Bible is the guardian of the church because in it is the source of the Christian life. The gospel is associated with the Bible in a way it is not with the church. Through its impact on men, the Bible creates the church.

The church is the community or fellowship of believers, those who are committed to God in Christ and who live by his mercy and power. Their community is anchored in a common faith in a common Lord; they meet together to hear God's Word preached and considered; they participate in the sacraments as particular and significant acts instituted in the time of the New Testament. In worship they give thanks for God's marvelous mercy, confess their sins, hope to be renewed in mind and spirit, hear the meaning of particular passages of scripture interpreted by ministers—all in the faith that God will make himself known for their daily existence.

Differences within the church are functional and vocational. There is no difference of status before God for clergy and for laity. The two reformers did not believe that everyone should function as a clergyman. They were much too insistent on order in the church to risk such anarchy. The concept of the priesthood of all believers did not mean that the clergy are superfluous. But utilizing the medieval concept of priesthood as the necessary mediation of the presence of God in Christ, Luther graphically showed how each man himself confronts God and neighbor as priest or mediator. Before self and God, there can stand no priest. Here one is his own priest. No one can have faith for another. It can only be his own. Likewise in relation to neighbor, no persons or groups can claim to be special channels of grace. We are all priests in mediating Christ to our fellowmen, neighbors in the deepest sense of the term.

In the life of the Christian, the priesthood of all believers means being a witness to God's redeeming activity and presence in every circumstance. This is the theoretical base for the concept of "vocation," which Luther stripped of its medieval hierarchical distinction. Now one can be equally a Christian in every decent calling; no calling is "higher" than another. The cobbler who exercises his calling with Christian responsibility is doing his task under God with the same significance as the minister who functions in the church. The difference between cobbler and minister is one of function. They stand equally under God, and both are called upon to think out their Christian faith, to nourish it, and to witness to others by being Christians in their tasks. The minister, to be sure, has a particular responsibility to expound the gospel and his faithfulness to that task will be a sign of the fulfillment of a proper vocation. He may know more of the intricacies of the Bible and of its meaning, but this will provide him neither with more faith nor with certainty in what he believes.

Early in the Reformation, the church was described as the place where the Word is rightly preached and the sacraments rightly administered. Calvin very clearly uses this formulation in the fourth book of the Institutes. In the Reformation churches preaching assumed an importance it did not have in churches which were primarily sacramental. The faithful exercise of expounding scripture was a real criterion for the adequacy of the minister, since the Word and its correlative, faith, were the basis of the life of the church. The minister was a steward of the mysteries of God. He could not give another man faith, but he was responsible for the faithful setting forth of God's redemptive message and in this way indirectly responsible for the life and vitality of the flock entrusted to him.

no Neither the preached nor the written word was in itself the Word of God. They became the Word of God when they became alive in the heart and mind of man through the Spirit. One came to the faith either through the written or preached word, usually the latter. Therefore preaching, as the explication of the biblical word, could be said to be more primary than sacraments.

Luther and Calvin insisted that the word be preached each time the sacrament was given. Preaching was for the imparting of faith, for instruction and for the confrontation with God's judging and redeeming word. The sacraments presupposed this faith. Therefore, one of the prerequisites of a proper sacrament was the faith of the believer. In addition, the criteria of a sacrament included an instituted sign or visible act (water in baptism and bread and wine in the Lord's Supper) and a spoken word of promise in connection with the acts (the forgiveness of sins) — these being founded in the New Testament. The application of these criteria required the reduction of the number of sacraments to two: baptism and the Lord's Supper.

Having rejected the medieval sacramental theories, Luther nevertheless found himself in controversy over the understanding of both sacraments. On the question of baptism, he found himself between the Anabaptists and the Roman Catholics. The Anabaptists (see Ch. III) rejected infant baptism because an infant could not be considered to have faith. It was believers who were to be baptized into the community. Luther was convinced, however, that faith is more than intellectual assent, and he felt that the Anabaptists had relegated it to that level. For him, faith includes a total commitment based upon the activity of God and cannot be confined to the age of reason or possible rational decision. Neither could he accept the magical view of baptism in the

medieval church, according to which grace automatically restored the grace lost through original sin. Luther resorted to the
idea of "infantile faith" as his way of stressing the importance of
faith against all magical theories. At the same time, this provided
him with a weapon against the Anabaptists, who in spite of their
emphasis on Spirit seemed to him to rationalize the religious
dimension by confusing it with consciousness. It is perhaps just
as well that Luther did not explain the term "infantile faith";
one can, however, understand why he came to it.

For both Luther and Calvin, baptism is the sacrament in
which, through God's promise and its acceptance in faith, man
dies to sin and is reborn in faith. This symbolism is accepted
even when faith is not a conscious possibility, and emphasis falls
upon the faith of the congregation in initiating the individual
into the Christian fold. It is the symbol and sign of the Christian's
forgiveness.

Controversy over the Lord's Supper was chiefly between
Luther and Zwingli, one of the great reformers of Zurich. Emphasizing God's promise in connection with the sacrament,
Luther assumed that the words, "This is my body," surely meant
no less than actual body. As a minimum he interpreted this to
mean that in faith God in Christ is present, in, with, and under
the elements, both in bodily and spiritual form. He did not
accept the medieval notion that the bread and wine are changed
into the body and blood of Christ, while remaining under the
accidents of bread and wine. But he did insist that Christ is
bodily present, even as he is spiritually present. Christ therefore
is not bodily sitting on the right hand of God. His body or his
spirit is potentially everywhere. Without this, Luther insisted,
Christ is not fully present. Calvin, too, emphasized bodily as well
as spiritual presence, but still maintained that Christ is seated at
the right hand of the Father in glory. Like Luther, he insisted on
the bodily presence as a way of affirming God's veritable presence
to him who believes it. Unlike Luther, he did not spell it out in
a metaphysical way. Actually, Luther and Calvin are very close
on this basic understanding of the Lord's Supper. It was Zwingli
rather than Calvin who influenced the reformed tradition at this
point. Zwingli emphasized that the Lord's Supper was estab-

lished in the New Testament through the rite in which Jesus declared "This do in remembrance of me." He did not say that one partakes of the elements simply in memory of Jesus whom one thinks significant in some way or another. He meant that through this act, instituted in the New Testament, the believer is graphically reminded of and participates in the total drama of God's redeeming activity in Christ. One is nourished in faith as he engages in an act which vividly recalls the total meaning of the life, death and resurrection of Christ. This act is a visible sign in which is telescoped the total gospel in a way words could not convey. The remembrance is a dramatic presentation of the whole of that which is at the basis of faith.

The differences in understanding of the Lord's Supper as exhibited by Luther and Calvin on the one side, and Zwingli on the other, are indeed vast. Luther was probably correct in his statement to the Zwinglian party that they were of a different spirit. Yet both spirits have been a part of Protestantism and have not necessarily been a different faith. The interpretation came together at the crucial point, viewing the Lord's Supper as a particularly instituted rite having to do with the forgiveness of sins.

c. Word over tradition

Such differences in theological formulation must be seen in the light of the reformers' insistence that the authority of the Word can be guaranteed neither by ecclesiastical authority nor by tradition. Neither Luther, Calvin nor Zwingli accepted the notion that tradition is finally decisive. They were aware of the dangers in breaking with the past. The most difficult taunts Luther had to bear were those which suggested that he was going against the practice and wisdom of the ages and setting himself up as the interpreter and custodian of truth. He finally insisted that his conscience was captive to the Word of God and that this was his authority over against all tradition. The problem was more difficult for Luther than for Calvin, since by the time of the latter, the initial break had already been made.

Luther and Calvin both studied and knew the church Fathers. They quoted Augustine most. Ideally, the Fathers were to be

understood as those who expounded biblical truth, who led men
to an understanding of the Bible. Actually, both of the reformers
(Luther particularly) felt that the Fathers generally led not to
the clarity of the gospel, but away from it. Even the councils of
the church could not be taken as finally authoritative or necessarily correct. Luther pointed out frequently that it was often a
council which called the results of a previous council heretical.
Calvin remarked that one ought to argue from scripture and that
from this perspective,

> councils would retain all the majesty which is due to them,
> while at the same time the scripture would hold the pre-
> eminence, so that everything would be subject to its
> standard.[18]

Tradition is not to be taken lightly, but it is to be corrected by
biblical truth. That is why Luther, while reluctant, did not
shrink from the *reforming* task. The reformers did not believe
they were starting a new church. They believed that they were
calling the church to a more adequate reflection of the gospel
which was its base. Moreover, they believed this is a continual
necessity. When, therefore, Rome would not reform, they felt
that it was no longer the church. They felt their work to be in
the tradition of the ages. But they were convinced that the life
of the church in each age is nourished by the biblical faith, not
tradition. The gospel itself is the only proper tradition, imper-
fectly but significantly reflected in a continuously reforming
church.

4. THE CHRISTIAN AND THE STATE

For Luther, the Christian finds his life in two spheres—the
spiritual and the temporal. Similarly, Calvin distinguishes between the inward and outward aspects of government, the former
referring to the inner life of the soul in its earthly pilgrimage, and
the latter to forms of external conduct. For both men, there is an
individual and a corporate ethic.

We have discussed the nature of ethics insofar as it concerns
the basis and direction of man's life (sect. 1, c, above). Here it is

---

[18] *Ibid.*, IV, ix, 8.

important to recall that Luther had such confidence in Christians that he believed they do not need the state themselves, but obey it out of love for the neighbor. For Luther, the state is a remedy for sin, preventing disorder and anarchy. In accord with his own understanding that the Christian is still sinner, it would have been logical to assume that the state, too, would still be needed if all men were Christians. Luther's statement must, however, be understood in an ideal sense; he never anticipated that it would be realized in this life.

Calvin emphasized progress in the Christian life much more than did Luther, but he insisted that Christians, too, need the state for the welfare and ordering of their own lives. The state is a remedy for sin. But even more, it exists as a place of concord, order and relative peace given by God for the well-being of the Christian in his earthly pilgrimage toward final redemption. Though related to sin, the state is a very positive blessing of God. One of its tasks is even to guarantee and protect pure religion. (Luther did not consider this a necessary function of the state, but he was willing to call upon Christian princes to reform a church which would not reform itself.)

For both reformers, the state is ordained of God and a gift for this life. Therefore, Christians are not to despise it but to accept it. They are to obey it and not interfere with its functioning. Men in authority are like gods under God, given the responsibility of order and concord in the world and the suppression of disorder and anarchy. Rulers ought, to be sure, to govern justly, and if they do not they will ultimately pay the penalty before God. They can and must be called to account by the Word of God, even the preached Word of God. But, Luther held, they cannot be actively resisted. In the face of injustice, the Christian can only suffer. He cannot rebel.

The difficulties of Luther's approach became apparent in the Peasants' Revolution (1524–25). Although personally sympathetic to the cause of the peasants, Luther wrote vitriolic attacks against them when they revolted. Partly Luther acted out of religious conviction. But other important factors also played their part. He felt that the peasants were confusing their cause with the Reformation. Further, he lived in an explosive period and, as

is usual in such times, had a much greater fear of anarchy than of
tyranny. Authority must be preserved.

Yet Luther's claim of loyalty to God against every tyrant is
unmistakable. Man's obedience to God is more ultimate than his
duty to the state. Therefore God must be obeyed above all else.
Perhaps because of the peculiar problems of his own situation,
Luther did not see the full implications of this position. (It was
just this claim to loyalty to God above all else which was used by
Norwegian Lutherans as the basis for their valiant resistance
against the Nazis.)

Calvin, no less than Luther, urged obedience to duly constituted authority, but he made at least two significant qualifying
statements which became of fundamental importance for posterity. Speaking of obedience to parents enjoined by the fifth commandment, he stated that they are to be obeyed "in the Lord"—
that is, as parents who do not demand what is contrary to God.
"If they [parents] instigate us to any transgression of the law, we
may justly consider them not as parents, but as strangers who
attempt to seduce us from obedience to our real Father. The same
observation is applicable to princes, lords, and superiors of every
description." [19] Thus, if any superior violates our religious obligations, we may refuse to regard him as a constituted authority. In
another passage, Calvin suggests how such an attitude might find
implementation. Resistance to evil rulers is not the right of private
persons but of lesser magistrates.

> For though the correction of tyrannical domination is the
> vengeance of God, we are not, therefore, to conclude that it
> is committed to us who have received no other command
> than to obey and suffer. This observation I always apply to
> private persons. For if there be, in the present day, any
> magistrates appointed for the protection of the people and
> the moderation of the power of kings, such as were in
> ancient times the Ephori, who were a check upon the kings
> among the Lacedaemonians, or the popular tribunes upon
> the consuls among the Romans, or the Demarchi upon the
> senate among the Athenians; or with power such as perhaps
> is now possessed by the three estates in every kingdom when
> they are assembled; I am so far from prohibiting them in
> the discharge of their duty, to oppose the violence or cruelty

[19] *Ibid.*, II, viii, 38.

of kings that I affirm that if they connive at kings in their
oppression of their people, such forbearance involves the
most nefarious perfidy because they fraudulently betray the
liberty of the people of which they know that they have
been appointed protectors by the ordination of God.[20]

Luther himself showed a similar understanding in changing his
support from the emperor to the princes in the struggle over
Roman Catholicism. He shifted his support when a number of
jurists declared that the princes were the duly constituted authority since the emperor no longer acted as such.

More important than such technical possibilities was the basic
religious affirmation that man's allegiance is to a sovereign God
above all sovereignties. Under such a claim, princes, kings and
empires frequently were resisted (and not only passively) and
not infrequently transformed. Political developments in England
and America particularly were related to this claim (see Chs.
V, VII).

The state was never considered an end in itself, and just
because it served primarily as a means toward another end,
neither Luther nor Calvin paid much attention to the form and
structure of government. Yet there is a passage in Calvin's *Institutes* which may not be altogether unrelated to the American
Constitution and the notion of the distribution of power.

> The vice or imperfection of men therefore renders it safer
> and more tolerable for the government to be in the hands of
> many, that they may afford each other mutual assistance
> and admonition, and that if any one arrogate to himself
> more than is right, the many may act as censors and masters
> to restrain his ambition.[21]

Here the plea for the distribution of power is not that all men
are capable of its exercise, but that men are not to be trusted with
too much power.

5. THE "LAST THINGS"

The reformers stressed obedience to the state, not for the
sake of power or of absolutist claims, but because it served an

[20] *Ibid.*, IV, xx, 31.
[21] *Ibid.*, IV, xx, 8.

interim purpose. All life is a pilgrimage destined to its final fulfillment in the kingdom of God. God's reign in the lives of individuals
is the beginning of that kingdom and the basis for affirming its
final consummation. Christians are pilgrims, but it is the faith of
pilgrims which is the basis for the resurrection and kingdom
hope. Because they know of the power of God now, they are able
to affirm the eventual advent of the fullness of the kingdom. In
Calvin's *Institutes,* the section on the resurrection stands at the
end of the material on the Christian life. This is a reminder that
it is the present faith of Christians which is related to the resurrection faith. Without the latter, faith would be in vain. But without present faith as its authentic basis, men believe in the kingdom because of fear. For Luther "the fear of the gallows" was an
impossible reason for being a Christian. Only he whose faith is
meaningful in the present is safely permitted to think of the future
life.

Neither Luther nor Calvin speculated on the nature of the
future life. Luther believed that God's kingdom would soon be at
hand. He interpreted the upheavals of his day to be the travail
and tribulation before the end. This mistaken historical judgment
does not, however, invalidate the affirmation of a kingdom which
in its fullness depends wholly on the act of God, and certainly not
upon the calculation of men.

The kingdom cannot be described.

> For though we are plainly informed that the Kingdom of
> God is full of light, joy, felicity and glory, yet all that is
> mentioned remains far above our comprehension and envel-
> oped, as it were, in enigmatical obscurity till the arrival of
> that day when He shall exhibit His glory to us face to face. [22]

It is more wonderful than the joy of present faith, yet that joy is
sufficient for the present. Luther and Calvin believed in the future
life, in the fullness of God's kingdom. But they were not obsessed
with it. Because their hope in its final reality was grounded in
faith itself, they confidently lived in the present world.

[22] *Ibid.,* III, xxv, 10.

III

Other Reformation Patterns

While Luther and Calvin (together with Zwingli) were laying the foundations for the development of the Lutheran and Reformed traditions (see Ch. IV), there were other Reformation developments in Germany, Switzerland, Holland, and England. Chief among these were the Anabaptist movement on the Continent and the English Reformation. Both of these were related to the work of the reformers we have discussed, but they also had independent roots. Their patterns of thought and institution were forged not only in opposition to the medieval church but also in contrast with the Lutheran and Reformed developments. For the Anabaptists, Luther and Calvin had not gone far enough in the restoration of the New Testament church forms; for the Anglicans, they had departed too far from the historical traditions of the church. Both of these movements thus represent distinctive (though not wholly independent) Reformation traditions.

1. THE ANABAPTIST TRADITION

During the very period in which Luther was thinking through the implications of the newly rediscovered faith, there appeared other men and movements who thought of the reconstitution of the church in ways much more radical. Many of these groups arose independently of each other. But common to them was the conviction that the presence of the Spirit of God in the lives of believers called for a drastic return to the church as it existed in the New Testament period. These groups sometimes disagreed sharply on the meaning of the Spirit's presence, and occasionally some engaged in excesses which gave a "bad" name to the rest. Most of the groups, however, were of a more stable nature and in the course of approximately fifteen years there developed a common Anabaptist tradition. We shall first consider the beginnings of the movement, and then the central tradition as it developed.

a. Anabaptist Beginnings and Struggles

One of the earliest manifestations of the radical Reformation spirit occurred in the city of Wittenberg while Luther was in seclusion at the Wartburg (1521). Here a group under the leadership of Andreas Carlstadt insisted that the reform of the church included the rejection of images and music as well as of the medieval understanding of the Mass. They believed that the former as well as the latter interfered with the worship of God through genuinely spiritual means. The stress upon the spiritual was carried further with the arrival of the Wittenberg "prophets" from the neighboring town of Zwickau. Insisting that God had spoken directly to them through his spirit, these men declared the Bible to be unnecessary. Moreover, they announced that God's kingdom was at hand in the reign of those who were genuinely spiritual. The ungodly would soon be destroyed.

Of an even more radical temperament than either Andreas Carlstadt or the Zwickau prophets was Thomas Müntzer. He emphasized the direct, unmediated presence of the Word and advocated the establishment of the kingdom by physical force if necessary. It was his spirit which was behind various revolutionary activities. More than any other individual, he was responsible for the identification of the peasants' struggle for greater justice with the Reformation cause. He considered that struggle to be the medium through which the reign of the Spirit would be realized and firmly established. (This identification was at least partly responsible for Luther's violent reactions to the Peasants' Revolt.) The present throes marked the dawning of the new day when power would be given to the saints for the destruction of the ungodly. It was inevitable that such advice and practice would meet with the determined opposition of princes and reformers, and that many innocent men would perish in the process.

The best-known attempt to use force as a means of establishing the rule of the saints in the city of Münster occurred approximately a decade after the Peasants' Revolt. Here a group of Anabaptists succeeded for a time in imposing their rule on the city and in establishing a society patterned according to their concept of the New Testament community. The goods of life were shared in accord with the practice described in the book of Acts, and the motivation for this was therefore primarily religious rather than social. The groups also instituted the practice of polygamy. (Luther, too, had not had a wholly good record on this problem, as his consent to the bigamy of Philip of Hesse indicates, though that consent was given grudgingly and under peculiar circumstances.) Aside from powerful sociological reasons for this brief venture into polygamy (notably the surplus of women over men in certain areas), two religious factors must be noted. First, the reconstitution of the faith was so thoroughgoing that even the traditional ethic of monogamy had to be examined. Second, some felt that precedent was at hand in the example of some of the Old Testament patriarchs. Although the practice in Münster led to immorality, it must be kept in mind that in principle polygamy was intended as an answer to the temptation of immorality. Here is a case where practice had the opposite effect of the intention.

The activities of Thomas Müntzer and the later events in the city of Münster were by no means typical of the Anabaptist movement, though they were largely responsible for many of the negative attitudes toward the entire group. There were others who believed in the imminent end of the present stage of history and the advent of the reign of the saints. But in contrast to the revolutionaries, they counseled patient waiting for the end (e.g., Melchior Hofmann). There continued to be many also who believed in the direct accessibility of the Spirit apart from the Bible, and who considered the scriptures unnecessary for salvation (e.g., Hans Denck). There were those who emphasized the individual relation to God without reference to community. Many of these extremists should be characterized as free spirits rather than

Anabaptists. Yet there were individuals within Anabaptist circles of similar tendencies. They became a problem, for although the Anabaptists insisted on each individual's faith, they did *not* generally understand this in an individualistic sense.

Alongside revolutionaries and individualists and men who stressed Spirit over Bible, stood a large number who desired reform from the perspective of a faith looking directly to the biblical tradition. Among leaders in this group were such men as the cultured Conrad Grebel and the distinguished scholar Balthasar Hübmaier. Their activities centered in several Swiss cantons and they came into conflict with Zwinglians in Zurich. There initially friendly disputations about the faith between Anabaptist and Reformed leaders turned into an outright campaign against the former, with the latter receiving the support of civil authorities.

Ostensibly, the point at issue between the Reformed and the Anabaptist groups in Switzerland (and generally elsewhere) was the latter's practice of baptizing persons who had already been baptized as infants. Hence the nickname Anabaptist (i.e., "rebaptizer"). Since the Anabaptists held that there could be no valid baptism apart from the faith of the believer, they rejected the notion that they "rebaptized." Infant baptism was no baptism at all. But this contention carried no weight with those who accepted infant baptism, and the latter were able to find legal basis for suppression of the Anabaptists in an ancient legal code of the Emperor Justinian, which forbade rebaptism.

At the heart of the conflict were different conceptions of the faith as expressed in the understanding of the church (these will be discussed in the next section). However, the excesses of some Anabaptist groups unfortunately fed fuel to the fire of those who already feared the radical emphasis upon the spirit. They saw in this a source of a new disorder equal in danger to that of the medieval church. The good moral character of many of the Anabaptists, including their leaders, was conceded by the opposition. But it was felt that the implications of their position led to disorder and threatened the orderly affairs of the newly emerging Reformation churches. In the course of events, Anabaptist groups were banished and persecuted, while most of the leaders became martyrs through burning or drowning. (The latter was a particularly taunting form of death because of its associations with immersion in baptism.) Few of the leaders of the Anabaptist movement died in bed. But in spite of uprootings, sufferings and the dangers of death, Anabaptist communities arose throughout north central Europe. In Bern, Basel, Strasbourg, Augsburg, Nuremberg, and Münster, there continued to be thriving communities, and numerous groups sprang up in south Germany.

But the core of the Anabaptist movement as it was destined to have its major impact upon posterity did not develop in either Switzerland or Germany. It came instead from Moravia and Holland. The chief leaders of movements which formed a definite Anabaptist tradition were Jakob Huter and Menno Simons. The Hutterites became a disciplined and continuing Anabaptist community in Moravia. Menno Simons was undoubtedly the most outstanding figure in the Anabaptist tradition, and the Mennonites in Holland contributed to the life of Protestantism in ways far beyond the confines of their own groups. Neither the English Baptists nor the Quakers can be traced directly to the Mennonites. But there were some points of contact. It is not too much to say that these Anabaptists provided a type of spirituality which had its effects upon all those who have come into contact with them. Later, the Mennonites in Holland surrendered much of their distinctive witness. The Anabaptist tradition continued with vitality in settlements in Poland, Russia, and Paraguay, but most of all in the Mennonite communities in Pennsylvania.

b. Tenets of Central Anabaptists

In the main stream of Anabaptist life and thought there was agreement that a reconstitution of the church according to the pattern of the new Testament must be effected without compromise at any point. Luther, for example, allowed many existing practices having no basis in the New Testament, provided they did not contradict the essentials of the faith. Not so the Anabaptists. This only proved that Luther, as well as Zwingli, had not gone far enough. They were "half-way" men who had made an excellent beginning but had not drawn the logical conclusion their position demanded.

Actually it was not a matter of drawing a conclusion.[1] We have to do here with a fundamentally different understanding of the church and the Christian life. That is why the Anabaptists form an independent Reformation tradition. Basic to the Anabaptist view is the conviction that the church is a voluntary association of Christians patterned after the New Testament. For the reformers, as we noted in the previous chapter, the church, too, is a community of believers in which faith is related to every aspect of its life. But there is a real difference between believing that faith is decisive for the church, and believing that the faith and life of Christians is itself a norm demanding a particular form of the church. In the sense that the Anabaptists drew the latter conclusion, they could claim that they, rather than the reformers, were carrying out a reformation only half-way completed by the reformers.

It is only as one understands the content of the statement that the church is a community of those who have experienced the living Christ that the genuine differences appear. Luther, Calvin, Zwingli, and the Anabaptists alike could make this statement. But the Anabaptists drew the further inference that a new pattern of life is at the heart of the New Testament, and that therefore the New Testament forms must be followed in every respect, including the order and practice of the church.

For the Anabaptists, then, the new life in Christ through the Spirit rather than justification by faith is the center of the New Testament faith and therefore of the church. The life of the redeemed, the presence of the Spirit in believers, is foremost. Not the Word of God as found in the Bible, but the experience of Christ's presence is the foundation of the church. The Spirit of Christ spread abroad in the human heart is more important than any endeavor to understand the content of God's disclosure, whether found in the Bible or expressed in theological statements. The New Testament is a book of the Christian life, and authoritative in that sense.

[1] One of the recurring sources of confusion in Protestantism is that those who stand in the Lutheran and Reformed tradition see only anarchy in the outlook of those who stress the Spirit and voluntary association, and that those who stand in the "free church" tradition prefer to view themselves as having carried the Reformation to its logical conclusion.

The Anabaptists vigorously responded to all problems from the conviction that all that matters is the manifest vitality of Christian saints. That conviction provides the clue to what they rejected and what they affirmed. They were not interested in how men became saints, but in the life of men now walking on a path leading toward perfection. That is why the struggle over justification was not central to their outlook and frequently appeared to them as theological bickering. They were interested in the "life" of the church rather than in its thought. Theology was considered a highly suspicious enterprise in which theologians spun out theses which were a stumbling block to those of simple but genuine faith. Anabaptists trusted farmers and craftsmen more than theologians. Those who were the regenerate constituted the church, quite apart from how they understood the relation of faith and works.

But theology was only one of the ways in which the Anabaptists saw the church as threatened by loss of its life. The church also lost its true nature when it was no longer confined to the regenerated and their own tests for membership in the community. For many Anabaptists, the adoption of Christianity as the religion of the empire (under Constantine) marked the "fall" of the church. Belonging to the church became no longer a matter of decision but of birth and social destiny. The vitality and very essence of the church as a voluntary association was destroyed. There were others who dated the fall of the church with the Council of Nicaea in 325. This represented the crystallization of trinitarian thought, precipitated by the intrigues of the powerful Roman empire and expressed through the speculation of philosophers. For others, it was the enforcement of infant baptism in 407 (with penalty for failure to comply).

Common to the different theories of the fall of the church was the contention that the true nature of the church as a voluntary, disciplined community of saints had been abandoned. To the Anabaptists, Luther and Calvin were not sufficiently clear exactly at this point. The reformers' hopes of community or territorial churches, enforced through the arms of the state, were themselves a part of the pattern which characterized a fallen church.

For the Anabaptists, the only possible church is a voluntary but disciplined community of saints patterned after the New Testament community. In this community there is no distinction even of function, between clergy and laity. Those who have the Spirit are Christians and therefore equally a source of Christian truth and action. The priesthood of all believers refers not only to each man's relation to God and to his priesthood to neighbor, as in Luther. It refers also to the equality of all men in the Christian community in respect to formal function. No man has any status not possessed by all. (Reluctantly, many of the Anabaptist communities did have to separate functions in such a way that some functioned as "clergy." But nowhere, except among the Quakers, has lay responsibility been greater.)

It was the community, chiefly through its leaders, which exercised the discipline required in the life of the church. The church was a voluntary and free association; but it implied a discipline and a way of life. Those who violated God's commands and did not exhibit the presence of the Spirit were warned, sometimes placed on probation, not infrequently punished, and occasionally barred from the community. But the church could maintain its discipline and life only by being a society "withdrawn." Therefore, Anabaptists were concerned primarily with fellow Christians, except in the case of missionary preaching (the object of which obviously was to bring others into the fold).

The purity of the community had to be maintained, both by internal discipline and by the inclusion only of those who are Christians by free decisions. Thus, the church must be a separate community, and in particular separate from the state. Most Anabaptists admitted that the state was a necessary institution for mankind and even for themselves, but they did not find it possible to assume any responsibility for it. For example, they felt that a Christian could not be a magistrate because he would contaminate and perhaps vitiate the witness he must make to the peace and order of the new life in Christ. Likewise, they refused to participate in war and to swear oaths of any kind. These acts violated the new life in Christ as exhibited in the injunctions of the New Testament.

It was the insistence upon the church as a community of the new life, patterned after the New Testament, which led to the Anabaptist view of baptism. Wrote Menno Simons:

> We are not regenerated because we have been baptized
> . . . but we are baptized because we have been regenerated
> by faith and the Word of God (I Pet. 1:23). Regeneration
> is not the result of baptism, but baptism the result of re-
> generation. This can indeed not be controverted by any
> man, or disproved by the Scriptures.[2]

Baptism is the indication that one believes in the forgiveness of sins and the new life in Christ. It is not a medium for either, but rather an expression of the acceptance of both. It is not absolutely necessary, being one of the least of the commandments given by Christ.

Such a view of baptism demands believers who have reached some degree of consciousness and maturity. Simons rejected Luther's concept of infantile faith. By definition, infant baptism is meaningless. Moreover, the Anabaptists could find no basis whatsoever for infant baptism in the Bible. Infant baptism, there-fore, violates the two criteria of the church, the voluntary nature of faith and the New Testament pattern. It places the cart before the horse; baptism must follow faith, not precede it. Baptism is not an instrument of grace; it is an expression of the fact of grace already visibly present.

The same logic applies to the Lord's Supper. In the words of Balthasar Hübmaier:

> That is the true communion of the saints, which is not a
> communion because the bread is broken; but where the
> bread is broken because the communion has preceded and
> been enclosed in the heart since Christ has come in the
> flesh. For not all who break the bread are partakers of the
> body and blood of Christ, which I prove by the traitor
> Judas. But those who are now in communion inwardly and
> in spirit, they may also use this bread and wine worthily in
> an outward way. . . .[3]

[2] Harold S. Bender, *Menno Simons' Life and Writings,* Mennonite Publishing House, 1936, 78.
[3] Balthasar Hübmaier, *A Form for the Celebration of the Lord's Supper,* in Harry Emerson Fosdick, *Great Voices of the Reformation,* 312–313.

In no sense does anything special happen in the elements of the Lord's Supper. It is the outward expression of a communion and community which exists, the fellowship of forgiven sinners who are saints. It is a rite of fellowship inaugurated in the early church. There is no presence of Christ in the elements.

Such are the main tenets of this Reformation tradition. It is related to the Lutheran and Reformed traditions, but definitely distinctive in its understanding of the biblical faith. The church is a creation of the voluntary, free association of believers, uncoerced by either hierarchy or state. Everything which threatens this way of life of the church must be rejected, not violently but through suffering if necessary. The faith of the Christian is nourished by the Bible. But more than that, the Bible provides a definite pattern for the expression of that faith through the discipline of the saints. In the Anabaptist tradition, the freedom of the Christian is combined with the utmost of discipline in community.

2. THE ENGLISH REFORMATION AND THE FORMATION OF ANGLICANISM

The Anglican tradition was explicitly forged in the context of English history, so much so that it is necessary to speak of an "English Reformation." There were, to be sure, important influences from the Continent, but both in the break with Rome and in the pattern of reform, the English movement was distinctive. More than any other of the churches with a Reformation history, Anglicanism bears the marks of a national church. In order to understand the ethos and development characterized as central Anglicanism, it is necessary to look briefly at the events of the English Reformation, with its unique intertwining of affairs of state and church.

a. From Reforming Activities to the Elizabethan Settlement

In England, as on the Continent, there were signs of unrest before the Reformation. We have already noted the activities of Wyclife (Ch. I). Remnants of the Lollard tradition still survived, and there were other religious associations such as the "Christian brethren" or "known men." In addition, the Renaissance humanist tradition was strong. One need only recall the names of such men as John Colet, the dean of St. Paul's, and Sir Thomas More, author of the famous *Utopia*.

More explosive than the foregoing was the relation of the English nation to both papacy and foreign political powers. The suppression by the papacy of some of the English monasteries (a practice later adopted by Henry VIII on a much wider scale and also mainly for financial reasons), with the revenue from sale of the properties going to Rome, raised the ire of many an Englishman. The assignment of Italian priests, many of whom were unable to speak English, was a further source of offense. In general, the English were tired of domination and interference by foreign power.

The spark which lit the fire was the refusal of the papacy to annul the marriage of Henry VIII and Katherine of Aragon. Although the papacy had waived canon law to permit Henry to marry the widow of his brother, it was unwilling to annul the marriage, primarily because of the risk of finally alienating the Holy Roman Emperor and King of Spain, Charles V (nephew of Katherine), upon whose good will the papacy had to depend at this time. Henry's concern for the continuation of his line and the stability of England had been expressed long before his fascination with Anne Boleyn. Since severe civil strife had been occasioned in an earlier time by lack of a male descendant for the throne, he was much exercised over the increasingly unlikely prospect of a male heir issuing from his marriage to Katherine. In order to effect an annullment, Henry broke the ties with Rome by a series of bold acts. Having deposed Cardinal Wolsey, he forbade appeals to Rome without the King's consent, and required through Parliamentary act that the clergy continue to function despite possible papal excommunication. In Thomas Cranmer, who had been sympathetic to the annulment and had suggested a university rather than canon law decision, the King found a ready Archbishop of Canterbury who might be the primate of all England. But the top position Henry reserved for himself. The Act of Supremacy (1534) declared: "The King's majesty justly and rightly is and ought to be and shall be reputed the only supreme head in earth of the Church of England called

Anglicana Ecclesia." Nevertheless, he was not a priest. He appointed, but could not consecrate bishops; he could defend the faith, but he could not declare dogma. But h` was head of a new national church.

Under Henry, however, "reformation" in practice or doctrine was not very extensive. He insisted on a Bible in every parish, with a chapter to be read each Sunday. The Ten Articles of Religion of 1536 made reference to the authority of the Bible and justification by faith, but made these no more central than in the medieval church generally. In fact, Henry himself approved of the use of images, invocations to the departed saints, the concept of purgatory and masses for those who still sojourned there, transubstantiation together with communion in one element only, celibacy for the clergy, private masses and auricular confessions.

These views were not shared by the then Archbishop of Canterbury, Thomas Cranmer, whose influence reached its height in the reign of Edward VI, only son of Henry VIII. Edward was still a young boy at the time of his accession (1547), and the regime was first under the protectorate of the Duke of Somerset, and then of the Duke of Northumberland. In both instances, the affairs of church were dominated by Cranmer and his associates, including many of the continental reformers who in this period found refuge in England. Among these were Martin Bucer, the Strasbourg reformer, and Peter Martyr, one of the early Lutheran theologians. It was during this period that the English Reformation was closest to that of the Continent. During the first protectorate, a general Lutheran outlook prevailed, and during the second, views reflecting both Luther and Calvin. The two prayer books of Edward's reign represent the two traditions. Although these views did not prevail, permanent changes dating from this period center in the abolition of considerable medieval ceremony and liturgical practice. Rome was declared wrong in faith, transubstantiation was decisively rejected, marriage of the clergy was permitted, auricular confession was abolished, and communion was administered to the people with both bread and wine. But during this period when the continental influence was at its highest, the episcopacy was accepted without question and pains were taken to guarantee adequate succession.

Edward, always in poor health, died after only six years on the throne and was succeeded by his older sister Mary, the Roman Catholic daughter of Henry's first wife. It was only natural that policy should be reversed. Many who leaned toward the continental reforms, including Cranmer, were burned at the stake. A ruthless attempt was undertaken to re-establish Roman Catholicism. But after five years, Mary died and was followed by Elizabeth, daughter of Henry and Anne Boleyn.

It was under Elizabeth's forty-five-year reign that a religious settlement was made which still gives form to Anglicanism today. Her motivations were undoubtedly colored more by the desire for order and peace in the church as a way to political stability than by definite religious convictions. She decided against Roman Catholicism and for a broad Protestantism. The extremes of both Rome and the continental Reformation were rejected. While holding a firm grip, Elizabeth seemed even to relax control by the state by taking the title of "supreme governor" rather than "supreme head" of the Church of England.

Only in worship did uniformity appear essential, and that for the well-being of both church and state. Nevertheless, there was some demand for minimal doctrinal statements. The promulgation of the Thirty-nine Articles, which were accepted primarily as a guide rather than as a binding rule of faith, served this purpose. These are broadly Protestant in tenor, with stress at various points on the positive use of the tradition of the church. The sufficiency of scripture for salvation and the authority of the church are equally stressed. The church has the duty of settling both ceremonial matters and controversies in faith, though in no case dare it decide upon a course contrary to God's Word. The church, therefore, has a responsibility for the Bible and its proper interpretation. The papacy, purgatory, indulgences, and the veneration of the images and relics are rejected as unwarranted by scripture and contrary to the Word of God. On the theological side, justification by faith is affirmed as against works, and the concept of single predestination is affirmed for the comfort of good persons and believers. On the Lord's Supper, transubstantiation is rejected, but the real presence of the body of Christ "after an heavenly and spiritual manner" is affirmed. The church is defined (as also by the continental reformers) as an institution in which the Word is properly preached and the sacraments rightly administered.

At the most, the Thirty-nine Articles have had a relative authority. Anglicanism has no doctrinal tests, and the Articles are viewed as but the setting forth of minimal aspects of the faith for the sake of direction in a period of history when foundations had to be laid. Even the enforced subscription to the Articles by clergy in the time of Elizabeth were based on this sort of consideration. The words of John Bramhall are instructive:

> We do not suffer any man 'to reject' the Thirty-Nine articles of the Church of England 'at his pleasure'; yet neither do we look upon them as essentials of saving faith or 'legacies of Christ and of His Apostles'; but in a mean, as pious opinions fitted for the preservation of unity. Neither do we oblige any man to believe them, but only not to contradict them.[4]

Although the Articles are included in the Prayer Book and have been revised from time to time, Anglicans have thought of them as an adequate expression of the faith in the particular historical context rather than as a binding rule of faith for the church. The Nicene Creed and Apostles' Creed, which are affirmed in the Articles, are considered more truly normative. But even these are not thought of as complete and exclusive dogmatic statements. Rather they are accepted as precise and concise summaries of the broad dimensions of biblical faith, more adequately understood in intention through recitation or song than in exegesis or analysis.

The Book of Common Prayer was of far greater significance than the Thirty-nine Articles, both for the Elizabethan settlement and for subsequent Anglicanism. Like the Articles, the Prayer Book was based on similar documents formulated under the previous reign but was given its distinctive form in the time of Elizabeth. It reflects the tendency to combine much of the ancient tradition of the church with some of the Reformation insights. Sometimes, the two aspects lie side by side, as in the following sentences from the communion service: "The body of

[4] John Bramhall, *Schism Guarded,* in More and Cross, *Anglicanism,* 186.

our Lord Jesus Christ, which was given for thee, preserve thy body and soul unto everlasting life. Take and eat this in remembrance that Christ died for thee, and feed on him in thy heart by faith, with thanksgiving." Nothing less than the genuine presence of Christ in the elements is combined with the Zwinglian concept of remembrance. The Communion service also retains the concept of sacrifice, but Christ is an oblation once offered.

The Prayer Book contains prayers and liturgical forms dating from the early history of the church. These were adapted to the new situation, and practices considered contrary to the Word were abandoned in true Reformation form. The whole work reflects an unmistakable biblical basis. Each service encompasses the full sweep of the gospel message. Moreover, through prescribed collects and scripture readings for each service, full coverage of the various aspects of the faith is guaranteed year after year. In this way a prescribed form is combined with wholeness and variety of content. No single religious idea is singled out for emphasis. The totality of faith is represented in dramatic form.

Through the Thirty-nine Articles, the Prayer Book, and further steps taken by Elizabeth to insure the episcopal succession, the main lines for Anglicanism were definitely established. The Elizabethan settlement was in many ways the thought and practice of the Edwardian period, but modified in the direction of greater stress on the traditions and forms which had developed in the history of the church. It was a broad Catholicism, qualified by inclusion of central Reformation concerns. The settlement was formalized by the Act of Supremacy, which reaffirmed the place of the Crown in matters of state and church against all foreign pressures, and the Act of Uniformity, which assured uniformity of worship and practice.

b. Further Development of Anglican Self-understanding

If the general direction of Anglicanism was settled during the early years of Elizabeth's reign, the full meaning of the new development had yet to be explored. Undoubtedly, Anglicans would have reflected on the implications of their distinctive community in any case, but this process was speeded by the appearance and rapid growth of a competing group, the Puritans (see

Ch. V). The challenge of Puritanism, beginning during Elizabeth's time, led Anglican thinkers to an acute awareness that their new experiment was rooted in a very old tradition and could be justified on various grounds.

Foremost among such thinkers was Richard Hooker (d. 1600) whose *Ecclesiastical Polity* was written with the Puritans in mind. The immediate question at issue was the primacy of the episcopacy and episcopal succession. At first the episcopacy had more or less been taken for granted in the new English church. But the Puritans could find no basis for it in the Bible. Many Anglicans thought they could. Hooker, too, was convinced that a case could be made for the primacy of bishops in the New Testament; but he also admitted the possibility of reading the record in another way, as the Puritan Cartwright and his followers had done. In contrast to the Puritans, he did not rest his case upon the New Testament alone. Tradition and reason, too, were criteria for the church and when they were added to the New Testament, the argument seemed incontrovertible. For over fifteen hundred years, argued Hooker, episcopacy had been the dominant form of church government. Moreover, it was reasonable. It made for decent and proper order in the church, and what made good sense was worth having.

Behind the defense of the episcopacy lay more than immediately meets the eye. It involved a different understanding of the gospel and its relation to church than that held either by the Puritans or the reformed bodies on the Continent. But this was also quite different from the Roman views.

Hooker's concept of law and reason drew much from the medieval tradition, particularly Aquinas. The nature of God, the structure of the world, and the order of the church formed part of a single whole in which the church completed and fulfilled the natural order. Continuity, rather than discontinuity, marked the relation of God and the world. But Hooker's view of redemption in relation to the church was nearer to that of the Reformation bodies than to the Roman concept. Thus Hooker looked to an essential tradition of which neither the Reformation bodies nor the Roman church was the true descendant.

This general position was further elaborated in the seventeenth century by the group of distinguished preachers and writers known as the Caroline divines (e.g., Lancelot Andrewes. Thomas Barlow, William Beveridge, John Bramhall, Gilbert Burnet, William Laud, Robert Sanderson, Jeremy Taylor, John Wilkins, and John Woolton). These men considered themselves neither merely Protestant nor Roman Catholic, but those who held the "Middle Way," as John Donne expressed it, or as those who held "the mean between two extremes," as Sanderson put it. Certainly the Caroline divines did not agree with each other on all points. But they represented a common perspective, and a faith in the distinctive character of Anglicanism as at once "Protestant and Reformed according to the Ancient Catholic Church." They denied the authority of Rome because they considered it tyrannical, and the emphasis on the Bible of the Puritans because they considered it bibliolatry and an offense against reason. Hence, like Hooker, they insisted upon scripture, tradition, and reason. They were united in a studied *via media*. Theologically, this meant an emphasis upon the early Fathers of the church (and occasionally the implication that the early period was a kind of golden age of the church). Aquinas was quoted extensively and when stripped of the distinctively Roman aspects, he was considered more congenial than Luther or Calvin. But the reformers, too, were quoted. The Caroline divines were interested in a balanced religious outlook, related to the practical concerns of life. If they did not usually push any religious affirmation to its logical conclusion or always relate it successfully to others, this was a defect of their virtue of insisting that the totality of the life of the church was more important than great emphasis upon one religious concept. Their goal was a theology comprehensive in scope, conducive to morality, and always related to the life of the church.

For many, the Caroline divines represent the central stream of Anglicanism. This is perhaps easier to see in retrospect than in their own time, since most of the writers worked in a period of political and religious upheaval. In the civil strife of the mid-seventeenth century, the whole concept of the English church was threatened, though the restoration of the monarchy safely re-established Anglicanism with greater strength than ever. This

re-establishment was only slightly modified in the revolution of
1688 by the granting of greater privileges for dissenters.

The security of the restoration brought problems of its own,
and first with the rise of the Latitudinarians. The term *Latitudinarian* was a nickname for theological liberals who emphasized
tolerance and the primary role of reason in the theological enterprise. They were convinced that theology based upon reason
could be demonstrated to be not at all contrary to revealed religion, and that, in fact, the religion of the Bible could be defended by appeal to reason.

The Latitudinarians made ascendant one element of the trium-
virate of New Testament, tradition, and reason, thereby distort-
ing the other two. The historical justification for their effort was
the need to be creative in a period calling for readjustment. The
new scientific discoveries demanded attention in the thinking
of the churches and the Latitudinarians sought to relate the new
knowledge to Christian faith by appeal to a common rational
framework. They were liberals in a period when religion was not
noted for that characteristic. They were among the first to advocate a genuine toleration which eventually triumphed in the
English scene.

At the same time, however, men such as Stillingfleet and Tillot-
son reflected scarcely any of the evangelical outlook of the New
Testament with its offer of mercy to sinful men. Both Lati-
tudinarianism and the later more extreme accent upon the "reasonableness of religion," as presented by Locke, belong to a basic
pattern in which the "rational" threatened the religious. By the
second decade of the eighteenth century, the stress upon reason
had made such inroads into Anglicanism that the Christian
evangelical witness had all but disappeared. The fluid tradition
had spread so thin that the waters no longer ran deep. Moreover,
it appeared to many that the ecclesiastical machinery fostered
rather than changed this situation. Thus, the eighteenth century
saw the rise of the Wesleyan Movement as an attempt to recapture for the English church the living experience of redemption
from sin (see Ch. VI). And in the nineteenth century, the Oxford
Movement sought to recall the church to its Catholic heritage (in
contrast both to an individualistic evangelicalism and to a

liberalism largely indifferent to the claims of gospel and church)
while at the same time rejecting Roman interpretations of
Catholicism.

In sum, Anglicanism is best understood as a broad stream,
guided by a sense for order and tradition as guaranteed by the
episcopacy and the Prayer Book. It asks no particular theological
understanding, and has never been a theological church. Seldom
has it had theological giants. It surmounted the crises of Reformation influences in its battles with Puritanism, and of Roman
claims in connection with the Oxford Movement. It lost much of
its vitality in the Latitudinarian Movement, but managed under
pressure to regain it. For many, these three instances at least raise
the question of how far the vitality of Anglicanism is dependent
upon more tightly knit religious groups which basically challenge
its understanding of the church.

In spite of this, Anglicanism can claim to represent a tattered
but never broken tradition of the entire church. It reads its history as one which ante-dates the Reformation and preserves the
significant elements in the life of the church since its inception.
It claims, too, that in England the church was under the rule of
Rome for a shorter period of time than on the Continent and that
it stands, therefore, for the genuine tradition in contrast both to
Roman church, which distorted the tradition, and to the Protestants, who too rashly broke it.

For Anglicanism, the episcopal succession is the symbol and
guarantee of the continuity of the faith in the life of the church.
Anglicans differ as to whether the continuity is to be considered
a continuity of the gospel symbolized by the line of bishops, or
whether the succession of bishops is itself the continuity (through
the laying on of hands since the time of the Apostles). The difference between the two ways of viewing succession is enormous.
Nevertheless, the agreement that the church is one in its continuity makes it possible for individuals who so differ to remain
together in a bond of fellowship. The sense of belonging to the
communion of saints throughout the ages makes it possible for
men of diverse outlook to live in the same church.

Anglicanism belongs to the history of the Reformation and to
the history of Protestantism. But few Anglicans accept either the

Reformation on the Continent or the English reformation as normative. They prefer to think of themselves as belonging to a total history, purified from time to time through various reformations. Most think of themselves as Protestant and truly Catholic at the same time. In accord with the *via media,* they consider themselves Protestant in respect to continual *re*-formation and Catholic in the sense of the tradition and continuity of the church. Having ventured these general remarks, it is safest, nevertheless, to leave the question of whether Anglicanism is Protestant to the self-understanding of each Anglican.

IV

The Reformation Churches

The Lutheran and Reformed traditions are frequently called the Reformation churches, since they stem most directly from the activities of the major continental reformers, Luther in the one case, Zwingli and Calvin in the other. Between them, they swept over most of Western Europe, and found their way to America, too. Here we can only outline the development, touching upon institutional and geographical expansion, and devoting most of our attention to the religious problems and outlooks of the two bodies.

1. THE LUTHERAN DEVELOPMENT

From the very beginning the Lutheran movement had the problem of determining its relations with the empire and princes on the one hand and of arbitrating differences of religious opinion within its own house, on the other. Precisely because the emperor had other urgent problems, he could not give time to stamping out the Lutheran "heresy." Lutheran churches prospered in this atmosphere to the point where they had to be accepted in one way or another. In 1524, the Diet of Nuremberg urged enforcing the decision of the Diet of Worms against Luther "insofar as possible." This qualification was itself a sign of the strength of the new movement. The second Diet of Speyer, in 1529, held at a time of a temporary setback for the Lutherans, accepted the principle of a territorial solution (see below). Moreover, pending a final solution in a subsequent meeting, Lutheranism should be tolerated where it could not be suppressed. Catholic minorities in such Lutheran communities should be given religious liberty, but Lutheran minorities in Roman Catholic areas were not to be granted liberty of worship. Against this decision, the Lutherans declared "they must protest and testify publicly before God that they could do nothing contrary to His word." It was this witness and protest from which the name "Protestant" was first derived (see Ch. XIV).

The last attempts at reconciliation between Rome and the Lutheran group occurred in the Diet meeting at Augsburg in 1530, and in the ecclesiastical council at Regensburg in 1541. For the first meeting the Augsburg Confession was drafted by Philip Melanchthon, who was the architect of the later Lutheran development. In the Confession, the common elements of the new group and Rome were featured, though the Lutheran view was frankly presented; justification by faith was affirmed and transubstantiation repudiated. The document did not bring unity nor did outright conflict result.

As at the Diet of Augsburg, the concept of transubstantiation proved to be a decisive dividing line in the Diet of Regensburg of 1541. In addition, some Protestants, such as Martin Bucer, would not grant papal dominion even if the other issues could have been resolved. The Inquisition followed, but it was impossible to stamp out the new movement. The only solution was the recognition of two faiths. This was accomplished through the principle of territorialism, viz., that the religion of a territory was to be that of its ruler. The two faiths were not to exist freely together. (One could always, and many did, move to another territory if the religion where he was turned out to be different from his own.) Moreover, the Peace of Augsburg of 1555 recognized only Lutherans and Roman Catholics. The exclusion of other Protestant groups later became one of the contributory causes of the Thirty Years' War.

By 1555, Lutheranism had established itself in Germany as one of the two major groups. In the same century, Lutheran groups were formed in East Prussia, Poland, Estonia, Hungary and Transylvania. Directly to the north, Lutheranism became the established faith in Denmark and Norway. The Church of Sweden rejected the authority of Rome and adopted Luther's theology but did not take the name Lutheran and maintained the episcopal succession. A century later, in addition to the congregation in the Dutch settlement of New Amsterdam in America, Lutheran congregations were organized among the Swedes in Delaware. It was the eighteenth century, however, before a wave of German Lutherans settled in Pennsylvania, and it was this group which firmly planted Lutheranism in the new world.

Lutheranism thus spread rapidly and extensively. The controversies which beset it did not seriously hinder its early development, since the new religious movement met the religious aspirations of countless men. The controversies, in fact, manifest the exceeding vitality of the new movement, though in retrospect many think that the particular alternatives hardly left a real choice. Some of the issues came into focus through actual and assumed differences between the prophet of the Reformation, Luther, and its systematic exponent, Melanchthon. These differences, which were nuances rather than fundamental disagreements, grew partly out of misunderstanding and partly out of temperamental and cultural leanings. Luther met every new problem on the basis of the gospel message and never consciously wrote or thought in a systematic theological form. His consistency lay in a determined attempt to relate everything to the logic of faith. Melanchthon, a man of broad cultural, humanist and classical interests, was more disposed to write self-contained tracts and to use the utmost of tact and mediation in every situation. The early edition of his *Loci Communes,* or "Common-Places in Theology," is a systematic discussion of the nature and implications of justification by faith. Although Luther rediscovered the power and meaning of the concept, he did not systematically discuss it as Melanchthon did.

The revision of the *Loci* and the Augsburg Confession gives evidence that Melanchthon's formulations were phrased in such a way as concurrently to mediate differences and to emphasize right doctrine and teaching. The latter could only be accomplished if the former was possible. In the controversies which developed later, the emphasis fell more upon correct doctrine, though not always in agreement with the views of Melanchthon.

Not infrequently, occasional and almost off-hand statements of Luther were tenaciously affirmed against Melanchthon. But whether in agreement or disagreement, the spirit of right thinking exemplified by Melanchthon increasingly formed a part of the Lutheran development. The seriousness of the demand for precise and rigorous thought is apparent in the renewed controversy over the physical presence of Christ in the elements and in the debates over various aspects of the Christian life.

1) The first controversy centered in the nature of Christ's presence in the elements of the Lord's Supper. Melanchthon, Calvin, and Luther rejected the Zwinglian conception of the Lord's Supper as a memorial or sign representing the drama of Christ's life and death. But on the nature of the presence of Christ in the sacrament, Melanchthon found himself nearer to Calvin than to Luther. All agreed that faith alone guarantees Christ's presence, but Luther also insisted upon the corporeal or physical presence of Christ in the elements (Ch. 11). He maintained that Christ was totally and genuinely present. He believed that spiritual presence alone did not sufficiently take into account the total nature and activity of Christ and denied the bodily character of the risen Lord. It was therefore significant for the development of Lutheranism when Melanchthon rewrote the Augsburg Confession to permit a "spiritual" interpretation. In the conflict which ensued, the conservative party won the victory and believed that Luther's views had been vindicated. Actually, their literal understanding of the bodily presence of Christ in the elements led them to miss the point of Luther's insistence. They shifted the emphasis from the *meaning* of the bodily presence to a mere factual assertion of its necessity.

2) The second controversy dealt with the implications of the activity of the Spirit for the understanding of man. It was agreed that God initiates and sustains faith. But what is man like in this process? Is he active or passive as the Spirit lays hold of him and directs him? The conservatives insisted that through the continuing presence of Christ in the believer, man is molded like a lump of clay. Melanchthon, e.g., contended that man was active and genuinely asserted himself as himself even when God's power laid hold of him.

The issue was complicated in the first instance because the extreme conservatives overstated their case. Flacius, one of their representatives, used the concept of the lump of clay in a more than figurative sense. He defined total depravity as the complete loss of everything which makes man a genuine person, including every capacity for good. Regeneration then meant the creation of a new self, completely unrelated to the old self. In this analysis, man could only be passive in respect to the activity of grace.

Flacius contended that he expressed Luther's views and quoted numerous passages in support. But it is doubtful that he was true to Luther's intent. Luther's statements on total depravity, the inability of man to determine his relation to God, and his accent upon the directing activity of the Spirit even in faith, reflect a religious confession based upon experience. He did not intend his statements to be understood as a doctrine simply of human nature, either before or in faith. He was concerned with man's situation before God.

The issue was complicated in the second instance because Melanchthon also only partially understood Luther's views, and accepted the battle lines as drawn by the conservatives. Although Luther's main point about the bondage of the will referred to man's situation before God, Melanchthon, too, understood this as a statement about the nature of man. Melanchthon, therefore, insisted both upon the initiating and sustaining activity of God and upon the activity of man. God and man are co-workers. (Theologically, this is known as *synergism*.) By such phrasing, Melanchthon intended to safeguard the priority of grace while affirming a dignified concept of man. It is difficult to hold such a position, and some of Melanchthon's followers emphasized man's activity so much that it was evident that they had shifted the accent too far in the direction of man. Such views were rejected, as were, on the other side, the views of Flacius.

Melanchthon's views were a compromise, designed to safeguard the gospel, rather than a creative solution. By accepting the problem as defined, Melanchthon lost the opportunity of confessing that one finds his truest self, including his activity and response, in the faith which lays hold of him. Instead, Melanchthon had to contend for a formal definition of human capacity, abstracted from the experience of faith.

3) A third controversy concerned the place of law and works in the context of faith. On the basis of justification by faith, Luther spoke in glowing terms of the new life in Christ, frequently without caution or careful definition. Sensing the need for careful thinking on this level, subsequent theologians took Luther's occasional and unguarded utterances at face value. Johann Agricola, for instance, rightly saw that Luther's understanding of the gospel demanded the abrogation of law. But he interpreted this to mean that one had no obligation to fulfill the requirements of God as laid down in the law and that good works were even detrimental to salvation. Such a position is called *anti-nomian*, since it emphasizes the life in the Spirit over against any stress upon law, commandment, or requirement. Although this interpretation arose from Luther's emphasis upon the freedom of the Christian man and the new life in the Spirit, it disregarded his concern that the law be fulfilled in the Spirit. The anti-nomians generally were men whose lives, lifted to new heights of achievement by the Gospel, were examples of Christian grace. On the other hand, the lack of concern for standards occasionally led instead to acts of license.

In opposition to this, George Major insisted that good works were necessary for salvation. He did not state that man was saved by works. He insisted upon justification; he merely added that good works were necessary for salvation. Thus justification and merit together defined the Christian concept of salvation. This obviously contradicted Luther. Melanchthon, who acted as a mediator in the controversy, suggested that one could not say that good works were necessary for salvation, but one must say that good works were necessary.

As an attempt at mediation, this expressed Luther's general position with some cogency, but the difficulty was that the nuances of meaning were not the same. There is a difference between saying that the central emphasis is faith, not without works, and that works are necessary. The former places works in the context of faith at every point and leaves the definition of their "necessity" in unavoidable suspension. Melanchthon only verbally escaped the conclusion that if something is necessary in faith, it is necessary for salvation. Even without that conclusion, his statement distorted Luther's concern by considering works apart from a genuine relation to faith. At the most, Luther's writings ascribe relative necessity to works by casting every reference to the activity of man into the context of faith and the fruits of the Spirit.

4) The fourth controversy concerned the nature of the righteousness of the Christian man. Generally, Saint Paul and Luther had declared that the righteousness of God is imputed to man, that is, ascribed to man though he does not actually possess it. Andreas Osiander insisted that man was genuinely made righteous in faith. In asserting that faith made a difference and that man entered into a new reality, Osiander was correct. But the insistence that even believers were unrighteous was so much a part of the Reformation that Osiander's view had no chance of success. As a believer, man may be more righteous than as an unbeliever. But in Luther's understanding, he is not yet righteous and needs to be covered by God's cloak of righteousness. He did not deny that the Christian was actually righteous *in contrast* to his former status. His main point, however, was that the unrighteousness which still characterized the believer made it impossible to think of righteousness or consider even degrees of righteousness. In the last analysis, men need God's righteousness ascribed to them, if they are to stand before him.

The preceding issues were settled in the Formula of Concord in 1577 along the lines indicated above. In all cases, it was a victory for the conservative wing. The Augsburg Confession (and Melanchthon's defense of it), the Formula of Concord, and the catechisms of Luther were assembled and became the Book of Concord. This became the doctrinal standard for Lutheranism in Germany (and continues to have tremendous influence among conservative Lutheran groups; among other Lutherans, only the Augsburg Confession and Luther's Small Catechism are the generally accepted standards).

For many in the seventeenth and eighteenth centuries, the Book of Concord was a veritable text book for the resolution of all problems. It was as indispensable as the Bible for being a Christian, since it contained the proper approach to and the interpretation of the Bible. Lutherans looked to it and to the Bible for all knowledge, including knowledge of the world. They built this wall around themselves in order to preserve the purity of Christian concepts.

In this development, Luther's stress upon the Spirit as the agent through which the Bible is and becomes the Word of God was considered too subjective. The Bible as Bible, understood through the Book of Concord, was synonymous with the Word of God. Faith in revelation meant assent to statements which had been given in an infallible form in a book. God's truth meant propositions about God. Thus the initial warmth and freedom of Lutheranism gave way to a stress upon statements derived from the Bible. And these were set forth with the rigor of a theological method in which sensitive spirituality was often lacking. Men were now more concerned with being correct than with the revivifying power of the Spirit. This kind of faith was subsequently challenged within the churches by the pietist movement.

2. THE REFORMED TRADITION

a. *The Spread of the Reformed Movement*

The Reformed groups early established themselves firmly in Zurich (where Zwingli was the leader) and the northern Swiss cantons. As a result the principle of territorialism was applied in Switzerland as well as in Germany. But in this situation the official recognition of the Protestant churches led to quite a different development from that in Lutheran Germany, and the contrast between the Reformed and Lutheran conceptions of the Christian life came clearly into view.

In Lutheranism, the individual in his relation to God was the paramount concern. Men expressed their faith in all their social relations, of course, but essentially through the existing social structures. In the "secular" realm, men continued to be subject to the ordinary demands of the community upon its citizens. But in the Reformed churches, there was a profound sense of the need for reordering the total life of the community into a truly

Christian society. No activity was to be omitted; all were to be claimed as the domain of God's activity and as the area for special, collective Christian responsibility.

The Geneva community (under Calvin's leadership from 1541 to 1564) is the best-known example of an attempt in Protestant history to apply this principle in thoroughgoing fashion. As a Christian society, Geneva was to be governed by the community of the elect. By intent and design Geneva was democratic rather than authoritarian. Authority in the church was distributed among pastors, doctors, elders and deacons. To the first belonged the ministry of the Word, preaching and the administering of the sacraments. To the doctors belonged the teaching function of the church, a ministry particularly to the young as the future pillars of the church. Responsibility for the visitation of the sick and aid to the poor fell to the deacons. Elders made up a court of discipline, charged with the responsibility of seeing to it that all men obeyed the precepts of the gospel (willingly or unwillingly). The Consistory, which was made up of clergy and laymen, but with lay members predominating, had the responsibility of supervising the corporate life of the community. Consequently, it was very important in the life of the city and not infrequently the subject of considerable debate. Whenever necessary, its decisions were enforced by the council of the city. This was in line with Calvin's notion that the state should not dictate to the church, but rather that the civil powers existed for the sake of maintaining and protecting the faith. The state must learn the true nature of the faith from the church, in order that life might be properly ordered. Being a magistrate was thus a Christian vocation and responsibility and included the responsibility not only for civil order but also for right religion.

The Geneva experiment is not easy for men of a later time to assess. The intolerance toward dissent (e.g., the execution of Servetus) and the rigid control through the Consistory over every detail of public and private life must be understood in their historical context (we are not speaking of justification or blame). The notorious execution of Michael Servetus does not tell us much about the uniqueness of Geneva—for this was not strange in a time when death was the accepted penalty for heretics who

refused to recant, and when religious uniformity within a given
territory was taken for granted (the affair of Servetus actually
involved more than heresy; it was in fact a direct challenge to
Calvin's leadership in Geneva). Geneva was also a haven for
refugee Protestants, and it was partly through the training of
such men that Calvin's influence spread so far. But central in
the Geneva experiment was the vision of a city in every way
dedicated to the glorification of God. It was this goal, together
with the assumptions that total Christian patterns of life could
be specified in detail and that the elect could safely be trusted to
enforce such Christian standards, which led to the iron collectivism of Geneva.

The Geneva pattern could not be applied in the other areas in
which the Reformed tradition arose and flourished. In fact, only
in America was it possible to carry out a similar experiment, and
then only for a time. In the other areas, there was considerable
opposition on the part of constituted authorities and no possibility
of taking over the control of affairs. This is partly why Geneva
became such a symbol and why Calvinists in other lands looked
half wistfully at Geneva. It was not that Geneva, under the
leadership of John Calvin, was itself so important. Rather,
Geneva seemed to represent the fullest expression of this type of
reform movement. In many other places the drive for the manifestation of the Christian concern in all areas of life had to be
content with personal morality and diligence and thrift in social
and economic affairs, rather than in the direct control of all life
through dedicated or friendly authority. The same drive which
lay behind the Genevan community was involved in the support
which industrious Calvinists gave to the new capitalist order.[1]

The most difficult place for the Reformed development was
France. Initially, the "Huguenot" communities met little opposition, but as they grew they increasingly became a problem in a
country which had accepted the principle of "one land, one
religion." They were persecuted extensively, but in the Edict of
January 1562 won limited toleration. Wars and intrigues followed, with the Massacre of St. Bartholomew's Day in 1572 being
a call for the elimination of all Huguenots. Over ten thousand fell

[1] See Ch. V, and especially Ch. XI.

in Paris alone. As a result of revulsion to this act, but primarily because of changes in the crown, the Edict of Toleration in 1598 granted Calvinism full toleration. But this was revoked in 1685 under the reign of Louis XIV, who insisted on one faith, one king, one land. French Protestantism continued as a definite minority group.

In the Empire, the spread of the Reformed faith was limited by the strength of the Lutheran bodies. Nevertheless, Reformed churches emerged among the Magyars of Hungary, and even more in the valley of the Rhine, particularly in the Palatinate. Among the latter, a controversy concerning the Lord's Supper resulted in a notable document, the influence of which extended far beyond the immediate issue. This was the Heidelberg Catechism, written by Peter Ursinus and Caspar Olevianus, a balanced statement, admirably suited for purposes of instruction. It was accepted by nearly all of the Reformed churches.

In the Low Countries, the Reformed tradition did not have any strength until about 1560. Before that, this had been a center of the Anabaptists and of Lutheran groups. For a period, there was considerable tension between the Protestant groups, though common fear of the Roman Catholic influence through the domination of Spain generally kept them from fighting each other. The Anabaptists, however, had been weakened by persecution and expulsion, and the Lutherans were not aggressive. In this situation the Calvinists won the ascendancy and also the favor of Prince William (probably because the concept of justifiable resistance by the lower magistrates appealed to him). Nevertheless, he was for some principle of toleration. In the long run the territorial solution prevailed. In the southern regions (Belgium) Roman Catholicism became the established religion, while in the North (Holland), Calvinism was established.

Scotland, next to Geneva, presented a situation in which circumstances and the genius of the Reformed faith combined to shape and form a people. Here, largely through the energies of John Knox, a people sympathetic to reformation were welded into a religious society dominating the land. A man who had suffered under the Inquisition and who had drunk at the Reformation fountains of Zurich and Geneva, Knox feared nothing, and openly and successfully challenged the Roman Catholic queen, Mary Stuart. He was able to forge a church which for generations influenced the destiny of the nation.

The Puritan movement also belongs to the Reformed tradition. But because it has an outlook distinctive to itself, we shall consider it in the next chapter. Many of the national groups discussed here found their way to the new world and brought their respective traditions. Even the Huguenots made a settlement. The Dutch Reformed Church arose out of the Dutch Calvinist development and the first congregation in the new world was in New York, then New Amsterdam, in 1628. In the early eighteenth century, the Scotch-Irish migrated to the new world. From them came the Presbyterian churches. The German Reformed groups came in large numbers after the first quarter of the eighteenth century.

b. The Development of Orthodox Calvinism

Most of the Reformed groups in Europe formulated confessions of faith. The Second Helvetic or Swiss Confession of 1566, written by Bullinger, was a doctrinal statement of great influence throughout the Swiss cantons. The Gallican Confession in France reflected a strong emphasis on predestination. The Belgic Confession of 1561 in the Low Countries has the earmarks of the influence of Geneva. Initially, the Scottish faith found expression in the Confession of 1560, written largely by Knox. This Confession remained the standard of faith until the completion of the Westminster Confession in 1647, which, though prepared in England, had been written with the collaboration of Scotch delegates (see Ch. V).

The confessions of faith served originally as guides and often as dikes against distortion. But increasingly, in the midst of controversy, men pointed to the confessions as correct Christian thinking. People were asked to believe the confessions, and the faith these were meant to safeguard often took second place. That was the beginning of Protestant "orthodoxy," which not infrequently substituted right thinking for the experience which lay behind all thought. (This is one of the reasons why later generations find it hard to realize the power of the confessions in their original situations or to acknowledge the religious faith which initially informed them.)

The development toward orthodoxy was accelerated through theological controversies in which the conservative groups were consistently the victors. One of the earliest instances occurred in Holland in the early 1600's. Here controversy was provoked through the vocal doubts of a pious Christian by the name of Koornheert who, though he did not reject the idea, was perplexed by the claim that God damned men from all eternity. Arminius, who had been asked to refute Koornheert, instead became convinced that the traditional view must be rejected. He then became the leader of the group which now bears his name. The brunt of the controversy was borne by a disciple of Arminius named Bisschop. Another important supporter was the well-known jurist, Hugo Grotius.

The tenets of the Arminians were expressed in a series of articles known as the *Remonstrance*. A Counter-Remonstrance, influenced largely by the conservative Gomar, was then written. While the controversy was settled in the Synod of Dort in Holland in the year 1618, an examination of the issues will give us a picture of the theological thinking of the period.

1) The first issue concerned the understanding of God's decree in predestination. The Arminians rejected the now prevalent view of predestination: that God decreed which individuals would be saved and which would be damned. This repudiation applied equally to what were later called "supralapsarian" and "infralapsarian" views of predestination. Supralapsarianism, the view held by Gomar, was the affirmation that before the creation of the world God had decreed who would be saved and who would be damned. In fact, this decision of God's was a reason for creation. God's decision concerning individual men had no reference to the Fall (lapsus) of man. The infralapsarians, on the other hand, related God's decrees to the Fall. In this view, God also made the decision about every individual prior to creation. But in so doing, he took into account the fact of the Fall before it happened. This view provided a rationale for assigning men to hell and put creation in a better light.

Having distinguished between the supralapsarians and the infralapsarians, we must now distinguish two types of infralapsarian thinkers. The "double" predestinarians held that God had directly willed both the salvation of elect individuals and the damnation of all others. On the other hand, those who held the concept of "single" predestination, contended that God had decided who should be saved but had made no decision concerning those who did not belong to the predestined. For all practical purposes, the latter were left to their own devices (which was hardly more tolerable than to be among the damned).

Brushing aside the preceding distinctions, the Arminians affirmed instead that the idea of a decree has reference merely to the serious nature of God's plan for the world. It is a statement of how God works, without reference to the precise destiny of any particular man. Defined in this way, the decree means no more than that God has declared that whoever accepts Christ will be saved and whoever does not will be excluded. It describes a general situation, the outcome of which is to be determined by each individual himself in accordance with his own decisions in faith.

The Arminians anchored the concept of predestination in faith and experience, but they reduced the decision of faith simply to a human, rational possibility. The holders of lapsarian theories, on the other hand, attempted to safeguard the priority of God's activity by ascribing all events and happenings to him. They lost the experiential character of faith and accepted a form of determinism as the basis of faith. Calvin, too, had had a deterministic understanding of the operation of God in relation to predestination. But he intended only one thing: the exclusion of works. His orientation definitely was from faith to predestination (see Ch. II). Now this was reversed. One moved from predestination to other problems, including that of faith. Whereas faith had once been the foundation of predestination, now predestination was the basis of faith.

The Synod of Dort did not transcend the choice between the rationalistic alternatives: either free decision to be a Christian or deterministic predestination. It adopted a view which was

neither clearly supra nor infralapsarian, though definitely associated with a concept of single predestination.[2] God's decree
before the foundation of the world was clearly affirmed. At the
same time, the concept of single predestination took the onus
of damnation out of the hands of God since God had not ordained
men for damnation. Actually, of course, the destiny of those
apart from the elect was not affected by the affirmation of single
rather than double predestination. In subsequent developments,
double predestination was reaffirmed in spite of the Synod of
Dort.

2) Closely allied with the preceding was the question whether
Christ died only for the elect or for all men. The Arminians, of
course, insisted that Christ had died for all and obtained forgiveness for all, though forgiveness could be effective only as a
man accepted Christ. The orthodox party insisted that Christ
died only for the elect. Convinced that what happens is what is
willed by God and that whatever happens is determined by God,
they insisted that Christ could have died only for the faithful.
Otherwise God would be frustrated since what he intended did
not happen. They gave expression to the universality and greatness of God, however, by declaring that God's grace would be
adequate for all men, though it was intended only for the
elect.

The Synod of Dort sided with the orthodox party. As in the
case of predestination, there was no sign of a new formulation
of the problem which might have avoided these two alternatives,
each of which leaves much to be desired.

3) Another issue concerned the understanding of faith in relation to the possibility or impossibility of rejecting God's grace.
Both Arminians and orthodox agreed that there is no salvation
apart from faith. On one level, they even described faith in the
same way. For the Arminians, faith was the acceptance of God's
intention for man; for the conservatives, it was assent to what
God had done. Thus both those who contended for human voli-
tion and those who insisted upon a rigid determination defined

[2] This is in contradistinction to the usually accepted opinion that the
Synod took an infralapsarian position, a judgment based on the fact that
historically the concept of single predestination had been associated only
with the infralapsarian position.

faith as a decision. From opposite positions, they came to decep-
tively similar affirmations of salvation by faith.

The problematic nature of this agreement became apparent in
the discussion of whether a person could reject God's grace. The
Arminians affirmed that man could, and if he could not, he was
no more than a puppet. Their prime theological interest was to
safeguard the meaningfulness of human decision. That of the
conservatives, on the other hand, was to place the will of God
above all else. The latter group naturally appeared in a better
light, though not necessarily in a better theological position. The
orthodox refused to distinguish between God's will to redeem and
man's acceptance. If God willed faith for any man, he had it.

Again, the Synod of Dort came down on the conservative side
and declared that "faith is therefore a gift of God, not on account of its being offered for man's choice, but because it is in
reality conferred, inspired, and infused into him. It is not that
God confers the power to believe, and then awaits the con-
currence or act of believing from the will of man; but he who
works in man both to will and to do, and indeed all things in all,
produces both the will to believe and the act of believing also."
(From this passage it is clear that the conservatives should have
disagreed with the Arminians on the nature of faith.) This statement is no longer a confessional statement of the overwhelming
experience of grace; it is a metaphysical account, abstracted
from faith, of the operation of God and of man's impotence. It
makes man into an object maneuvered by God.

4) Can the man in whom God's grace is operative possibly
lose it? The Arminians tentatively answered "Yes," pending
further study of Scripture. This was in accord with their concern
for the volitional nature of man. The conservatives insisted that
one could not fall from grace. Just as a man could not resist
grace, he could not lose it. To say that he could, would mean that
God was defeated in specific instances. That was intolerable
from the strict Calvinist position.

Again, the Synod of Dort took the conservative position. But
the alternatives, as in the previous instances, confused the issue
as the Reformers had seen it. No one deliberately departs from
grace, and he who stands under its power can reasonably expect

to remain under it. But this hope is based in the sustaining and trustworthy activity of God. This was the truth in the orthodox system, though distorted by a deterministic view of God's nature and activity. Nevertheless, it does happen that men do not remain in the state of grace. This was the truth of the other side, in which the activity of God and man were not simply identified.

On every level, the Synod of Dort defined the will of God in such a way that what God wills and what happens were virtually identified. Only the Fall as such was excluded from the divine decree; all else, including the results of the Fall for human life and destiny, was the outworking of God's immutable will.

It was this general outlook which dominated the Calvinist tradition for at least another century. There were significant developments on the problem of predestination, the interpretation of Scripture and miracles, found in the writings of such men as Danaeus (1588), Dusanus (1599), Bucanus (1609), Polanus (1623), Crocius (1636), Martinius (1609), Cocceius (1648), Van Til (1704), and Heideggerus (1696). But in the general perspective we have outlined, we can see the basic concern of later Calvinist theologians. We suggested earlier that although the Synod of Dort affirmed single predestination, it was followed by a theological development in which double predestination was predominant. The rationale for this development lay in an increasing emphasis upon the glory, majesty, and honor of God. Calvin, too, had stressed the majesty of God, but as grounded always in his justifying activity. In the later tradition, God's honor and glory *per se* become the dominant motif of interpretation. The concern was to express this at every point.

At the root of the discussions of predestination was always the bewildering problem that the mercy of God becomes a reality for some, but not for others. It was assumed that all men deserve nothing else than damnation, but the question remained of God's purpose in election and rejection. The later Calvinists' way of meeting the problem was through the concept of double predestination, understood as a declaration of the absolute sovereignty and glory of God. God is God. Since God sends some to eternal life and some to eternal damnation, he is a God of glory, majesty and power. Heideggerus, for example, declared that God's glory is expressed more clearly through the concept of damnation than through the idea of man's just death for his sins. "The supreme end is the glory of God reprobating;—the subordinate end is the righteous condemnation of the reprobated to death for their sins." [3]

This is double predestination with a vengeance. It is infinitely different from the views of the mystics and of the early Luther, for whom faith was so wonderful that they proclaimed their willingness to be damned for God's sake; that is, to accept his plan for them. That was a declaration of faith in which the possibility of damnation is overarched by the experience of faith. For the Calvinists, double predestination is considered without reference to the confession of the believer. Calvin's movement always from faith to predestination (in order to guard against a doctrine of works) has been lost. Now rigid determinism is accepted as a doctrine in its own right.

In the interpretation of Scripture, Luther and Calvin in principle distinguished between the Word of God and the Bible. Word and Bible were brought together through the testimony of the Holy Spirit. To later Calvinists, as to Lutherans, this opened the door to purely subjective interpretation. Their fears had been partially fostered by the extremes of some of the Anabaptist groups (see Ch. III), which claimed the direct presence of God through the Spirit apart from Bible. In reaction, the orthodox abandoned the notion that the Bible contained or might become the Word of God in faith, in favor of an unqualified identification of Word and scripture. Already in the second Helvetic Confession of 1566 it was declared that the "canonical Scriptures are the actual true word of God." Any question of the identification of the Bible and the Word of God was rejected outright. So wrote Wolleb: "the query whether the scriptures or sacred books are the Word of God is unworthy of a Christian. As in a school we do not dispute with one who denied first principles, so we ought to adjudge a man unworthy to be listened to if he denied the first principles of the Christian religion." [4]

The Calvinists did not reject the Holy Spirit; but the Spirit

[3] Heinrich Heppe, *Reformed Dogmatics* (London: George Allen & Unwin, Ltd., 1950), 187.
[4] *Ibid.*, 15.

was now the agent of God's authorship of the biblical record. Inspiration no longer included participation in the reception and experience of revelation. The book as such was revelation, because it was written under the Spirit. Nevertheless, many disputes arose concerning the relative activity or passivity of men in the actual writing. Those who believed that the biblical writers were active could at least account for the diversity of style in the Bible since if God simply dictated it, one would expect him to use the same style throughout. But even those who pled that the biblical writers were active as well as passive never doubted for a moment that the content of the Bible was literally the Word of God. So the Bible was the Word of God from cover to cover.

Such an understanding of the Bible included literal acceptance of miracles. These depicted God's activity in the world, and in debate served as crucial evidence of the truth of Christianity. Miracles were understood as acts of God which could not be accounted for in the natural scheme of things. Their contrast to the natural order made them most important. Thus a miracle could be defined as "a singular work of God, beyond the order and above the power of the creatures, for confirming divine truth." [5] This view of miracle held sway among the conservative groups until such time as men could no longer find these Christian evidences in an ordered world, and until the whole concept of miracle was recast in the early nineteenth century, notably through the work of Schleiermacher (see Chs. IX and X).

3. THE SPIRIT OF ORTHODOXY

The developments we have described in this chapter are generally characterized as "Protestant orthodoxy." The word *orthodox* means "correct belief," and as applied to individuals or groups usually denotes conformity to accepted standards. Thus where the goal is orthodoxy, the precise definition of truth is all important.

It is therefore understandable why the movements we have described are called orthodox. On many levels there was a discernible shift from religious thinking which always arises out

----
[5] *Ibid.,* 204.

of the experience of faith to a stress upon proper and right
thinking. This is most clearly seen in the development of the
understanding of predestination. The dynamic religious thinking
of Luther and Calvin was arrested by a concern whether or not
particular formulations were true to Luther or Calvin. Frequently, this concern led to statements which differed greatly
from the spirit of Luther and Calvin.

This tendency was accentuated by the necessity of making
statements in the midst of controversies. (We have already indicated that the alternatives in the controversies were so phrased
as to make the problem incapable of solution.) Religious truth
and propositions about religious problems were identified in such
a way that the latter became the criteria for the former. Men
were asked to assent to statements of truth. Instead of statements
reflecting an experience of encounter with truth, truth now was
tantamount to the statement itself. Hence theological formulations became the norm of Christian truth, including that of the
experience of God through the Bible. Whereas Roman Catholicism insisted that the church was the interpreter of the Bible,
orthodox theology now tended to be the custodian of biblical
truth. Theology came before the Bible, as the key to its interpretation, rather than after it, as its explication.

The spirit of this approach is reflected in the second term
which is frequently applied to the movement as a whole, "Protestant scholasticism." The term scholastic is used because of definite
analogies to medieval scholasticism. Assent to truth in proposi-
tional form marked both periods. There was similarity also in
emphasis upon a natural knowledge of God, supplemented by
revelation (and, in the case of Protestants, also corrected by
revelation).

There is a contrast, however, between Protestant scholasticism
and medieval scholasticism which is important for the understanding of the former. In the classical medieval period, rational
propositions about God and rational discourse about revelation
were in conformity with the climate of opinion of the period.
Reason made room for revelation and revelation took account
of reason. Theology stood in a positive and creative relation to
the culture. In contrast, Protestant scholasticism had to argue

its case. It was confronted by the shaping of a new "scientific" view of the world which stood in sharp contrast to the biblical scheme, and by a philosophical trend which was almost exclusively rationalistic. The orthodox theologians felt compelled to set themselves against these views, and could see no creative relation to them. But in this encounter, Protestant scholasticism did not escape the spirit of rationalism itself. It was, in fact, akin to the new rationalistic currents both in temper and in method. It was no wonder that the dissatisfaction with philosophical rationalism should also bring dissatisfaction with this type of theology.

Such dissatisfaction expressed itself in Pietism and in a kind of general revulsion against orthodoxy. The revulsion was accentuated by the impact of the Thirty Years' War, which to many appeared as a gross spectacle of religious groups pitted futilely against each other, fighting for particular theological interpretations unworthy of defense.

Nevertheless, the type of thinking which was represented in Protestant orthodoxy took seriously the nature of the theological task. It set for itself the rigorous discipline of trying to think from a Christian perspective at every point. Seldom has the task of saving the center of Christian theology against encroachment from outside been taken so seriously.

V

Puritanism and Related Movements

1. THE PURITAN OUTLOOK

The term *Puritan* refers to a particular Protestant outlook expressed in the late sixteenth and seventeenth century in England and New England. Denominationally, the Puritans comprised primarily Presbyterian, Congregational and Baptist groups. In religious viewpoint, most of them represented a vital Calvinist tradition. But whether Calvinist or not, they were marked by an intense experience of the living God, nourished exclusively by the Bible and expressed in every thought and act.

a. Biblical Foundations

For the Puritans, the Elizabethan settlement appeared as a half-way house between Rome and Geneva. The appeal to tradition, church authority and reason obscured the only proper basis for the life of Church and society alike. Puritans believed in the sole sufficiency of the Bible. Only the Bible could be taken as a guide for faith and life. The biblical word, strictly adhered to, provided an adequate criterion for all problems.

The authority of the Bible had two facets. In the first place, it was only through the Bible that one obtained and experienced knowledge of the God who is related to every aspect of man's

99

life. The Puritans did not mean that the Bible disclosed the
inmost nature of God. This remained hidden. Even the Bible
pointed to the incomprehensible being of God. But incompre-
hensibility does not mean unknowability. In the faith nourished
by the Bible one did know that God is in control of everything
and that he predestines some to salvation and others to damnation. His activity was known, but his rationale a mystery.

In the second place, the Bible was a document which reflected
the organization of the early Christian community. There church
order and the vitality of the faith went hand in hand. The organization of the church was not a hindrance to the depth of
faith, as the Puritans suspected it had become in Anglicanism,
but a natural manifestation of faith. Puritans were divided in
their understanding of the constitution of the New Testament
community. But they were agreed that the true order of the
church was given in the biblical community of faith. Church
order expressed faith and therefore no supplemental criteria,
such as reason or tradition, could be used. (Later in the chapter
we shall show in some detail how this understanding was expressed in English history.)

b. Experienced Predestination

The Puritans believed that God ordered everything in the
world. At the same time they asked men to be active Christians
whose lives would show forth the glory of God in the transformation of life and society under his name. They were at once the
most predestinarian and the most activistic of Christians. This
paradoxical combination provides the clue to the understanding
of the Puritan ethos.

Like Calvinists generally, Puritans believed that nature and
history, the world and man, were governed by God. Providence,
God's continual sustaining and ordering activity, and predestination, his governance of human destiny, were virtually identified
as the determination of all things by God. God was behind everything which happened. Even sin could not be excluded from his
providential activity, though he was not held accountable for it.
The guilt for sin was man's, because of the Fall.

But such affirmations could only be made by those who were

already believers called by God. Unlike orthodox Calvinists who
moved from predestination to faith, Puritans grounded predestination more integrally in the experience of the believer. Only
he who was a believer could say that God's predestining act was
the cause of his faith. Predestination was not a general proposition about all men. Determination by God made sense only to
the believer. It was a category used by the faithful to account
for their faith. It pointed to the mystery of election, grounded
only in the God who controlled and ordered all. The view of
God as the governor of all things belonged to the Puritans'
experience and accorded with their understanding of the Bible.
It was not strange or alien to their own existence. Although God
controlled everything, he was not a tyrant. There was a profound
difference between the majesty of God, however fearful, and
tyranny. Only he who had not taken God seriously could think
of the latter. Moreover, the God of majesty had already revealed
himself as merciful. Hence God's activity, in which the concept
of predestination was anchored, was already weighted, among
the faithful, on the side of his gracious activity. (As we saw, this
had been the original basis for the declaration of God's predestining activity.)

The Puritans considered themselves among the faithful but
emphasized the mystery of election. Hence they never questioned
God's justice. Sometimes they rationalized it, as when with St.
Augustine they stated that since no one deserved to be saved,
there was no injustice in the election of some. At their best they
insisted that the mystery of God would eventually be disclosed,
but in the meantime one must simply accept it.

However much Puritans believed that God controlled all events,
they never interpreted this as a sign for relinquishing the responsibilities they felt called upon to assume. If God had called them,
they must do his work. God demanded things of the elect. To be
called by him was serious and demanded the redoubling of one's
activities. To relax would be not to be serious. Those who believe that a concept of predestination leads to quietism do not
understand, as do believers, that it is God with whom they are
dealing. Predestination means that God has laid his hand upon
men for a purpose. Believing with all their being that God justi-

fied through faith, Puritans went on to assert that justification
was but the first stage, followed by sanctification, or the new life
in Christ.

As a result, many Puritans believed that the activity of Christians in the world was a mark of their election, a sign to themselves and to others that they were among God's chosen. The
validity and certainty of faith was shown in the actuality of the
new life, dedicated to doing everything under the rule and for
the glory of God. "By their fruits you shall know them." This was
a dictum which the Puritans applied to themselves. All things
must be undertaken for God, and only in such activity could one
gain reasonable certainty that he was not deluded in his faith.
Necessary as justification was, it alone did not give assurance
of one's election. The believer's experience of justification must
be followed by actual holiness. (It was the fear that one might
not really be among the righteous which sometimes manifested
itself in self-righteousness.)

The Puritans were aware of a real psychological problem.
Often those outside the churches, with little or no experience of
God, appeared more responsible and were better men, judged by
outward standards, than those who confessed that justification
and sanctification came through the merciful activity of God.
The problem was intensified because the Puritans had an
uncanny sense that the outward was a sign of the inward. Could
one be sure where he stood, particularly when some unbelievers
did so well? The result of such questioning was only a more
resolute attempt to live one's life as if only God mattered and
as if one could not do enough in the world under his rule. Thus
predestination, which was such a comfort to Luther, became the
most baffling problem for the individual Puritan. Although the
Puritan never dreamt that he could be perfect, he nevertheless
did expect clear signs of his election. And where signs are expected, one is never certain whether the signs which appear are
clear enough.

The anxiety caused by this problem was eased in a later stage
of Puritanism through the notion that one could not lose his election. This did not mean that one could do as he pleased; it was a
responsible statement made in the context of faith. This was a

way of saying that God had an unending concern for his own and that man need not be so preoccupied with himself. The impossibility of losing one's election should have been asserted when the faith was vigorous. It was actually suggested when Puritanism had lost much of its vitality.

More to the point for subsequent history was the continual assertion of the faithful that as long as man struggled under God as a believer, he could trust God to see him through. Many Puritans believed that whoever did not struggle or fight the battle of life was among the lost. Inactivity was a sure sign that a man was not a believer, no matter what his profession of faith. This is why the Puritans spoke of the warfare of life. If there was peace for them, it was in the midst of ceaseless activity under God. As long as one strove under God, there was some hope that he might be among the elect.

It was not easy to resolve the tension in the souls of men who believed in the all-determining nature of God's activity and yet found in their own activity in faith a clue to what God had in store for them. The difficulty was that the Puritans had accepted a concept of predestination which, though grounded in faith, was understood in deterministic categories. If one defines God's relation to the world in terms which make him responsible for all that happens, including how it happens, it is impossible to reconcile this with one's own responsibility in any relation to God. It is only possible to correlate the two when predestination is conceived, not in deterministic categories, but in terms of the mystery of God in his activity. Predestination then means that the world and man are safely in the hands of God and that even one's faith is grounded in him. Determinism, on the other hand, makes man into a puppet.

Having inherited the concept of a deterministic predestination from the Calvinists, the Puritans did not sufficiently challenge it from the standpoint of their faith. They challenged it only by emphasizing, in a way which the Protestant scholastics did not, the activity of man at the same time. The activity of the Christian was considered a sign of his election. But this was not a device for solving the problem. It was something genuinely felt. Puritans believed in an experienced predestination.

In order to give expression to both the activity of God and the activity of man, some Puritans, particularly in New England, had recourse to the concept of a covenant, between God and man and among men in the churches. In the Bible there was a covenan between God and Abraham, and then in the New Testament there was a new covenant. A covenant, of course, is a compact. Religiously speaking, however, it is not a compact between equals but between an initiating God and a responding people. All promises and responsibilities are cast into that framework. The terms of the covenant therefore imply that God has been faithful in the exercise of his freely announced obligations; thus it is the task of man to keep his. The idea of covenant gave a way of maintaining great stress upon the will and responsibility of man without abandoning an equal stress upon the controlling and determining activity of God. The covenant correctly emphasized the initiating and continually triumphant activity of God. Though it did not solve the problem of their relation, the concept of covenant at least made it possible to emphasize both the priority of God and the activity of man. Some Puritans did stress activity so much that they shifted the emphasis to the point where it was felt that once the process of sanctification had started, man contributed to his salvation.

c. Ordering All Under God

The concept of covenant also focused the pervasive Puritan concern for ordering all life under God. This was the ethical side of the covenant, expressed in the Bible in both individual and social terms. Each individual had responsibility under God and no one could take his place. But the covenant also involved a people meant to live in community under God. God's plan for the world had a social nature; it included the participation of individuals in a common unity which sustained and gave meaning to all. It involved a holy community sustained by God but expressed by men dedicated to doing all things in accord with his will and for his glory.

We shall never be able to grasp the spirit of the Puritans unless we try sympathetically to enter into the perspective of men committed to the belief that everything is to be understood and ordered from the standpoint of the divine. This may be the aim of most Christians; but never before or after Puritanism has it been so consciously or self-consciously expressed. Self-consciousness frequently hindered the realization of the ideal. Nevertheless, the intense cultivation of that motif had important consequences for individual and social life of the time.

This dominant Puritan concern led to a high degree of sobriety and sombreness toward life. But this was not a dour pessimism. It was rather a deliberate "sitting loose" to the things of this world. The Puritans believed that nothing in human existence held a meaning in its own right and continually sought for its meaning under God. Since God had destined the elect for a life beyond, the achievements as well as the sorrows of this life were not ultimate. Loyalty to God meant that nothing in this life deserved final allegiance. Human existence was to be transformed insofar as possible by the might and power of Christian men; beyond this was the assurance of a God who could be trusted to bring the history of the world to its fulfillment.

Nothing was excluded from this outlook. Card playing was denounced not merely because it seemed to foster gambling, but primarily because it was a frivolous activity. All energies were to be devoted to the service of God. Puritans read good literature, classical and secular as well as religious. Many were outstanding scholars and men of culture. But even such pursuits must not be allowed to side-track men from the main business of life. They, too, must serve God. Joyful human associations, including the imbibing of wine (the tee-totalism of a later generation should not be blamed on the Puritans) and dancing, were accepted, provided they contributed to the well-being of the pilgrim traveling through this world under God. All such things were good, but they were not to be used for their own sake.

In economic life this outlook was conducive to the utmost thrift and industry. Money and goods were neither to be wasted nor trusted. When thrift was coupled with the zealous activity of Christians who saw in diligent performance of their work a service of God, and in success perhaps a sign of election, a combination was produced which could powerfully affect the economic developments of the age. Many Puritans belonged to the rising business class, and through their efforts and thrift undoubtedly accelerated the pace of the expanding capitalist development.[1] At the same time, the strong sense for responsible employment of all activity under God did much to check the most flagrant abuses of the emerging capitalist order.

Since no segment of life fell outside the purview of responsibility to God, the Puritans naturally hoped to organize all social and political life along Christian patterns. For this, Geneva remained a model. As we shall see in the next section, such a dream was short lived in England and for that matter in New England, too, though it was more successful in the latter place.

Much more important for political development was the fact that the Puritans' faith led them to challenge tyranny and abuse of power, whether in state or church. God was sovereign and as members of his legion they were unafraid of any earthly powers. When God alone is sovereign, all other powers are subject to restraint. Unrestricted power can be granted to no one. With this sense of responsibility to God alone, Puritans provided the spiritual foundation for a democratic society. This was the case even though many Puritans were so interested in establishing a society which reflected God from top to bottom that they did not see this implication of their faith. Nevertheless, workable democratic structures have arisen primarily in lands influenced by Puritan traditions.

2. THE MAJOR PURITAN BODIES

Puritans were by no means agreed on the proper pattern of church order. But they were agreed that such questions must be answered by a strict adherence to the biblical record. The Puritan religious outlook itself determined the understanding of the church. The issue with the Anglicans was not merely one of bishops versus presbyters in the church. The roots of the difference were as deep as the types of spirituality manifest in the respective traditions. It can be characterized as the difference between a rigorous adherence to the patterns of the Bible on the

[1] The relation between Calvinism and the rising capitalist economy has been studied in detail in Max Weber, *The Protestant Ethic and the Spirit of Capitalism*, and R. H. Tawney, *Religion and the Rise of Capitalism*. See Ch. XI.

one hand and, on the other, a more urbane and carefully considered view of the church as a part of the ongoing character of God's incarnation with historical and theological significance alongside of, though based upon, the Bible. Most Anglicans did not rest the case for bishops entirely upon the Bible, but also upon the dominant tradition of the church and upon its basic reasonableness. By contrast, the Puritans insisted that the Bible was the only place in which the norm for Christian living could be found, including church order. It was not enough to say that a church pattern does not contradict the Bible; rather, only that order is permissible which is specifically founded in the Bible.

However differently they understood that order, even in the New Testament, Puritans were agreed that it was neither to be sought nor substantiated elsewhere. To their opponents this looked like a kind of biblicism, that is, an exclusive and narrow stress on the Bible; this, they felt, made the history of the church unimportant. The Puritans, on the other hand, insisted that they were returning to the church in its original state.

In spite of this common intention, the Puritan development was diverse. In the first place, there were differences of understanding and approach. In the second place, historical developments in England and New England were different and virtually determined the respective patterns. In England, after the first major Anglican Puritan group came the Presbyterians led by the Cambridge professor, Thomas Cartwright. This group believed that the Genevan experiment and the Presbyterian pattern in Scotland represented the New Testament concept of the church. But the aim was not severance from the established Church of England. Rather, that church was to be purified and purged of the remnants of Roman corruption. These men believed that in the Church of England the ministry was neither rightly constituted nor properly educated, that medieval ceremonies still clustered around the sacraments, and that the prayer book had too many remnants of the Mass. In short, the church must abandon its half-way house between Geneva and Rome.

The Puritan Presbyterians called upon Parliament to change the Elizabethan settlement in order to make a truly reformed church. They, too, believed in a national church, dominating the entire land. And if neither Queen nor bishops were ready to reform, then Parliament should. But the Queen insisted on keeping the religious settlement as it was. Thus, Presbyterians took other steps. They organized groups of ministers who met together to study and expound the Bible. Sometimes laymen were also included. Although the Queen insisted on the suppression of those groups, the Presbyterians actually took the additional step of trying to introduce their principles of church government from within the Church of England. Ministers of Presbyterian persuasion were ordained to episcopal orders, but would not accept a congregation without its express approval. They called themselves pastors rather than priests, and in various areas met together to exhort each other in faith and practice. They insisted upon regular ministers who preached, taught, administered the sacraments, and admonished and corrected believers whenever necessary.

Although the Presbyterians were the largest body of Puritan dissenters, there were other groups whose outlook was considerably different. Closest to the Presbyterians was a group of Independents or Congregationalists who also wanted to purify the church without separating from it. But their understanding of the church was characterized by an emphasis upon the local church as an independent body of believers, subject neither to presbyterian nor episcopal system. Having a similar understanding of the church, but convinced that no good could come out of staying in the Church of England, was the group known as Separatists. They characterized the Presbyterians as those who tarried for the magistrates to undertake reformation. Their outlook was expressed in a tract by Robert Browne entitled "A Treatise of Reformation Without Tarrying for Any." The separatist program defied church and state alike. It was a declaration that matters of church could not be dictated by magistrates. The church was not a church of the land or nation, including all who are born into it. It was truly the community of believers who entered into a covenant on the basis of their profession of faith.

Congregationalists and Separatists differed on the way the

reformation of the church should proceed, whether from within or by separation. But on the nature of the church, they were mainly in agreement. Profession of faith was the *sine qua non* for church membership. Yet not everyone who decided to be a church member was permitted to be a part of the church in the fullest sense. Only those whose profession met the testing of members in good standing could be admitted to the full rites of the church. No accident of birth sufficed; not even one's own decision. The church was based on a covenant of believers, dedicated to making sure that the church expressed the spirit of its Lord. Hence, entrance into such a community required the approval of the other covenanted members.

Such communities of faith operate in particular places. By definition, in this way of thinking, the church is the local church. Hence the term "Congregationalists"—those who believed that the church is the local, functioning body. There is no church in the abstract, no such thing as a combination of churches forming the church. The church is always a concrete community and in the aggregate one can only speak of churches. This does not prevent a number of communities from undertaking joint projects; but in theory that would be only the concurrent action of individual churches. (In New England such common concern was expressed in the plans for an educated ministry and resulted in the founding of various educational institutions.)

Since the church was the local church and it was the believers who made the decisions, there was a tendency toward democracy in the congregations. But responsibility was still heavily focused on an educated clergy. Congregationalists were wary of untutored and untrained clergy. They distrusted emotion, though not vitality, and placed a premium upon learning. The polity (or church order) of Congregationalists, therefore, reflected an attempt to institute a structure in which all believers were on an equal footing, but which nevertheless placed particular responsibilities in the hands of a selected number. Such a particular procedure obviously made religious and practical sense. It took into account the fact that in Christ there are no essential distinctions, and yet there are differences in calling and training. The difficulty, however, for Congregationalists was that although this pattern might be in accord with the spirit of the Bible, it could not be found directly in scripture.

In addition to the Congregationalists, Baptist churches also emerged out of the separatist tradition. The first Baptist church was probably organized by John Smyth while in exile from England in Holland. This group migrated back to England under Thomas Helwys, a follower of Smyth. In spite of certain religious affinities and some possible direct relation with the Anabaptists in Holland, the Baptist movement was nourished primarily by the Separatist tradition in the English scene.

Generally, Baptists, in contrast to Congregationalists, were non-Calvinistic Puritans (though there were some Calvinistic Baptists, known as Particular Baptists). They preferred to steer a course between the concepts of free will and predestination, but were not interested in working out how this could be accomplished. Their strength did not lie in theological astuteness. Their interests were elsewhere. They were concerned with the church as a gathered community, with the corollary of believers' baptism, and with the separation of church and state. Like the Congregationalists, they believed that the church was a covenanted community in which men were on an equal footing, served each other, and assumed each other's burdens. For the Baptists, however, this implied a more rigid democratic structure. Among some Baptists anyone who had the Spirit could be the minister, provided he was called and elected; in other Baptist groups, minimal educational qualifications, as in Congregational groups, were required. Certainly democratic structures do not exclude the education of ministers. But many Baptist and sectarian groups insisted that education was wholly irrelevant to the operation of the Spirit. Men were not only theoretically but actually equal in the Spirit. Baptists knew all too well that education has a way of producing class levels, even in a community of grace. Many belonged to the lower economic strata of society and acutely sensed any drift toward social differentiation.

Like the Anabaptists, the Baptists came to the conviction that believers' baptism was essential. If the church was the community of those who were believers and had made a covenant together, then baptism must be at an age when one could enter

the covenant by responsible decision. Certainly the form of baptism, immersion (which was not required originally), was less
important than the emphasis on decision and faith as the key
to the rite. Baptism was not a sacramental means of grace, but
an "ordinance" symbolizing a regeneration which had already
taken place.

Unlike the Anabaptists, the Baptists accommodated themselves
to the demands of the state and supported it in the duties of
citizenship up to the point where religious liberty was involved.
Congregationalists, too, were for religious freedom, unhampered
by magistrates in any way. But among English Congregationalists,
this was not so much conviction as necessity. They had no other
choice, with Anglicans on the one side and Presbyterians on the
other, both determined that there must be a national church.
For the Baptists, on the other hand, the separation of church and
state was a matter of deep religious conviction. Since the church
was a strictly voluntary association, its very nature was destroyed
by any governmental decisions respecting its life. One danger of
any alliance between the two was a loss of vitality in the church.
This could only be maintained where the church itself was a
"gathered" group of real Christians, as opposed to state churches
which sought to include all, and by reason of accident of birth
rather than Christian conviction.

While separation appeared essential for the sake of vitality, it
seemed no less important for genuine liberty of conscience in
matters of belief. Baptists were convinced that doctrinal tests
violated the rights of men whose consciences under God led to
different convictions. Perhaps this principle was partially reinforced by the fact that Baptists did not accept the prevailing
Calvinism of Presbyterian and Congregationalist alike. But it was
no more than reinforced, since freedom of religious belief and
expression was a matter of fundamental conviction among Baptists. Their understanding of God and his relation to man demanded it.

In America, this faith first found expression in New England.
Roger Williams, who came to New England as a Puritan turning
Separatist, now became a Baptist in conviction and is credited
with founding the first Baptist church in the new world in Provi-

dence. Essentially a searching man in religious matters, and banished from the New England Puritan community, he established religious toleration in his own area. He, too, believed in a Christian society, but one in which the church influenced the community through the quality of its life and not by means of laws. The separation of church and state, which is the heritage of America, was contributed to largely by Roger Williams and the Baptists. It obviously did not mean the separation of religion and culture.

For Baptists, the principle of individual decision in relation to God meant complete freedom for each man in his faith. Because of this, church order belongs to the individuals who are Christians and not to clergy. Further, because the life of the Church is the life of individual Christians, there can be no imposed liturgy. Prayers express a man's faith and therefore ought to be extemporaneous.

3. SEVENTEENTH-CENTURY DEVELOPMENTS IN ENGLAND

In England those of Presbyterian persuasion continued to hope that eventually their notions of reform might gradually be realized in the Church of England. Even some Congregational groups who did not believe in separation joined in this hope. When, with the execution of Mary Queen of Scots, it became clear that James of Scotland, King of a Presbyterian stronghold, would be the successor of Elizabeth, hopes ran high. Upon his ascension to the throne, the Presbyterian clergy sent a restrained petition to the king, calling for the reform of the church but carefully pointing out that they were not schismatics seeking the dissolution of the state church. To their great disappointment, the King decided in favor of the Anglicans. Not only were the dreams of the Presbyterians destroyed, they were to enter into a period of enforced uniformity and intense opposition. A group of Separatists migrated to Holland to escape persecution and to gain freedom, and some of them later sailed to America and founded the Plymouth Colony.

With the succession to the throne of Charles I and the increasing influence of William Laud, one of the most powerful and

intensely Anglican of all English bishops, opposition to dissent
expressed itself in an extremely vigorous policy on the part of
both church and state. Complete conformity to Anglican practice
was demanded, and countless Puritan preachers were deprived
of position and not infrequently prosecuted. Because of this policy, many Puritans, most of whom were not separatists but of
Congregationalist leaning, left England and founded the Puritan
settlement in Salem, Massachusetts.

In the immediately ensuing years, Anglicans sided with the
King, even when he dismissed Parliament in 1629. But when the
Long Parliament was convened in 1640, the Presbyterians were
in the majority. Laud was cast into prison and the arbitrary
actions of the King resulted in civil war two years later. Episcopacy was abolished and the Book of Common Prayer forbidden.
Parliament called the Westminster Assembly for the purpose of
effecting a new and proper church order. Under the influence of   ) Solemn
the Scots, whom Parliament definitely needed on its side in the   / League
war, it was insisted that the pattern for the new order be in line / + Covenant
with that of the best Reformed churches. Present in the assembly
were eight Scottish commissioners, lay members of both houses
of Parliament, five Independent ministers, and a few of Anglican
leaning. But dominating the entire assembly were the Presbyterian divines. Under their influence the Westminster Confession
of Faith was formulated.

An examination of the Confession would require restatement
of many of the religious affirmations described earlier. The
material will not be repeated. It is important, however, to note
that the general spirit of Puritan theology, however similar the
particular affirmations, is different from that of this highly
Calvinistic confession. When one reads Puritan writings, one
catches a sense of vital and living faith. Earlier in this chapter,
we noted the strong experiential quality of Puritan thinking. The
Westminster Confession, which for a long time informed Presbyterian thinking and which is still subscribed to in large segments
of the Presbyterian church, is a concise and formal statement of
points to be accepted. As an example of clarity and theological
precision in confessions, it is a masterpiece. Yet it is a Puritan
document curiously devoid of the usual vitality of Puritanism.

Perhaps this was inevitable in the kind of semi-creedal writing which characterized it. Like all such formulations, it suffers when the faith which underlies it is not evident to those who read it. In this instance, the damage is particularly telling, since the theology of Puritanism, apart from its experiential basis, is especially difficult. More than anything else, the Westminster Confession is responsible for later negative attitudes toward Calvinism.

The catechisms prepared by the assembly were in fact more representative of the Puritan spirit than was the Confession. The Directory for Public Worship likewise exhibited this spirit and hewed a path between a "prescribed liturgy and extemporaneous prayer." The schemes for church order, including ordination and discipline, had no chance of implementation because of the opposition of the non-Presbyterians who, in the changing political scene, became more influential.

Many Independents or Congregationalists (who had held a congregational understanding of the church combined with a Calvinistic view of the relation of religion to all of life) had not been separatists but became so under Presbyterian pressure for uniformity. John Milton was convinced that the "new Presbyter is but old Priest writ large" and that out of Westminster one could not expect toleration. In the Commonwealth and Protectorate under Oliver Cromwell, who had defeated Charles I, the Presbyterians were unable to assume control as they had expected. Cromwell himself was an Independent and insisted upon toleration for many of the religious groups. But he did not accept the principle of separation completely. Rejecting both Presbyterian and Anglican domination, he yet insisted upon some control of church order and payment of clergy by the state. Through local Committees of Ejectors, unfit clergy to the number of over six thousand were deprived of their positions, while through a national committee of Triers, the vacancies were filled from among Presbyterians, Independents and Baptists. Since the primary criteria for incumbency were a godly life and trustworthy political opinions—obviously those which would not threaten the new regime—a considerable number of Anglicans remained. In this way, Cromwell worked out a system which comprehended diverse elements, while maintaining national control. Although Quakers had no clergy and therefore did not fit into this scheme, they, too, were tolerated by Cromwell and were comparatively unmolested (see section 5).

This settlement lasted no longer than the life of Oliver Cromwell. His son Richard had neither the understanding nor forcefulness of his father. Presbyterians and Royalists alike longed for the restoration of the monarchy. In the Long Parliament and in the Convention Parliament, which was to work out the details of the recall of Charles II, the Presbyterians had a majority. Their intention was to work out a system which would include Presbyterians and Anglicans in one national church. Had they insisted upon this as the basis of the recall, rather than on subscription by Charles II to a nebulous statement granting liberty to tender consciences, they might have been more successful. As it was, the political settlement was made and the King, with the support of the Anglicans, dismissed the Convention Parliament, and the newly elected Cavalier Parliament, composed primarily of Royalists and Anglicans, re-established Anglicanism more securely than ever. Exiles returned and suppressed Anglicans came back to life. As one writer has put it, Archbishop Laud was more successful in death than in life, for now his dreams were realized.

From this point on, the Presbyterian hope of belonging to a national church in England was completely shattered. Now Presbyterians shared the lot of Independents and Baptists. In the Act of Uniformity of 1662, episcopal ordination was required and all clergy had to subscribe to the revised Book of Common Prayer. It was a serious offense even to attend a service which was not conducted in accord with the Prayer Book. Now the Puritans were definitely forced out of the Anglican fold into the role of "Protestant" dissenters; and severe penalties were attached to dissent.

Not until the advent of William and Mary, who came to the throne partly through Protestant support, did the picture change. The Act of Toleration of 1689 was "An Act to exempt their magistrates' Protestant subjects dissenting from the Church of England from the penalties of certain laws." However, such Protestants had to be trinitarian, and their places of meeting had to be registered. Clergy had to subscribe to the doctrinal, though not liturgical, aspects of the Thirty-nine Articles. Not until 1779 was the authority of the Bible substituted for the Thirty-nine Articles, and not until 1813 were non-trinitarians tolerated. From the time of 1689, however, toleration of dissenters was never withdrawn. The Church of England was the established church, but the ideal of encompassing the diverse elements in one national church had been given up.

4. PURITANISM IN NEW ENGLAND

In America, the goal of Puritanism was more nearly realized. Plymouth Colony had been founded by Separatists coming from England after a sojourn in Holland. Salem was established by Congregational groups who fled under the period of Laud. Within ten years' time over twenty thousand men and women came to the latter colony, including such distinguished divines as John Cotton, John Davenport, and Richard Mather.

The relations between Plymouth and Salem were friendly, but New England Puritanism was formed more by the latter than by the former. In the new situation in America, Puritans set out to do what had become impossible in England. The Puritan ideal of ordering all under God was combined with a congregational view of the church. Most of the New England Puritans were non-separatist Congregationalists who had hoped to reform the Church of England from within. They felt that they were doing just this in America. The church was to be made up only of professed believers, covenanted together in local churches, but dominated by the Calvinistic ideal of a society ordered in worship and in all realms of life by a single religious understanding. This was a hope which emerged out of the English scene, but which became effective only in America.

The combination of emphasis upon the local church and upon uniformity in worship and life throughout the body politic was centrifugal, and potentially explosive. It accounts for some of the problems of the New England community. Where churches were independent bodies of believers, both they and the Christian life of the society could be threatened by an alien body politic. In principle, the churches were protected by the Charter which the

Puritans had wrung from Charles I before leaving England. But those who made no profession of faith more and more predominated in the new communities, and it was clear that their control of society might be fatal to the Christian idea of uniformity and of a Christian society. To keep this from happening, Puritans saw to it that only churchmen could be freemen or voters. And since only those who professed their faith and were found to be true believers were admitted to the church, this procedure was decidedly effective.

Under the pressure of internal problems, it became necessary to modify the stress on the local church in the direction of some over-all control. The local body remained the only true "church," but associations of clergy arose to deal with matters which affected the life of all the churches, such as education and the combatting of divisions within the churches. For example, the separatist views of Roger Williams, and the remarks of Anne Hutchinson, and later still the coming of Quakers, demanded more than local treatment. Moreover, criticism from Puritans abroad concerning the exclusion of Presbyterians from full communion could not be answered by a local church. Nor could individual local bodies effectively protest against the separatist views which came to dominate English Congregationalists after 1640. Further, the loss of the Charter in 1684 made it more important for the church to have an over-all structure.

For a number of reasons, therefore, associations of churches and clergy developed early. Although the theory remained that such associations were merely consultative and practical, for all practical purposes they determined policy. While the Cambridge Platform of 1648 reaffirmed the congregational principle, it was itself the product of ecclesiastical forces which partly belied the principle. Thus New England Congregationalism, in order to maintain its Calvinistic ideals in relation to society, moved administratively closer to a Presbyterian conception of the ordering of the church by bodies more inclusive than the local church. But it never gave up its conception that the local church alone is the church.

The New England churches did, however, have to make concessions to the loss of vitality in the second generation of Puritans in America. Those who came to America already professing their faith and those who initially joined the Puritan group in America maintained the enthusiasm of the original movement. But of many in the second generation, those born and reared in the new world, one could not say the same. They were born and baptized in the church but seldom had the experience which led to public and adult confession of their faith; thus they never entered into the covenant. They were good men who believed in God, but had little of the intense zeal of their forebears. Through a compromise known as the Halfway Covenant, such persons were barred from Holy Communion and from voting on spiritual matters. But in other respects they were members of the church and exercised the rights of citizenship. This was a device to guarantee the on-going life of the Puritan experiment in uniting church and state. But it proved also to be a sign that much of its life had waned.

5. THE QUAKERS

The Quakers were the most distinctive of the movements related to Puritanism. They arose out of the religious unrest of England during the period of Cromwell and stood for a radical kind of reform within Christendom which contrasted sharply with Protestant, Anglican, and Roman patterns alike. They preferred to think of themselves as the third way in Christendom, over against Roman Catholicism and Protestantism.

Small groups of "friends" (as they called themselves) first met in the Lake district of England, and the movement spread throughout England. One of the foremost protagonists of the Friends was George Fox, who went up and down the length of England, disputing the beliefs of Christians, not infrequently interrupting sermons to challenge what was said and turning the challenge into a sermon itself. Fox felt called upon by God to gather people to the truth from out of the steeple-houses, as he called the churches:

> Now the Lord had shewed me, while I was in Derby prison, that I should speak in steeple-houses, to gather people from thence; and a concern sometimes would come upon my mind about the pulpits that the priests lolled in. For the steeple-

houses and pulpits were offensive to my mind, because
both priests and people called them the house of God, and
idolised them; reckoning that God dwelt there in the outward house. Whereas they should have looked for God and
Christ to dwell in their hearts, and their bodies to be made
the temples of God; for the Apostle said, 'God dwelleth not
in temples made with hands: but by reason of the people's
idolising those places, it was counted a heinous thing to
declare against them.[2]

Such conduct was hardly likely to be tolerated in a period not at
all convinced of the value of tolerance. In spite of persecution,
the movement grew. The essential seriousness of Quakers—so
named because they quaked at the Word of God—soon won the
respect of many and even a degree of toleration under Cromwell.
In America, they suffered at the hands of the Puritans, but had
freedom in Rhode Island (though Roger Williams considered
them wrong) and in Pennsylvania, the colony started by Quaker
William Penn with the principle of toleration as one of its
cornerstones.

The fundamental tenet of the Quakers was that God is directly approachable and experienced by men as within themselves. They spoke of the light within, or of Christ within, even
of God within. God's spirit was immediately present and discernible to all who sought him in sincerity. His truth and way of life
could be directly apprehended.

To those Protestants who did not share this conviction, this
appeared as a direct denial of everything biblical. The Puritans
found sin rather than God within. Quakers, in contrast, insisted
on the essential goodness of men. Puritans felt that the emphasis upon immediate revelation of the Spirit within led to uncertainty as to knowledge of the true God, disclosed in the Bible.
They suspected that the Quakers belonged to the mystical tradition and had no adequate criterion of truth. (To be sure, the
Quakers were in a heritage related to mysticism, though they
were not directly its heirs.) Barclay in his *Apology* was quick to
point out that "neither tradition nor the Scriptures, nor reason
which the Papists, Protestants and Socinians do respectively make

[2] George Fox, *Journal* (New York: E. P. Dutton & Co., Inc., 1948.
Everyman's Library), 49.

the rule of their faith are in any whit more certain." Roman
Catholics disagreed about tradition. The Protestants contended
over the meaning of the Bible even as they idolized it. And the
Socinians, a late sixteenth-century rationalistic group, disagreed
over the results obtained by reason. In contrast, Quakers felt that
what emerged out of their own seeking was both more definite
and consistent.

Early Quakers felt that they were carrying out the logical
implications of the Reformation. Not infrequently, they quoted
the reformers themselves. Both Jesus Christ and the Bible were
important, but in no case should they be in the way of the believer's direct apprehension of God. In Jesus of Nazareth the
love of God was historically manifest, and in the eternal Christ
present in man he is continually accessible and available. The
Bible is an account of the historical manifestations of this love
and it contains much truth which is important for men. But as
such it is neither the word of God nor truth. Truth can be found
directly by those who wait quietly for the Lord. The Bible itself
bears witness to such truth discernible within. Man needs to discover and rediscover this truth as the source of his life, letting
nothing else pull him aside.

The stringent emphasis upon the truth within gave discipline
and order to the lives of Quakers. In this respect, they were a part
of the Puritan ethos, in which life was ordered from top to
bottom by the truth as perceived. For Quakers, a life, simple and
elegant in its dignity, was more important than all thought.
Plain speech and simple clothes were adopted. Integrity in all
things was prized above all else. A life given in suffering was
more important than all striving, since it witnessed to the truth
and peace of God.

Since God was found directly within, it was the responsibility
of each to discover and profess the truth. For Quakers, this
implied a distinctive pattern of worship. The Quaker meeting
was a place where each, in the presence of the others, meditated
silently upon God's presence and spoke only as he felt called to
do so, whether on God's presence itself or on the meaning of
his presence for some problem. Such directness excluded an
organized ministry as well as a special church building, or a

liturgical order of worship. Quaker organization existed only for the sake of convenience in coming together, in keeping records, and in taking care of other details of their common activity. All decisions involving action were jointly agreed upon, not by vote, but by a kind of consensus which the secretary recorded as the sense of the meeting. Until a consensus could be safely affirmed, nothing was recorded.

In the world at large, Quaker concern early manifested itself in the alleviation of suffering and in philanthropic works. Most Quakers also have believed in non-resistance, and remained impartial in the conflicts of nations with each other. Although this at times proved embarrassing, as in the Revolutionary War, it frequently made them emissaries of relief and reconciliation across the chasms which have torn the rest of the world.

VI

Revival of the Evangelical Spirit

Movements of the spirit not infrequently lose their vitality through inertia or through suffocation by alien forces growing up within or infiltrating from without. When this happens, a movement either lingers on and eventually dies, or is reborn. Even churches do not escape this historical pattern. Their only justifiable claim to existence in the face of such an historical destiny is that their concern for the gospel frequently becomes the means of rebirth. Such was the pattern in the evangelical movements which swept through Germany, England, and America in the eighteenth century.

In Chapter IV we noted how the Lutheran churches increasingly emphasized right belief, and made assent to theological formulations the basis of the Christian life. They had unwittingly assumed the spirit and argumentative nature of rationalism. This made Christian faith exceedingly formal and forbidding to those who rightly sensed that the New Testament emphasized justification and the new life in Christ as the basis for all Christian living and thinking.

In England, on the other hand, the vitality of faith was seriously weakened by the alliance with "natural religion." This led to formalism in the churches and to a partially "secularized" clergy. The net result was loss of the sense that religion touched the total human being. It appealed to the head without captivating the heart. The work of John Wesley and the Methodist movement successfully revived a faith which moved the hearts of men.

The situation in America was similar. Puritanism had lost much of its religious power, while the form and structure of its theology remained intact. In the previous chapter, we noted that the theology of Puritanism at its height was undergirded by a profound and vibrant faith. With the decline of that faith, Puritan theology resembled the orthodox developments in Europe, against which pietism reacted. Theological formulations which no longer reflected an experiential base might be correct: but they became monstrous when individuals who themselves had lost the power of faith continued to insist upon them. A contributory cause of decline was the Arminian influence which had also penetrated to America. It was part of a general tendency to stress reason above all else in matters of religious doctrine.

Pietism on the Continent, Methodism in England, and the great awakenings in America shared in a common pattern. Connections between them can be traced. Wesley visited a pietist community on the Continent and read the pietist writings. Whitefield, originally associated with Wesley, was the most noted preacher in the American awakenings. Interesting as these connections are, however, the movements were largely independent in origin. The existence of the movements, rather than their derivation from each other, accounts for the connections. In their various situations, they arose to arrest current developments by an emphasis upon the experience of the living Christ in the hearts of men.

1. THE PIETIST MOVEMENT

The pietist tradition began in German Lutheranism, through the work of Philip Spener and his disciple, August Francke. Both were concerned to revitalize the Lutheran Church, whose insistence on right doctrine seemed to make no place for experiential faith in the living Christ. Spener and Francke organized small groups of Lutherans who met together in private homes for the mutual enrichment of their faith. These were to be a leaven in the church, quietly bringing life into its structure.

The *collegia pietatis* (associations of piety), as the little groups were called, nourished their faith especially in common study of the Bible. They dedicated themselves to the love of God in Jesus Christ, made known and experienced by the believer as he read and examined the New Testament. In this sense, they considered themselves the heirs of the Reformation. But in emphasizing the new life in Christ, they also felt they were bringing the Reformation understanding of justification to its fulfillment. The believer was not only justified; he lived a new life. He must be holy and as nearly perfect as possible. Perfection, however, was not interpreted as sinlessness; it meant definite progress in the Christian life. Such progress would be evidence of an undeviating allegiance to spiritual reality in contrast to the worldliness of the time, including that of the church and its clergy.

Pietists were under no illusions about how much they might accomplish. They did not expect much in this life. But the small communities in the midst of the churches were considered to represent truly the saved and redeemed community. As the redeemed, they did not pine for the end of the world, though many of them expected it momentarily. Rather salvation was already present in their communities. Because of this the churches could be transformed, but they had no hope that the world as such would be changed. They were concerned with the living presence of Christ in the hearts and wills of individual men. Where two or three were gathered together in the spirit, a community within the larger community of the church was born. In the terminology of a later time, the pietists were disciplined "cell" groups who experienced and practiced the presence of Christ.

By intention, pietism was lay minded. The concept of the priesthood of all believers now became a religious focus for insisting upon the responsibility of every man for his neighbor. Men not only studied the Word together, they exhorted each other toward faith and reminded each other of their responsibilities. They were examples to each other. Unfortunately, though they proclaimed the experience of forgiveness, they were often not themselves excellent examples of men who forgive. While insisting that the presence of Christ introduced warmth and feeling in life, they were nevertheless unbending toward those who had gone astray.

Thus, pietism was both personal and impersonal. It was personal in the sense of awakening each man to the unique and direct way in which the Spirit of Christ can transform human life. It was impersonal in that excessive emphasis upon the new life made many impatient of professions of piety which still exhibited marks of worldliness. To be in Christ meant to reject that which was not of Christ, and to have no traffic with it. It was inevitable that those not in sympathy with this outlook felt judged rather than exhorted, and suspected a bit of unintended self-righteousness.

The genuine warmth of pietism stemmed from the gospel itself. The movement should not finally be judged by how it reacted to what it disliked. Tired of the theological speculations of the Protestant scholastics, pietists pointed to the practical and penetrating power of the gospel as it affected the wills and hearts of men. Theological disputes were considered irrelevant, and detrimental insofar as they were responsible for the loss of vitality within Christianity. From the standpoint of new life in Christ, doctrinal differences were unimportant.

The truth in this contention was that theology had lost its vitality and was no longer an adequate representation of the faith. It had become a substitute for faith. Nevertheless, every confession of the presence of Christ has theological implications, even when these are not explicitly stated. And this was no less true of pietists. They tended to gloss over the depth of sin. Although they asserted that men needed to be justified, they quickly moved to sanctification, or the new life in Christ. The miracle and mystery of faith was side-stepped by an emphasis upon the availability of faith to all who would make the decision. And those who could say that they had experienced Christ cultivated his presence as if he could not and would not be absent from consciousness even for a moment.

The intention of pietists was to revitalize Lutheranism without changing any of its religious conceptions or organizational structure. They did not realize how their own distinctive emphasis was often at variance with fundamental tenets of Lutheranism. This was sensed more by orthodox churchmen than by pietists, and there was frequent opposition on the part of the former. Generally, however, pietist groups remained in the churches. Only occasionally did they have a separatist tendency. Usually, they thought of themselves as the leaven in the dough.

In one important instance, the pietist movement did result in a separate religious body. Count Zinzendorf, a German nobleman whose pietistic tendencies were confirmed by contact with Francke, offered his estate at Herrnhut to the remnants of the Bohemian Hussites. The latter, suffering under persecution, gladly accepted. Originally, Zinzendorf paid little attention to the group from a religious viewpoint, but soon found himself both their patron and religious leader. The unwillingness of most of them to become members of the Lutheran Church made it inevitable that they be consolidated into a distinct community. They became known as the Moravians, a name derived from the province of their origin.

Herrnhut became a center whose influence went far beyond its own confines. Christians from all over Europe visited the community to learn the secret of the Christian life in this community of grace. But even more important than this was the intense missionary consciousness of the community. Missionaries were sent throughout Europe, even to Greenland and the West Indies. Under the leadership of August Spangenberg, a settlement was made in Georgia. Several years later some of the Moravians in Georgia moved to Pennsylvania. Zinzendorf, on a visit to America, named this settlement Bethlehem, and it is still the center of Moravian influence in America.

The impact of the pietist movement, both within the churches and in the Moravian communities, was extensive. The University of Halle and later the University of Tübingen became centers of pietist influence. Through these especially, many of the promising minds of the future were shaped by the pietist tradition and continued to exhibit many of its qualities even as they spoke against the movement. Men as diverse as the philosopher Immanuel Kant (see Ch. VII) and the theologian Friedrich Schleiermacher (see Ch. IX) bore the traces of pietist upbringing and learning. For men disillusioned by theological bickering, religious wars, and rationalist patterns of thought, pietism offered a religious dimension which touched the center of life. It provided a source of vitality in a period in which men were dissatisfied with old ways of thinking and were searching for new directions.

2. THE EMERGENCE OF METHODISM

a. The Cult of Reasonableness in England

After 1689 both the Church of England and the Protestant bodies settled down to a period of comparative security. The battles had been fought and a religious settlement had been reached. But the new and unchallenged stability in the church was itself open to the possibility of stagnation and loss of vitality. Within the Church of England a rationalistic form of religion increasingly manifested itself. This was already latent in the Caroline Divines, who had emphasized the role of reason and morality as a component of the religious life. It was more evident in the Latitudinarians, who had tried to reconcile the faith with broad philosophical and scientific assumptions by showing the reasonableness of faith. But in the case of Caroline Divines and Latitudinarians, the struggles with the Puritans over the nature of the church kept the rationalist elements from becoming dominant.

However, with this battle over, the forces whose motto was reasonableness came to the fore. To them the controversy between Puritans and the Anglicans was itself justification for appeal simply to reason in settling religious disputes. As on the Continent, theological argument seemed like sterile and irrelevant bickering to men who believed that the fight was over non-essentials. They thought that an essential reasonableness ought to prevail in matters of religion and maintained that, after all, Christianity was essentially a reasonable religion.

The relation between the church and the new faith in reason had three important phases. In the first phase the supernatural character of the Christian revelation was maintained and declared to be in accord with reason. Prophecy and miracle were the supernatural evidences of the truth of Christianity, and this fact itself was essentially rational. Nothing was considered more reasonable than that Jesus was the Messiah, though the proof of this was found in prophecy and miracle rather than in reason itself. The pre-eminence of Christianity over all other religious views was still assumed and proclaimed as being in line with both reason and revelation. Such an outlook found itself at home within the church.

The second phase was also characterized by the harmonizing of Christianity and reason. Christianity was seen as an instance or illustration of the "natural religion" of mankind. Natural religion meant simply those religious tenets justified by reason and found in religions generally. Almost a century earlier, Lord Herbert of Cherbury had announced five principal tenets of such a religion. They were: that there is a divine being, that this divine being is to be worshipped, that proper worship consists in moral obedience and piety, that obedience is to be rewarded and disobedience to be punished, and that reward and punishment continue after this life.

It was now declared that at heart Christianity believes just this, though it has special forms of worship and practice. Moreover, since the beginning of time men have accepted these fundamental religious tenets. Thus Matthew Tindal could write a book called *Christianity as Old as Creation.* In essence, Christianity is older than Christ, since Christ recalls men to the religion which is as old as creation. The mission of Christianity is to republish the religion of nature, to call men back to a religion which they obscured through sin.

A considerable number of Anglican clergy held this view even as they read the Book of Common Prayer and administered the rites of the church. But there were some who did not follow such views. Bishop Butler's *Analogy* was written particularly to refute the views of Tindal, by pointing out that there were as many difficulties and obscurities in natural religion as in revealed religion. But he did not succeed in winning adherents among the men who were convinced that the way to true religion lay simply in reasonableness and clarity.

The third phase was testimony to the strength of those who believed that religion must be reasonable above all else. The second phase had already meant abandoning crucial points of the faith. Now there appeared outright opposition between Christianity and a form of natural religion called deism. In many respects, the antagonism centered in the understanding of the Bible. Those interested in reason attacked the miracles of the Bible, including the resurrection, as mythological. And by mythological, they meant fanciful and devoid of truth. (As we shall see, modern Protestants have to thank groups of this type for the early development of the biblical criticism which is now taken for granted.)

We need not concern ourselves with this third phase of the problem. Nor need we treat the first and second differently insofar as they relate to the spiritual life of the Church. Whether certain religious affirmations were declared to be supernatural and defended essentially by reason, or whether certain supernatural aspects were shunted aside in favor of a fundamental core which Christianity and natural religion had in common, made little difference. Both promoted an attitude of indifference. Certainly neither seriously touched the hearts or lives of men. That had to happen apart from all arguments. The spirit of rationalism was met by another spirit, namely, the Holy Spirit, as it laid hold of the lives of men.

b. The Nature of the New Spirit: John Wesley

Vitality never completely leaves the church. But the secure position of Anglicanism and the invasion of the rationalistic spirit combined to sap its life. The formal structure of Anglicanism, both in its hierarchy and its Prayer Book, further made it particularly susceptible to the loss of inner vigor.

The resurgence of a vital Christianity resulted from the labors of a handful of men, chief of whom were John Wesley, Charles Wesley, and George Whitefield. The greatest preacher among them was undoubtedly Whitefield, noted for his preaching both in England and America. Charles Wesley is primarily known for the hymns which he bequeathed to a circle infinitely wider than the Methodists. But it is John Wesley who was responsible for creating the distinctive Methodist movement.

John Wesley was the son of an Anglican priest of high church leanings and of a devout mother. He was a distinguished student and was elected a fellow at Oxford. There he became the leader of a group originally organized by his brother Charles, for the purpose of study and discipline so that the lives of the members might properly be directed to God and his salvation. This group became known as the "Holy Club" or as the "Methodists," both originally being terms of derision.

Soon Wesley was sent to Georgia as a missionary. En route to America, he was much impressed by the faith of a band of Moravians in the midst of a terrible storm. In Georgia itself, things did not go as well as expected, though Wesley worked prodigiously. The natives were less prone to accept Christianity than the "noble savage" described in the literature of Europe. The settlers, on the other hand, found Wesley's high churchmanship and rigorous demands not at all to their liking. His inability to decide between celibacy and marriage, though he had given some reason for a young lady to believe his intentions were matrimony, did not help his situation.

The truth is that, although a priest of the Church of England, Wesley had not yet found himself. And he knew it. Upon his return to England, Wesley one evening reluctantly went to a religious meeting in Aldersgate Street. It turned out to be the event which changed his life. In Wesley's own words:

> In the evening I went very unwillingly to a society in Aldersgate Street, where one was reading Luther's preface to the *Epistle to the Romans*. About a quarter of nine, while he was describing the change which God works in the heart through faith in Christ, I felt my heart strangely warmed. I felt I did trust in Christ, Christ alone for my salvation; and an assurance was given me that He had taken away my sins, even mine, and saved me from the law of sin and of death.[1]

This was Wesley's surrender to the forgiving, revivifying power of God. Now he had experienced God's presence and power much as the Moravians whom he had so admired.

The significance of Wesley's conversion, as that of his brother Charles three days before him, was that now he had experienced in his heart what he had vaguely believed in his mind. He had known about God's grace and presence; but now he had ex-

[1] *John Wesley's Journal,* Philosophical Library, 1951, 51.

perienced it. He had known that he could not come to God through work, but now he knew that he had been trying to do so nevertheless. From this he was now free; and he knew how free others might be who also shared this faith. Such men under the power of God could transform a world and march on to perfection.

This experience, together with the faith which grew out of it, is the point for understanding Wesley's subsequent thinking and behavior. Wesley did not think new thoughts as a result of his conversion. He did not even let the old ones go. He related them to his new experience and transformed them in this way. The rigor of the holy club at Oxford was never lost. It became part of the intense ethical concern that all life be lived in the service of God, much as in Puritanism. Card playing and other amusements were rejected because they could not qualify under the rule of utilizing all one's time and energies under God. Drinking, which in the England of this period was an acute social problem, was particularly rejected. (It was perhaps inevitable that succeeding ages should forget the reason and only remember that certain acts were proscribed.)

The semi-mystical writings of men such as William Law and the pietist tradition were also a definite part of the religious heritage of Wesley. But the nuances were distinctive. Wesley found Law's writings too mystical and not sufficiently based on Jesus Christ. But he was forever impressed by their depth and warmth of faith. The pietistic Moravians had attracted him ever since his trip to Georgia. Shortly after his conversion, he visited the Herrnhut community. It left an ineradicable impression upon him. Nevertheless, he found the members of the community, much as Law, too subjective in their faith and therefore not sufficiently based in Christ. Moreover, they appeared too complacent, assuming that piety would automatically produce fruit in personal and social life. For Wesley, faith must express itself in a definite pattern and direction. The difference can be illustrated by reference to the social scene. Neither Wesley nor the pietists challenged the *status quo*. Economically and politically, they were conservative. But Wesley's sense for meaningful discipline and direction had tremendous social consequences. His dictum, earn all you can, save all you can, give all you can, was formulated as a part of his faith, expressing the needful components of activity, honesty, frugality and charity in the Christian life. It fostered economic development and supplied a conscience in the midst of it. Methodists as a result were often in the forefront of reform movements relating to the new industrialism.

Basically, the content of Wesley's newly discovered faith was the intimate experience of the empowering presence of Christ. Nothing else mattered. Wesley's singular devotion to Christ and what might be accomplished through him lay behind his concept of "Christian perfection." Perfection, for him, meant nothing else than full devotion to Christ, expressed in every act. It is important to stress the element of devotion rather than the acts. At times, Wesley did speak of perfection in terms of perfect acts or an achieved pattern of life. But when he did, he usually denied, as did Calvin, that perfection is a possibility for the Christian. Usually, Wesley referred to singular devotion to Christ as the essence of perfection. It is "simplicity of intention and purity of affection," guiding the life and work of man. If, as a result, the Christian's life is almost morally perfect, Wesley's real point was still that perfection refers to the power of the ever-present Christ so to transform the nature of man that he will do nothing but good and pure acts. Perfection is the state of being in Christ. Christ fills and permeates one's being, just as the blood stream sends vitality through the human body. Perfect acts are but the consequence of this presence and are not to be considered apart from them. Where perfect acts are themselves the norm, living in Christ is secondary. This would be utterly foreign to Wesley's intention.

Perfection is living in the presence of Christ and sin is failure to live in the fullness of that presence. At times Wesley's enthusiastic description of the life in Christ led him to make affirmations about moral perfection which appeared to shift the base from which he spoke. In the same way, his opposition to particular flagrant violations of God's will led him to denounce these in such a way that it sometimes seemed as if sin meant simply particular sins. Nevertheless, his fundamental orientation was clear. Wesley's insistence that activity emerges out of grace was thoroughly in the Reformation tradition. But he gave this insight a distinctive turn by his emphasis on the life of experienced grace, zealous moral endeavor, and growth toward perfection. He considered the new life in grace so important that he relegated many other aspects of the faith to a peripheral position. It was not that he rejected these; on the contrary, Wesley was quite satisfied with the general theological tradition of the Thirty-nine Articles and the Prayer Book. He was simply concerned to emphasize certain elements in the tradition which had been neglected and were essential to a vital church. It was just this powerful concern with inward experience and moral living, however, which gave the Methodist movement its distinctive character—and this could and did often lead in later generations of Methodists to subjectivism and legalistic moralism, in which the larger theological background of Wesley's work was omitted.

Wesley did reject the concept of predestination. If God is just, he cannot foreordain men to damnation. The issue of their destiny must remain open. Anything less destroys the freedom of man, even the freedom which belongs to the sinner. Man is not a machine; he is an essentially moral being, whose activities have implications for his future.

Yet Wesley did not believe that man redeems himself. Although he believed in the uniqueness of man and insisted on safeguarding his freedom, he had a deep sense for the catastrophic and fateful character of the Fall. He insisted that nothing but God could rescue man. Apart from grace, man could do nothing good. But the Fall did not destroy man's nature as a responsible being. And God's grace was continually given to sinful men, making it possible for them to respond to his call. This was not the grace of faith, but the prior grace which enabled men to make the decision of faith. It was the ground of the freedom from which one might begin.

Wesley contended that those who nurtured this prior grace could expect God to respond with his presence. Their seeking in grace was the precondition for God's full redeeming activity. Man was not justified, however, by this prior grace or by his seeking. He was redeemed through the empowering reality which came to him in the midst of his search. He was justified by the fresh activity of God. But this came only to those who freely responded.

The advent of justifying grace could be sudden, but it could also be experienced as a moment in a gradual process of growth in grace. Justification was simply the forgiveness of sins. Sanctification, on the other hand, was the process of growth initiated by justification. It was the increasing presence of the grace of God in the human heart. But it was likewise the act of men expressing in works and discipline the new life which had come to them. Grace and works thus belonged together, mutually reinforcing each other. In fact, Wesley did not reject the notion of "saving works," provided they were understood as emerging from the regenerative power of the presence of Christ. Nothing was more characteristic of Methodism than the insistence that the Christian grows in grace and increasingly exhibits the perfect qualities of Christ.

c. Results of the New Spirit

In the power of such a message, Wesley found himself traveling the length and breadth of the English land, preaching whenever occasion presented itself. He declared: "I looked upon all the world as my parish; thus far I mean, that in whatever part of it I am, I judge it meet, right, and my bounden duty to declare unto all that are willing to hear, the glad tidings of salvation." [2] Nor was such preaching in vain. He, like George Whitefield, found ready audiences wherever he went. Men were longing to hear a redemptive message which warmed the heart and imparted new life. They were ready for a religion which made a difference in their lives.

Whitefield was undoubtedly the greater preacher of the two. But it was Wesley's genius for "follow up" and organization which created the Methodist movement. He established societies which met together separately to hear the Word and encourage a strict discipline. Wesley even issued tickets which needed renewal from time to time if one was to remain in good standing. In this way, he exercised control in order to increase genuine spirituality.

[2] Norman Sykes, *The English Religious Tradition,* 65.

Later he organized Methodist groups in "classes," each group consisting of twelve with a class leader. Aside from providing a convenient way to collect necessary funds, this device also helped to strengthen control over the societies. Increasingly, Wesley found himself not only preaching but also supervising the Methodist groups scattered throughout the country.

Contrary to his expectations, Wesley's work was not well received in the Anglican Church. The clergy would neither cooperate nor participate. As a result, Wesley had to depend upon a number of lay preachers. Nevertheless, the work prospered and Wesley found it necessary to organize the societies in ways which made it virtually a separate denomination. This was not his intention. Yet as the years went by, he had come to hold that in the New Testament, a presbyter was the same as a bishop, and because of the need of clergy, he began to ordain, first for America and then also for England. This made the position of Methodism within Anglicanism even more precarious.

The result of Wesley's work was that deism and natural religion were effectively challenged in the church. New vitality had entered into Anglicanism. But equally important, Wesley reached thousands of individuals who were never touched by the established church. In the increasing concentration of workers in towns as the industrial revolution progressed, Methodism was always near at hand, offering a spiritual experience and a new discipline. Unlike Anglicanism, it did not have to wait for an act of Parliament. Nevertheless, Methodism in England remained within Anglicanism until after Wesley's death. By that time, it had prompted evangelical stirrings within the Church of England which continued to manifest themselves for some time in spite of the break with the Methodists.

Wesley had also sent missionaries to America. Some worked in the New York area, others in the South where they were greatly helped by the current awakenings. Greatest among the missionaries was undoubtedly Francis Asbury. During the Revolutionary War, Asbury favored the American cause while Wesley counselled neutrality. By the end of the war, American Methodists were restive and felt that the demands of the gospel in a new world needed greater zeal, flexibility and mobility than associations with Anglicanism would allow. By this time Wesley was in agreement on the desirability of a separate American church. But both Coke and Asbury, set apart by Wesley to be superintendents, believed that they must also be independent of John Wesley. Out of this feeling, supported by Methodist groups, came the Methodist Episcopal Church in America. It began inauspiciously, but soon was one of the leading denominations in America.

3. THE GREAT AWAKENINGS

The "Great Awakening" is a term often used to describe the eighteenth-century rebirth of religious vitality which manifested itself in America in the Middle Colonies, in New England, and in the South, particularly in Virginia. Actually, there was no single great awakening, but a series of awakenings scattered in time and in space and relatively independent of each other.[3] It is more difficult to sift out the circumstances occasioning these than those of either pietism in Germany or Methodism in England. But their situation was not dissimilar to that of the European movements. Formalism in the Reformed and Presbyterian Churches in the Middle Colonies, and in Puritanism in New England, certainly played its part.

The first stirrings of the awakenings occurred among the Dutch Reformed in the Middle Colonies in the 1720's. It was inspired by the emotional preaching of Theodore J. Frelinghuysen who demanded a conversion of the heart as the basis for life in the church in place of the formal piety of his listeners. It was not much later that similar manifestations of awakenings occurred in Northampton, Massachusetts, and from there spread sporadically throughout New England.

There were special factors in the New England scene. This was the home of the Puritan experiment. Increasingly, its vitality had disappeared while the shell of orthodox views still lingered on.

---

[3] Because of this, we have accepted the term great awakenings, which was first suggested to us by Professor Robert T. Handy. We are also indebted to him for the term "great revivals" to cover the various expressions of vitality in early nineteenth-century America (See Ch. VII). This phase, in contrast to the term "Second Awakening," suggests both the diversity of the movement and its greater stress on emotions. We are also indebted to Professor Handy for other suggestions concerning the American scene.

Instead of fashioning a Christian society, Puritanism found itself surrounded more and more by the unfaithful. Within the churches themselves there was a spirit of rationalism, represented significantly in an increasing interest in Arminian views. Judging by the fact that Arminianism was so frequently attacked by the preachers of the awakening in New England, it was undoubtedly one of the chief occasions for the awakenings. But this was only part of a general development in the direction of stressing that which is "reasonable" in religious formulations. Predestination, the person of Christ, and the nature of redemption had been the central focus of orthodox formulations. A more reasonable interpretation tended to make such doctrines more palatable, but both these and the orthodox formulations had become matters primarily for intellectual debate. They were articles to be believed rather than expressions of a living faith. A similar rationalist tendency manifested itself in stress on human decision and responsibility in the covenant relation, rather than on the initiating activity of God. The choice was either Puritanism devoid of much of its vitality or rationalized versions as a substitute. Neither touched the heart as well as the head.

Theologically, Jonathan Edwards represents the revitalization of Calvinism under the new conditions. He attempted to make Calvinism relevant again to the social forces of the time, but without its previous theocratic orientation. Moreover, his theological thinking was undertaken in the context of new philosophies in Europe, such as that of Locke (though he did not succumb to their religious presuppositions). In his battle with the Arminians, he attempted to recapture the living experience of God in Christ which had once informed Puritanism.

In these enterprises, Edwards showed intellectual acumen and considerable originality. He was a theologian for the time and probably the greatest theologian America has produced. But his effect on posterity was greater through his association with the awakening in New England than through his theology. The awakening in New England started in his parish. His sermons on a judging, redeeming God, though read from manuscript and without emotion, hit the hearts of people and not infrequently were received with great emotion. Edwards tried his best to distinguish between genuine and spurious conversions, and to guide those whom he could. As in Northampton, so in congregation after congregation in New England, men found themselves surrendering to the experience of the mercy of God in a new and intensely emotional way.

Among the Presbyterians in Pennsylvania, New Jersey, and New York, the awakening was spearheaded by the Tennents, father and son. But the man who did more than any other in spreading the awakenings throughout the colonies was George Whitefield, whom we mentioned in connection with the Methodist movement. He was virtually the one link between the awakenings. Both Edwards and the Tennents welcomed him.

Whitefield's tour of America was no less successful than his preaching in England. Even Franklin was forcibly impressed by him. Part of the secret of his success, apart from his own personal ability and charm, was his insistence that the power of the gospel was greater and more important than the traditional denominations. Men redeemed by the activity and work of Christ are Christians without reference to their denominational affiliations. Preaching in Philadelphia, Whitefield declared: "Father Abraham, whom have you in Heaven? Any Episcopalians? 'No.' Any Presbyterians? 'No.' Have you any Independents or Seceders? 'No.' Have you any Methodists? 'No, no, no!' Whom have you there? 'We don't know those names here. All who are here are Christians—believers in Christ—men who have been overcome by the blood of the Lamb and the word of his testimony.' Oh, is this the case? Then God help us, God help us all, to forget party names, and to become Christians in deed and in truth." [4] With such eloquent and direct pleading, centered in the simple conviction that the experience of Christ would release a man from his afflictions and make him into a Christian, Whitefield affected the lives of thousands. It is estimated that thirty thousand people were brought into some form of Christian experience through the work of Whitefield and fellow evangelists.

But the awakening was not accepted everywhere with enthusiasm. In the Middle Colonies it became the occasion for a split between two factions which were already in disagreement. The

[4] William W. Sweet, *The Story of Religion in America*, 206.

Old Side Presbyterians felt that the Confession of faith and proper action by clergy and synods were the only safe marks of the Church. They already distrusted the New Side Presbyterians, many of whom were trained either in New England or in the Log college instituted by one of the Tennents. When the New Side joined in the awakening, the Old Side decided that this was the last straw. The New Side insisted that only a converted man was a true minister, no matter what his education or credentials. The Old Side responded by having the pro-awakening New Brunswick Presbytery forced out of the Synod. This split lasted only for the years 1741–1758.

In New England, too, opposition developed on the part of clergy who were appalled at the display of emotion in the awakening and at the impolite conduct of many revival preachers. A militant group formed under the leadership of Charles Chauncy. Over against the new movement, he defended sobriety and reason in matters of religion. Jonathan Edwards, admitting the excesses of the awakening, took issue with Chauncy and maintained that the whole man must be involved in the Christian experience. Unfortunately, his warning to the revivalists was not heeded. They went their way, the conservative theologians claimed Edwards as their spiritual leader, and the position maintained by Chauncy eventually developed in Unitarianism.

The awakening in the South was largely influenced by the North. Among Presbyterians who had settled in Hanover County, Virginia, the awakening had slowly begun under lay leadership through the reading of sermons of Whitefield and some of Luther's writings. But it came to prominence only after the arrival of William Robinson, sent to this area by the New Brunswick Presbytery of the New Side Presbyterians.

Although there were Baptist groups in the South early in the eighteenth century, many came directly from New England under the impact of the awakening. The regular Baptists in New England had not been sympathetic to the awakenings, but many individuals and even separatist churches became Baptist because the emphasis upon decision and voluntary association associated with the awakening made them feel most at home. Many migrated to the South where they carried on their interest in evangelism. Among the Baptist groups in the South, the awakening had a strong "revivalistic" tone and the enthusiasm engendered caused them to be the victims of persecution. Their calmness in the midst of attack, plus their growth in maturity under it, caused their numbers to increase and brought respect where there had been ridicule.

Thus the awakenings made their impact along the entire Eastern seaboard. The contributions which they made outlasted the awakenings themselves. In the long run, their effects were perhaps more indirect than direct. It was too much to expect that the intensity of religious experience inaugurated by the awakenings could last more than a few decades.

The movement made a great contribution to education. Many of the colleges and universities grew out of the need to prepare clergymen to serve a revitalized church. Princeton, Rutgers, Brown, and Dartmouth were some of the more significant universities created as a result of the religious impact of the awakenings.

Of greater importance still was the psychological impact of a religious movement which cut across denominational boundaries. In Europe, the pietist movement and Methodism were more confined to special denominational groups. In America, geographical proximity and the intermixture of divergent groups were favorable to movements cutting through traditional lines. This tendency, so evident in the awakenings, was truly the beginning of a process which gave a distinctive character to American Protestantism.

VII

Trends in America and
on the Continent

1. THE SHAPING OF AN AMERICAN TRADITION

Almost imperceptibly Protestantism in America lost its European stamp and assumed forms appropriate to the new world. In many cases, the early forms had differed from European patterns only because the new situation made possible the achievement of goals desired in the old world, but frustrated there. New England Puritans after all wanted to institute an experiment denied them in England. Baptists in Rhode Island and Quakers in Pennsylvania, had hopes that their religious convictions might find freer expression in America than in Europe.

It was inevitable that some of the clashes which occurred in Europe should also arise as the respective groups found themselves in the new world. The conflict between Puritan Congregationalists, Baptists, and Quakers in New England is but one example of this. Nevertheless, the resolution of such strife in America was different from Europe. In the new world a tradition emerged in which the various churches were entirely on their own and free from governmental restriction or support. There was neither conflict nor union between state and church, yet the churches profoundly affected the society in which they lived. In Europe, on the other hand, the pattern continued to be that of a state church favored and supported by government. Adjustments were made which permitted other religious groups to function, though usually at a disadvantage.

It is our present task to delineate some of the religious and historical factors which went into the formation of this distinctive American Protestant tradition. We have already mentioned the importance of Puritan theology in challenging all claims to absolute power and have hinted at the role this played in the revolution and in the formation of the American nation (Ch. V, section 1). We have also mentioned the role of the Baptists, who in principle insisted upon the separation of church and state. The contact across denominational lines engendered by the great awakenings has also been noted. To these must be added deism, the impact of later revivals, the frontier situation, and the practical impossibility of a state church. These factors, when seen in the context of American history, produced free, national churches, but no national church.[1]

a. Protestantism and the Founding of the Nation

By the time of the crisis which led to the American Revolution, much of the enthusiasm of the awakenings was gone, except in the South where the awakening had begun somewhat later. In spite of this, the impact of the churches was not seriously diminished. Clergy of Congregational and Presbyterian persuasion in New England and the Middle Colonies were predominantly on the side of the colonies. Moreover, they had prepared the soil of resistance for many through their preaching of a sovereign God who stands over all other sovereigns. They were the heirs of a history in which men had defied magistrates before, because of the higher loyalty to God and sometimes for the sake of the liberty of conscience which they demanded for themselves and others. Governments, like men, served a higher law than themselves. When they did not do so, it was necessary to resist and replace them. Thus, such men counseled resistance, not on the basis of national feeling but in the name of the liberty and justice demanded by a sovereign God.

[1] Toleration in Maryland was for a specific purpose and did not decidedly affect the American pattern.

Methodists and Anglicans had the greatest difficulty during the Revolution. Their churches were dependent on the mother country. In New England the Anglican clergy had already pled for bishops from England. Fulfillment of this request would demand an act of Parliament. But to the other churches in New England, such an act was foreign interference which violated the spirit of the original Charter. Nor had Presbyterians and Congregationalists forgotten the difficulties caused by Bishop Laud. It is clear why New England Anglicans vigorously favored the Royalist cause. In the South, on the other hand, Anglicans favored the Revolution. They considered the importation of bishops as an infringement of the rights of local vestries. Thus, the Anglicans were divided. Quakers and Moravians, traditionally pacifist groups, suffered most since they were distrusted by both sides.

The Declaration of Independence represented a current of thought derived largely from sources other than the churches. It affirmed certain natural rights, belonging to all men by virtue of their created being. It was essentially equalitarian. The views in the Declaration showed primarily the influence of French thought upon the more elite in American culture of this period. They were derived also partly from the writings of John Locke, whose political theories and views of man reflected a secularized Calvinistic background. Men who held these views were generally religious, but mostly as deists who had little concern for the churches' institutions and theologies, believing that all religions at heart affirmed the same truth, the existence of God and the goodness and equality of men. Jefferson, the writer of the Declaration, was such a deist. Not infrequently, deists were also members of churches. This was especially true among Anglicans, who seemed to have no difficulty combining deism with the Prayer Book. Two-thirds of the signers of the Declaration of Independence were Anglican laymen, essentially deist in their outlook.

The churches supporting the Revolution had no difficulty accepting the Declaration of Independence. John Witherspoon, the Presbyterian divine who was president of the College of New Jersey, now Princeton University, signed it. To be sure, the churches were concerned with liberty and freedom under God, rather than with "natural equality." Moreover, their understanding of man was not that of the deists. Their arguments for equality took account of sin as well as dignity. For some, of course, the rationalist currents within the church made the document itself theologically correct. For different religious reasons men found themselves together in a common struggle, accepting a common declaration of independence. The roots of independence therefore were varied. Religious and so-called secular forces coalesced in the formation of the American nation. Although men often had different motivations and reasons for what they did, they found themselves united in common actions and plans.

With victory came the independence of all the churches. Methodists and Anglicans declared their freedom from the mother churches and proceeded to organize along lines which would fit into the new nation. The Methodist group, as we noted, declared its independence of John Wesley and organized itself as the Methodist Episcopal Church. The Anglicans had the problem of obtaining duly consecrated bishops, and when no one would ordain Samuel Seabury in England because he could not take the oath of loyalty to the crown, he was consecrated by three Scottish Anglican bishops. Later, Parliament authorized the consecration of bishops for America through the Church of England, and in 1789 the group in America was formally constituted as the Protestant Episcopal Church in the United States of America.

The independence of the American nation did not cut off associations with European churches. But it did definitely end a period in which connections and influences were sought, even if only to affirm that what men had hoped for in Europe had been accomplished in America. Henceforth, the churches in America were to set their minds and energies to the tasks at home.

The relations of the churches to each other and to the state awaited solution. In some of the colonies, one religious group was still favored and supported by taxes, usually either Puritan or Anglican churches. Although other groups could not be kept out, they had to pay taxes for the support of the group successful in being established in the state. Hence, toleration was at a price. In Pennsylvania there was the greatest freedom and liberty in religion from the beginning. In New Jersey, Delaware, and Rhode Island, toleration and freedom were widespread. There was

neither establishment nor the payment of taxes for any religious
groups.

In other areas, similar developments were less a matter of
principle than of sheer expediency or necessity. Frequently the
religious groups in the areas were diverse and no single group
could gain control. In New York, e.g., establishment did not succeed, though full toleration and freedom did develop eventually.
In Virginia, a struggle for religious liberty was led by the Baptists, together with the Hanover Presbytery, against the tax supported Church of England. We have already noted that for the
Baptists, as well as the Quakers, separation of church and state
was a matter of religious principle. The Hanover Presbytery, as a
product of the awakenings, was sympathetic to the principle of
the church as a voluntary association and thus also opposed to all
encroachments by the state. Most of the Presbyterians favored
taxation for all religious groups. Jefferson and Madison agreed
with the Baptists and fought against establishment of any kind.
The battle was won. While Pennsylvania had not supported any
religious group from the beginning, now a state had actually
cut off previous support, ruled out establishment, and made all
churches equal before the law.

The Virginia enactment became a model for national policy.
This was not by accident since James Madison had been so active
in the Virginia fight. Included in the Constitution and the Bill
of Rights were the following sentences: "No religious test shall
ever be required as a qualification to any office or public trust
under the United States . . . Congress shall make no law respecting an establishment of religion, or prohibiting the free
exercise thereof." There was opposition to these clauses in the
Constitution and several states continued to have established
churches for some time (the constitutional statements, of course,
did not refer to *state* actions).

Both Madison and Jefferson greatly influenced the religious
outlook in the Constitution. But the roots of this separation between church and state were many. One important fact was the
sheer religious diversity of the new country, with no church in
a position to assert effectively a claim to establishment. Also
significant was the influence of the Baptists, with their traditional

strong opposition to the idea of a state church. The Quaker experiment in Pennsylvania provided an important precedent. The great awakenings should not be overlooked, since they changed the complexion of many of the churches in such a way that voluntary association and free decision, rather than community inclusiveness, marked the essence of the church. The deists, too, played a significant role. Convinced that most of the difficulties between religious groups were petty, they were in favor of a solution which placed none of them in prominence. Again, non-Christian forces helped in the formation of a state of affairs beneficial to the churches themselves.

In other respects, too, the Constitution reflected the meeting of Christian and non-Christian forces. Unlike the Declaration of Independence, its argument for checks and balances and for equality was partly based on the dangers of misuse of power. It safeguarded liberty and equality through a system which presupposed the possibility of both baseness and dignity.

Historians will have to settle the question (if it can be settled) whether the system of checks and balances came chiefly from Montesquieu or indirectly from John Calvin (see Chs. II and V), possibly through John Witherspoon to James Madison. Certainly at the time of the drafting of the Constitution, the Protestant influence on America was less than at the time of the Declaration of Independence. Yet the Constitution accords more with the prevailing Protestant concept of man. One cannot escape feeling that here, as in the Declaration of Independence and the struggle for religious liberty, Christian and non-Christian forces coalesced in a common end.

For our purposes, the important point is that the conceptions of religious liberty and of the separation of church and state gave the theoretical base for a distinctive kind of Protestantism. It became actual for all the churches during the next half century.

b. Through Infidelity to the Triumph of the Churches

A new nation had been formed. The exhilaration of achievement momentarily gave way to the letdown which almost invariably follows a newly won security. The spirit of the time was not favorable to expansion on the part of the churches.

Morever, in the last decade of the eighteenth century deism had suddenly become a powerful force in opposition to the churches.

By the middle of the eighteenth century, the tide of deism and natural religion had been effectively combatted in England by the Methodist movement. But it was only beginning to appear in the new world at this time. Only after the great awakenings did one find deists in America in appreciable numbers. They were neither anti-church nor aggressive in their outlook. Many of them belonged to the churches. They were what one might call gentle deists and came generally from the upper classes.

Beginning approximately at the time of the Declaration of Independence, a type of deism appeared which was militant in spirit and pressed for the victory of reason over the superstitions of the churches. This movement became powerful after the founding of the nation and the publication of Thomas Paine's *The Age of Reason*. Such deism taught men to rely upon themselves instead of on the churches. God, it held, is the creator, and the author of the moral law in the universe. Men must obey this law: breaking it brings punishment. But he who follows the moral law will discover the kindness and goodness of God, known directly in nature. The Bible, on the other hand, depicts a God of war and cruelty and caprice; even in the New Testament, it degrades human dignity. Truly this was a religion of rational self-confidence.

Some of the milder deists were shocked by this outlook. But it was propounded by one who had himself participated in the glorious French Revolution, and this was the period of the height of influence of French culture and ideas upon the American scene. Deist literature was widely disseminated. Deist societies were founded, the first of which was under the leadership of a former Baptist minister, Elihu Palmer.

The deist outlook was influential even when it was not accepted outright. It appealed to self-reliant men who had just created a nation. It appealed to men on the frontier who daily had to depend on nothing else but themselves for food and security. Lexington, Kentucky, became a center of deistic thinking. It appealed to many who had come to America for reasons of economic gain. It appealed to college students who were no longer impressed by theological thinking, whether Calvinist or not, and who found great difficulties in accepting the Bible as the Word of God.

This was a low period for the churches. Less than ten percent of the populace were church members. But there came new awakenings or revivals in the church. Already in the last decade of the eighteenth century revivals were spreading through New England colleges and churches. Timothy Dwight, the new president of Yale, almost single-handedly stemmed the deist tide in a university where there was hardly a theological student. Lyman Beecher made eloquent pleas for the truth and vitality of Christianity over against the deist "infidelity." Beecher also successfully limited the expansion of the Unitarian movement (see Ch. X). The New England revivals had emotional overtones, but they were not characterized by emotional outbursts. Without fanfare but with earnest conviction, the revival preachers effectively returned life to the churches and substantially increased their membership.

While this was happening in New England, the influence of the churches was weak on the frontier. Frontier towns were small and isolated. It was impossible to provide either clergy or churches for all of the communities. Congregationalists and Presbyterians, who insisted upon an educated clergy, were particularly hard pressed. In an effort to meet the need, they counseled communities where both Congregationalists and Presbyterians had settled, to form a single church and call a minister from either group. Methodists were generally more successful, since they organized small groups in "classes" with a lay leader in charge, just as Wesley had done. "Classes" and Methodist communities were then visited by a Methodist minister who traveled an extensive circuit of such groups. But Baptists were generally in the best position. In addition to having fought for political and religious freedom, they did not have the burden of a highly educated ministry. A Baptist preacher was one who felt the call. Once the decision had been made, preaching could begin. Moreover, such preachers usually were of the same social class as the people to whom they preached.

The preaching of most of these groups took on a "revivalistic" pattern. Individuals were confronted with God's terrible judgment upon the sins of indifference, infidelity, and immorality. These were painted in graphic pictures which brought fear and dread to the mind of listeners. When this was accomplished, the preacher pointed to the forgiveness of God for those who repented of their sins and were born anew by his spirit. This was a form of exposition uniquely effective in the life of the frontier.

At the turn of the century, such revival preaching was increasingly successful. But since families sometimes had to come from distances too great to permit them to return home on the same day, a new pattern of "camp meetings" developed in which the families brought provisions and stayed for several days of preaching and meetings. The most notable of such meetings were at Gasper River and Cain Ridge in Kentucky, the latter sponsored jointly by Methodist and Presbyterians.

Revivalism spread from Kentucky and Tennessee into the Northwest Territory. Its peak was reached by 1806. However, in the third decade of the nineteenth century, it sprang up again in the East, primarily in New York State through the preaching of Charles G. Finney. The influence of Finney's "new measure" revivals was widespread in American Protestantism.

However revivalists may be judged by a more sophisticated society, they did succeed in stemming the deist tide within and without the churches. It must not, of course, be forgotten that they were helped by a reaction to French influences after the excesses of the French Revolution. This did not, however, play a large part on the frontier. There the revivals alone won the victory.

The revivals had done much to revitalize and consolidate the life of the churches. They helped to establish the strength of the churches in a situation where there was neither state support nor interference. And churches generally now had the security to which free churches had been unaccustomed.

c. The American Church Tradition

Early in the nineteenth century, American Protestantism had thus worked out a distinctive pattern both in theory and in practice. Even the churches which had hoped for direct support from the state, or which hoped to dominate the life of the society through governmental recognition, either had voluntarily altered their position or had been forced to do so. There was to be no territorial or state church. This meant that even the traditional churches had become "sectarian" in the sense that each church now was composed only of those who freely professed their faith. Voluntary association had been a distinguishing mark of those groups sometimes called "sect-type" churches, in contrast to the churches which sought to be co-extensive with the community. Now all American churches were sectarian in the broad sense of the term. Religion was now a matter wholly of conscience and decision. One did not belong to a church simply by virtue of his place of birth, though he might stay in the church in which he was nurtured. But he could also freely change denominations, as many did and continue to do.

This was a necessary solution in the American scene. But it was also in line with the spirit of the awakenings. There was a stress upon individual decision, an opposition to governmental influence, and a disregard for denominational lines. The individual's relation to God was the crucial point for religious thinking. This tended to make American Protestantism individualistic in its outlook.

The general pattern of American Protestantism had several corollaries. In the first place, denominational consciousness was never to be as great in America as in Europe. In spite of deep splits, some of which came out of the revivals themselves, denominations were generally not as isolated from one another as in Europe. Second, the stress upon individual decision under Christ provided an atmosphere which, connected with other factors, was not conducive to the development of theology. There was, in fact, a suspicion of theology. The revivals placed an emphasis upon "essentials," upon the presence of Christ, not upon theories about him.

Third, several new but related developments set a pattern for the future. Aware of the continual need for a trained and educated clergy, churches created a number of denominational colleges, chiefly west of the Appalachians. The need for Bibles and literature led to the formation of Bible societies dedicated to the distribution of scripture. Tracts also appeared in increasing numbers, no doubt because they had been put to such good advantage in the propagation of deism. Sunday schools first made their appearance in this period. All of these agencies were directed to improving the understanding of a populace which was influenced by the religion of the heart. It is a credit to the awakenings that their more thoughtful adherents saw the necessity of directing this vitality and zeal into channels which would help preserve and consolidate the gains which had been made. Many of these developments will be discussed in the next chapter. As we shall see, they clearly testify that the separation of church and state had not meant the separation of religion and culture.

2. EUROPE: FROM ORTHODOXY TO ENLIGHTENMENT

In the early decades of the eighteenth century, orthodoxy and pietism were the two main Protestant currents on the Continent. Although pietism represented a reaction against orthodoxy, it did not succeed in influencing or softening large sections of the churches. In some areas both in Europe and America, orthodox developments continued well into the nineteenth and twentieth centuries. Charles Hodge, the most eminent professor of the newly organized Princeton Theological Seminary, was a follower of François Turretin, one of the foremost orthodox Swiss theologians. The older orthodoxy found perpetuation unto our time, not through Princeton Theological Seminary, but through such groups as the Orthodox Presbyterian and the Bible Presbyterian churches. In Lutheranism, orthodox thought continued into the present through the Missouri Synod Lutherans.

Predominantly, however, orthodox thought underwent changes, particularly on the Continent. In three phases of theological thinking, a general transition took place from orthodoxy to the Enlightenment. At first glance, one might think simply of contrast between these two, since orthodoxy was concerned with specifically Christian doctrine and the Enlightenment with religion in general. There was a kinship between the two, however, in the rationalistic spirit which dominated both; and as in philosophical thought generally, the rationalistic spirit gave way to a faith in an active, practical reason, so, too, there was a change in Protestant thinking which transformed and ended the orthodox development.[1]

a. From a New Scholasticism to a New Religion

Until the time of Christian Wolff (d. 1754), orthodox theologians reflected a rationalistic spirit but did not consciously relate their thinking to the new philosophical currents. Theirs was a scholasticism whose roots were planted more in medieval categories of thinking than in the newer state of opinion.

In Christian Wolff we see a man who considered himself quite orthodox and believed that the new philosophical outlook, particularly as seen in the philosopher Leibnitz, provided essentially the same truth as Christianity. Proper philosophy and theology lead to the same conclusions in most matters. Thus, following Leibnitz and the rationalist tradition, one can use the traditional proofs for the existence of God and ascribe attributes to him which are in accord with reason. Life itself is rational and ought to be directed toward virtue. Through virtue one's life is fulfilled and rewarded by God.

Wolff believed that the heart of orthodoxy was no different from this. To be sure, there were certain items not found in reason which were supplied by revelation, such as the Trinity, Christology, and grace. But these were above reason, not contrary to it. Miracle may be possible. If so, it means the interruption and the restoration of a natural order created by God. The Bible is rational and rational criteria must be used to substantiate its claims. God is righteous, holy, and good. Nevertheless, sin is a fact. Therefore, atonement is both rational and necessary.

Wolff seriously attempted to safeguard the essentials of the Christian faith. But the spirit of rationalism was so strong in his own approach that it, rather than the Christian substance, was determinative. Given the rubric under which he worked, it is remarkable how much of the traditional orthodox outlook he was able to maintain. To many in his own day, the enterprise ap-

[1] In certain respects the change was quite similar to the growth of natural religion and deism in England at a slightly earlier time.

peared impossible. The pietists were up in arms and had him removed from his professional position. And the philosopher Kant directed his attack against the rational proofs of God's existence as elaborated by Wolff.

The second stage in the movement from orthodoxy to Enlightenment was represented by what may be called the "transitional" theologians. Although they were not of the same mind on many points, they represented an attempt to improve the orthodox system by a new position which took seriously the new currents of thought but accepted neither Wolff nor the pietists. Frequently, theirs was a position between pietism and rationalism. Included among such theologians were Buddeus, Walch, Mosheim, Baumgarten, and the illustrious son of François Turretin, Jean Alphonse Turretin.

Like Wolff, the theologians in this group believed that revelation does not contradict reason. But they did not accept the tight philosophical system of Wolff. They reflected a rational, but not a rationalistic spirit. They were concerned with that which is reasonable. Some of them were influenced by English deist literature which had found its way into Germany. Like the deists, they were opposed to any system of thought which is essentially rigorous in what it asks people to accept, as in the systems of Wolff and of traditional orthodoxy.

Many of these men were intrigued, too, by the increased knowledge of other religious traditions, including those of the East. Convinced that Christianity in its Protestant form is pre-eminent, they nevertheless were searching for a rubric which encompassed the variety of religions and the natural religion of reason. Moreover, they were bothered by the divisions within Protestantism and by what they take to be quarrels about non-essentials.

Turretin's *Discourse on Fundamental Articles in Religion* represented one way taken by the transitional theologians in the light of these concerns. Turretin distinguished between that which is made known by the light of nature and that which is revealed. To the former belongs the knowledge that God is and that he rewards those who seek him. From this statement, believed Turretin, other consequences could be drawn, none of which disagreed with revelation. As a Protestant, however, he believed that revelation is necessary for salvation, and that the implications of revelation are necessary articles of belief, if one is to escape damnation. But he immediately added that these are necessary only to those to whom the gospel is preached and who are endowed with sufficient faculties to receive them. Thus Turretin found a way to stress the distinctiveness of revelation, but escaped making it normative for everyone.

In Christian history, Turretin found many contradictory statements as to what is fundamental. He concluded that the fundamentals are few and that men have fought mainly over non-essentials, such as predestination. Let men confess that they are free, that God rewards according to works, and that God is in control of everything. But they need not make any of these points into a necessary article of belief. For Protestants, there are criteria. These consist in the Word and in prudence. In respect to the Word, men may err and therefore cannot claim complete truth for their views. Man may hold convictions, but they must be tolerant. They must not confuse their interpretations with the total truth.

In this way, Turretin believed that he maintained Christian truth, while accepting the canons of tolerance and reasonableness. The Christian substance still had meaning for him, though its outmoded forms did not. He did not foresee that the canons of reasonableness which he proposed would not help to preserve a more thoughtful and convincing Protestantism, but would instead tend to become a substitute.

This happened in the third phase of the transition from orthodoxy to the enlightenment through the "innovating" theologians. This group included such men as J. F. W. Jerusalem, J. J. Spalding, J. S. Semler, J. A. Ernesti, and Joh. David Michaelis. They believed that revelation was genuine, but that its content at no point was beyond that of definite accord with reason.

Reason, however, was not understood by these men in a wholly formal or rationalistic way. It referred rather to that which makes practical sense, reason as an internalized, functioning reason, genuine to oneself. Formerly, the activity of reason had been construed as the participation of thought in a universal rational structure in the nature of things. This had been the view of Wolff and of rationalism in general. Now reason was understood as personal and inner, functioning as an expression of the self, practical and partly expressed in moral terms.

Revelation had now been reduced to that which is comprehensible to such a reasoning self. It was no longer a mystery beyond reason. Hence a new criterion had been found for looking at Bible and church alike. For some in this group, the early church alone stood out as an example of revelation and reason unencumbered by accretions. The Roman Catholic and Protestant orthodox positions reflected the addition of incidentals which obscured the real center of the church. Some of the "innovators" pushed into the Bible itself, seeing there, too, beginnings of developments which betrayed reason and revelation in the practical sense. The genuine elements in the Bible, according to Semler, are the moral truths taught by Christ, through which we improve our lives. This is the Gospel behind the gospel. We must therefore return to the true revelation which is included in the Bible and which is essentially akin to natural religion. The world view or cosmology of the Bible was now no longer essential to the faith and could be laid aside in favor of its moral truths. Thus, the ordered Newtonian world no longer needed to be repaired or broken by a God of miracle. Evidences from miracle and prophecy, upon which unfortunately churchmen, philosophers and scientists alike had depended, were now replaced by the self-evidence of reason. Moreover, such a procedure made it possible to maintain that there was truth in the Bible in spite of its contradictions. (Semler was one of the first to see the real implications of some of the contradictions and differences of viewpoint in the Bible. He suggested interpretations which became the basis for much of later biblical criticism. It must be recalled that he did this in a period in which such pursuits were extremely suspect. See Ch. IX, sect. 2.)

For the "innovators," revelation was still real and related to the Bible. But its content was not different from that of natural religion in general. What was said in the church was therefore not really different from that which thoughtful men were saying outside the church. Thus, in these theologians, Protestantism had moved from a new form of scholasticism to a new religion. The aim was understandable, but the distinctive substance of faith was gone. In these men, Protestantism had become the victim of the enlightenment.

b. Enlightenment and the Need for New Directions

In the preceding section, we indicated how the Enlightenment moved into Protestant thinking and effectively ended orthodoxy. Where the Enlightenment view was accepted, concern for revelation had ended. If revelation disclosed no more than man naturally can know of God and his relation to the world, it was certainly dispensable. English writings on natural religion and deism were now read by German scholars, though their effectiveness in England was already being challenged by the Methodist movement. (The Scottish philosopher David Hume had also called natural religion into question by doubting that there was a stable human nature which was the same everywhere. Without a human nature which was constant, there could be no fixed truths of religion open to everyone. But Hume was not taken that seriously by the Enlightenment, except by Kant.)

Nevertheless, the German enlightenment figures did not slavishly follow the dictates of natural religion. Natural religion was itself too formal in outlook and based on a fixed and static concept of reason. Men such as Lessing were more concerned with a practical religion for man, grounded in virtue and the good life. All religions at heart, he felt, were based on such practical interests. Their workability or helpfulness in the common good was the only criterion of their worth. That which helped humanity was enlightened, and that which hindered was superstition. Under the common God, all men must reach forward toward a new humanity.

Enlightenment religion had cast off the "shackles" of the past. It no longer felt bound by theological or liturgical formulations of previous ages. These had enslaved men. Now a man dared to think for himself, to take the cue for his life from what he directly observed and experienced about himself and his world. This new feeling, apart from whatever content was applied by various individuals, was itself religious in nature. It was a devotion to truth wherever it might be found. But hand in hand with this concern went the conviction that such devotion would lead to the best of religion and humanity. Only among a limited number of French thinkers was there a strong anti-religious protest. Essentially, the enlightenment was religious, with great hopes for the present and the future. It declared its independence of what bound men in the past, though it had not always emancipated itself as much as it thought.

It is not difficult to see that such a spirit left no room for a distinctly Protestant outlook. In fact, Protestant thinking had lost whatever unique character it had. The transition from orthodoxy to the Enlightenment had been made within and without the churches. It was time for a new beginning.

This was made by the philosopher Immanuel Kant. It is not our task to go into his philosophy here, except insofar as it affects the Protestant development. Kant, too, rejected the orthodox development; he also rejected the rationalism which paralleled and influenced it. Rationalism's claims to knowledge were too broad. Hence, Kant began, in the *Critique of Pure Reason*, by limiting *knowledge* to the experienced world. He did not deny the existence of "noumenal" reality, which lay behind the phenomena which we experience directly; but this was not given to us in perception. Nor did he deny the reality of *a priori*, universal concepts of reason; but these were to be understood as patterns of the mind, brought by us to experience and used in organizing the data of perception. Therefore, claims to knowledge must be limited to the experienced world, shaped by the rational structures of mind. Within these proper limits, knowledge could be certain, philosophy could be rehabilitated (in spite of Hume's attack), and the scientific (i.e., Newtonian) picture of an orderly world could be given philosophical certification. Obviously, claims to knowledge of God through "pure reason" were quite impossible, and Kant systematically attacked the traditional proofs for God's existence (and in a way which many have felt conclusive).

Nevertheless, religion could yet be established on a sound basis. It, too, belongs to reason, but to a different kind than that which we employ in the domain of knowledge. Its ground is practical reason, in contrast to "pure" or theoretical reason. Practical reason apprehends the moral law within. A concept of duty or law is universal in all men, and therefore valid for all. Right action always proceeds from the motive of obedience to this law, rather than any desire for happiness or satisfaction. All activity ought then to be based on the universal law of duty and morality which was the law of self and of the universe.

Kant knew of the tensions which beset men and lead them to activity counter to their moral nature. In fact, Kant's description of radical evil was more penetrating than most theological analyses. But Kant found it impossible to believe that evil could not be broken by the deliberate act of man. He maintained that this must be possible by a herculean effort of will. Otherwise the world would not be moral and therefore would be meaningless. Above all else, Kant was convinced that this is a moral world.

Sensing, nevertheless, that men do not fully succeed in this world in living in accord with the moral law, Kant argued that we are justified in postulating immortality as the necessary extension of time requisite for the final perfection of virtue. Kant had rejected the idea that happiness could be a proper motive for action—duty was the only right motive. But he was still convinced that the virtuous man must somehow be the happy man. Since man must not act from the desire for happiness, and since happiness and virtue do not seem to be commensurate in life, Kant concluded that we must postulate the existence of God to guarantee the proper correlation of virtue and happiness.

Such a reconstruction of the religious in connection with the ethical was more in line with the tradition of natural religion than with the prevailing currents of the Enlightenment. In some respects, Kant's views on religion were not so much an advance as a return to a tradition in which men insisted on establishing the religious by way of the moral.

More important for Protestant history was the influence Kant had on subsequent generations. The general outlook of the Enlightenment, including Kant's views on religion, convinced the Protestant theologian, Friedrich Schleiermacher, that a new start was necessary. But even his efforts at a new beginning, which we shall consider in Ch. X, were partly determined by Kant's own attempt to overcome the Enlightenment. Instead of relating the domain of religion to the ethical realm of Kant's second critique, he drew from the *a priori* categories of the first. For Schleiermacher, religion itself was a unique realm of experience, related to but not determined by knowledge or ethics. Only in this way could Protestant theology begin again. Albrecht Ritschl, on the other hand (see Ch. X), believed that Kant had begun a path in the second critique which opened the way for the revival of the Protestant Reformation.

Protestant theologians were to struggle for some time to conserve the gains of the Enlightenment, and at the same time recover the religious depths and particular Christian witness which they felt were lost in the Enlightenment. In the groping for new ways of thinking about the biblical message in relation to contemporary currents of thought, Kant's work played an important role. His distinction between knowledge and faith, however differently interpreted by theologians, continued to inform much of Protestant thinking.

VIII

A Century of Protestant Expansion

1. CHARACTERISTICS OF THE CENTURY

The beginning of the nineteenth century marks the onset of a new and formative period in the development of Protestant Christianity. This was an era of profound intellectual ferment, in which forces both within and outside the church combined to pose new problems for Christian thinking and to shape new perspectives for the understanding of the faith. We have already looked at one of the central features in the transition from eighteenth- to nineteenth-century modes of thought—viz. the critical philosophy of Kant (see Ch. VII). But equally important were the continuing influence of pietism and romanticism, the development of new tools for the study of the Bible, and the rapidly accelerating advances in the sciences of nature and society. The nineteenth century was also a period of striking institutional and geographical expansion in the Protestant churches. And this was a time of almost continual flux in the relations of church to society, brought on to some extent by the further growth of nationalism in Western Europe and America, but more especially by the social upheavals attendant upon the rise of an industrial society.

The over-all significance of these nineteenth-century developments has been given the most diverse interpretation. Perhaps nowhere has the point of view of the historian been more influential in determining his understanding of history than in the estimate of the role of religion in the nineteenth century. For some, this is the time of the great decline in the influence of Christianity (and particularly of Protestantism) in the West, so that by the early part of the twentieth century the part played by religion in molding men's thought and action could safely be ignored. For others, the nineteenth century was a time of great advance for Protestant Christianity because of its remarkable numerical, institutional and geographical expansion.

On the whole, most judgments on the nineteenth century have been less extreme than the two just mentioned. The importance of these extreme and contradictory views lies in their witness to the actual diversity in the religious trends of the century itself. On the one hand, there were important tendencies which seemed to indicate a serious weakening in the vitality and influence of the Protestant churches (and no less of Roman Catholicism and Eastern Orthodoxy). There was the powerful tendency toward formal separation of religious institutions from the political institutions. This trend was already apparent in the Bill of Rights of the Constitution of the United States, which forbade the federal government to make any church the official religion of the land (see Ch. VII). It was reflected in the English reforms of the 1830's which limited the traditional prerogatives of the Church of England. And it was prominently expressed in anticlericalism in predominantly Roman Catholic countries, e.g., in the liquidation of the papal states in Italy in 1870 and in the separation of church and state in France in 1905. (It should be remembered that many Protestants look with grave suspicion upon any established church. Thus the trend toward separation of church and state is seen as a significant advance rather than a reverse for the church.) Again, the support and control of education was taken over increasingly by the state and ceased to be primarily a function of the churches.

A less tangible though equally important development was the increasingly sharp distinction between the "religious" and the "secular," so that the life of faith becomes a thing apart from the world of government and of commerce, and the decisions of faith have little direct relevance to economic and political decisions. At the same time, the church seemed often to be so tied to racial, economic and national consciousnesses as to have no independent life of its own. Thus there arose charges that the church was simply the "opiate of the people" and the tool of class interests.

Particularly in the latter half of the century, the progress of science—notably biology, but also geology and anthropology, and later sociology and psychology—opened a veritable Pandora's box of questions as to the credibility of the traditional Christian world-view and of the biblical account of the origin of the world and of man. Perhaps more important, the successes of the scientific method suggested that here at last was found the means to all truth, and religious claims to truth might now be left behind.

Moreover, the industrialization of the West, both by its successes and its failures, contributed to a sense of the irrelevance of religion. The new miracles of production and technology, together with the discoveries of science, led to the belief that the era of plenty was at hand and that man could be the master of his environment without dependence upon divine assistance. On the other hand, to the great and growing body of industrial workers, the message of the church seemed increasingly irrelevant, for it did not speak to the difficulties which had been created for them by the age of the machine.

These are only some indications of the unfavorable tendencies with which nineteenth-century Protestantism was confronted. And it is not altogether strange that some have thought that the church was indeed waning in vitality, and that the adjustments in Protestant thinking toward the new sciences, the new philosophies and a changing society, were merely steps toward the ultimate dissolution of the faith itself.

But judgments of this sort rest upon only a portion of the evidence. For on many other counts, the nineteenth century was a time of the most vigorous activity and greatest growth in Protestant history. In terms of numbers and geographical extension, this century has not unjustly been called "the great century" of Christian expansion. This expansion was signalized particularly by the missionary movement, which we shall look at more carefully later in this chapter. Also, as a concomitant of the westward growth of the United States, the percentage of church members in the American population rose from less than 10 percent in 1800 to over 40 percent in 1910 (and to 58 percent in 1951). The religious revivals at the beginning of the century set a pattern which continued through most of the century in the British Isles and the United States. Methodist "circuit-riders" and traveling Baptist evangelists went steadily westward with the American frontier, and the success of their work accounts for the present numerical pre-eminence of the Baptist and Methodist Churches in the United States.

Moreover, if the development of institutional structures and the proliferation of new organizations are signs of life and strength, then the nineteenth century was a period of amazing Protestant vitality. This does not mean so much the appearance of new denominations—though in the United States that process continued apace in consequence of the revivals, of secessions from established denominations, of transplantation of European national churches through immigration, and of social cleavages (as in the division of several major bodies into Northern and Southern branches over the issue of slavery). More striking organizational developments are to be found in the church-sponsored or church-inspired movements which frequently cut across denominational lines and whose functions were supplementary to the work of the parish churches. This was peculiarly though not exclusively characteristic of Anglo-Saxon Protestantism, and was an expression of the vitality of the faith in establishing relevance to new situations.

Thus, a common characteristic of many of these movements was their direction toward particular groups and interests. Such were the Student Christian societies, which grew rapidly toward the end of the century and joined in the World's Student Christian Federation. Similarly, in Germany, France, Britain, the United States and Canada, such organizations as the YMCA and YWCA sought to provide new programs for spiritual, intellectual, social and physical growth, free from the traditional church patterns and denominational differences. These groups were mainly concerned to work in urban areas in universities and colleges. Within the denominations, a host of young people's societies were formed (e.g., the Methodist Epworth League, the Baptist Young People's Union, and the Luther League).

The Sunday schools, as we saw earlier, made their first appearance in the late decades of the eighteenth century (in England), and were designed to give religious and moral instruction to the poor and to teach the young to read the Bible. As the movement spread, the Sunday School became the characteristic Protestant method of religious instruction. The concern for Christian education was further revealed in the scores of denominational colleges which were founded in the United States during the century, as well as in the establishment of theological seminaries for the further training of the ministry (at least twenty-five seminaries were founded in the United States between 1808 and 1840). Interdenominational Bible societies (such as the American Bible Society, which has become increasingly important) had the dual aim of evangelism and religious instruction, gaining wide support in their efforts to make the Bible universally available.

We remarked earlier on the tendency toward the separation of the "religious" from the "secular" interests of life, and the separation of church and state. But there appeared also in this century a new and profound sense, on the part of the churches, of their responsibility for the well-being of the social whole. Evidence for this is found in the religiously inspired humanitarian and social reform movements, ranging from organizations concerned with particular social evils (such as the temperance and anti-slavery groups) to general philanthropic enterprises, and to efforts to Christianize the whole of the social and economic order (as in the occasional Christian socialist programs or the much more important "social gospel" movement).

Finally, the new vitality of nineteenth-century Protestantism is seen in the theological ferment of the period, beginning especially in Germany but spreading throughout the Protestant world. Measured simply in terms of sheer productivity and liveliness of debate, the century ranks with the most vigorous of Christian history. And for freedom and creativity of thought, it can be paralleled only by the early centuries of the church and by the Reformation.

What has now been said concerning the apparently contradictory trends in nineteenth-century Protestantism indicates something of the complexity of the century and the impossibility of simple generalizations regarding the development of Protestantism in the period. It also serves to suggest some of the central streams of development which must be examined in greater detail. Out of the variety of expressions of nineteenth-century Protestantism, we shall single out in succeeding chapters those broad trends which seem most significant for revealing the nature of Protestantism and the further development of its understanding of the Christian faith, and of that faith in relation to the world.

These general tendencies can be summarized under three main heads: 1) the growth of the Protestant missionary enterprise; 2) the rise of "liberal" theology; and 3) Protestant reactions to the social and economic change of the century, particularly as these are seen in the rise of the "social gospel." These developments, which were going on more or less simultaneously, were closely interrelated; and while they will be treated separately, it should be remembered that they are but aspects which have to be taken together if we are to understand the total movement of Protestantism in the century.

Moreover, since we are not primarily concerned in this book with institutional developments, we need pay relatively little attention to denominational differences. The external forces which helped to shape Protestant thought and life in the nineteenth century were not respectful of traditional church divisions, and newer trends in Protestant thinking seem to have been quite independent of denominational emphases. Indeed, one of the most marked developments of the century was a decline in concern for theological differences among the denominations and the consequent cross-fertilization among Protestant theological systems. It is fair to say that by the beginning of the first World War, "liberal" Presbyterians, Methodists, Episcopalians, Baptists, etc., were much closer to each other in religious outlook than they were to the extreme conservative or "fundamentalist" Christians within their own denominations. We shall thus largely pass over intra-denominational developments. These are no longer of primary importance for the understanding of the Protestant movement.

2. THE MISSIONARY MOVEMENT

The nineteenth century was the period of the greatest geographic spread of Christianity. The foremost American historian of the expansion of Christianity, Kenneth Scott Latourette, has asserted that, "Never had any other set of ideas, religious or secular, been propagated over so wide an area by so many professional agents maintained by the unconstrained donations of so many millions of individuals. . . . For sheer magnitude it has been without parallel in human history." [1] In this process, the Protestant churches, and especially the British and American churches, provided the chief impetus and the bulk of the resources.

The beginning of large-scale Protestant missionary activity is popularly dated from the publication in 1792 of a small book by a British shoemaker, school teacher, and preacher, William Carey, entitled *An Enquiry into the Obligations of Christians to Use Means for the Conversion of the Heathens*. Notice, in this title, the phrase "to use means." These words sum up Carey's opposition to a view that since God is omnipotent and has predetermined who are the elect, he will save whom he chooses without the assistance of human effort. Against this notion, Carey's view, which rapidly came to characterize nineteenth-century Protestantism and provided a primary stimulus to missionary activity, was that the New Testament command to "preach the Gospel to every creature" and to "make disciples of all nations" was directed to Christians of the present time as much as to the original apostles.

It would be quite incorrect to suppose that there had been no Protestant missionary work before the end of the eighteenth century. There had been numerous earlier efforts, though mainly in colonial areas. Sir Walter Raleigh had been zealous for the introduction of Christianity in his colony. Wesley had in his early life gone out a missionary to the Indians in Georgia. And among the Moravians, whole communities of families had devoted them-

[1] K. S. Latourette, *Anno Domini*, 169.

selves to the propagation of the faith, chiefly in Greenland and
the West Indies. Mainly because of the Moravians, Germany was
the chief source of missionaries prior to 1800. An English missionary society was formed as early as 1649, and two other groups,
which are still in existence, were organized at the beginning of
the eighteenth century (the Society for Promoting Christian
Knowledge, and the Society for the Propagation of the Gospel
in Foreign Parts).

But in general, it must be concluded that before the nineteenth
century, Protestantism was not characterized by very great concern for missionary work in foreign lands. The forerunners of the
modern movement were few and ill-supported; they were largely
confined to colonial areas; and they were often abortive because
they accepted converts without adequate instruction and failed
to develop native pastors and leaders. The early, scattered efforts
are significant mainly as exceptions to the usual pattern. Of
Protestant migration there was much, and of evangelistic effort
where the church already existed there was much, but of attempts
to transmit the gospel to those outside the Western European
cultural milieu there were few.

The question arises, why was this so? And to this, several
answers must be given. For one thing, most of the early Protestants had been indifferent or opposed to the idea of foreign
missions. Often, it was held that the New Testament instruction
to go to all nations applied only to the original disciples, and in
the minds of some the doctrine of predestination seemed to make
human efforts to convert the heathen both unnecessary and pre-
sumptuous. Moreover, the energies of the Reformers were wholly
absorbed in the work of reforming the church; and in subsequent
years, the intense theological disputes in Protestant scholasticism
and the internal wars in nations which were part Protestant and
part Roman Catholic (e.g., France, Germany and the Netherlands), occupied the center of attention. Another deterrent was
simply the lack of organization. For a thousand years the monastic
orders had carried on the principal Christian missionary activity,
and Protestants, opposed to the religious principle underlying
monasticism, had no practical means of performing the missionary
functions of the monks. Thus, for purely practical reasons, the

idea of foreign missions seemed often to be extravagant, foolish, and hopeless. Anyway, there was enough to be done in converting those at home.

Another sort of factor was the economic and political context of the Protestant churches. During the first century of Protestant history, it was the Roman Catholic countries of Spain and Portugal which dominated the commercial and imperial expansion of the Western European peoples. This was the age of the great Roman Catholic missionary activity, symbolized especially by the work of Francis Xavier and Ignatius Loyola. Protestant peoples came less widely into contact with non-Christian cultures. Not until after the defeat of the Spanish Armada and the emergence of the British and the Dutch as colonial powers were the new continents open to Protestant missionaries. So also, there were specific elements in the nineteenth-century situation which contributed to the growth of Protestant missions: the general peace and prosperity of the century; the close relation of Protestantism to the economic and political liberalism of the period; the greater flexibility with which Protestantism was able to adjust to the changing intellectual climate; the important role played by Britain, and later the United States, in the commercial expansion of the time; and perhaps most important, the powerful spirit of optimism and confidence which was so deeply a part of the nineteenth-century temper.

These socio-economic elements are undoubtedly of great importance in understanding the rise of the Protestant missionary movement. But it would be much too simple a reading of the evidence if we were to assume that this is all there was to it, that the inner movements of Protestantism simply reflected contemporary social changes, or that the missionary impulse was only the tail of the kite of economic and political expansion or cultural domination. Essentially the new concern for missions sprang from an impulse within the life of the church, and the correlation of cultural and religious factors in the nineteenth century was probably less close than in the preceding centuries.

As we noted earlier, previous Protestant evangelistic work had been largely confined to the sphere of Western cultural influences, but now an attempt was being made to carry the gospel to men of every land and every culture. And there was certainly no simple correlation of commercial and religious expansion. At the beginning of the nineteenth century movement the East India Company, acting for the British Government, vigorously opposed the entrance of missionaries into India. In the United States, the mushrooming of the missionary enterprise was all out of proportion to the relatively slower development of the commercial and political influence of the nation. It was not until after the First World War that the United States became a major power in world affairs, whereas in the nineteenth century she had already, with Great Britain, played the dominant role in the promotion of missionary work. In general, the growth of American foreign missions paralleled the rapid growth in wealth, population and territory of the nation. But one of the factors which most sharply distinguishes the missionary enterprise of the nineteenth century from that of the preceding centuries, is the extension of the work far beyond and quite independently of all direct commercial or political interests.

Here again, then, as in the case of the Reformation, we see a religious revolution in the midst of social change. The missionary movement can be accounted for only if we see in it a genuine rebirth of religious vitality, which we shall also find expressed in the theological vigor and the growing social concern of the century. It is this in which we are primarily interested, though we need to remember that the impulse to foreign missions would not have developed in the way it did apart from the general social and economic character of the time.

We see, then, at about the beginning of the nineteenth century the appearance in Protestantism of a new and pervasive impulse to carry the gospel to all men and of a new vision of the possibilities of such an effort. Whereas earlier the prevailing attitude of the major churches had been that missions were unnecessary and hopeless undertakings, voices were now heard on all sides proclaiming the duty of all Christians to share in the conversion of the peoples of the whole world. The Word of God spoken in Christ was a word addressed to all men, and those who had heard the word were to be the means by which it would reach the ears of the "heathen." The gospel was not the private possession of the European peoples. Nor was it proper to say, as the president of a Baptist conference told William Carey when he first made his proposal for a missionary society, that when it pleased God to convert the heathen, he would do it without Carey's help.

The tenor of the new movement is vividly expressed in many of the hymns of the period. For example, the following, by Reginald Heber (d. 1826):

> From Greenland's icy mountains,
> From India's coral strand,
> Where Afric's sunny fountains
> Roll down their golden sands;
> From many an ancient river,
> From many a palmy plain,
> They call us to deliver
> Their land from error's chain.
>
> Can we, whose souls are lighted
> With wisdom from on high;
> Can we to men benighted
> The lamp of life deny?
> Salvation, O salvation!
> The joyful sound proclaim,
> Till earth's remotest nation
> Has learnt Messiah's Name.
>
> Waft, waft, ye winds, his story,
> And you, ye waters, roll,
> Till, like a sea of glory,
> It spreads from pole to pole:
> Till o'er our ransomed nature,
> The Lamb for sinners slain,
> Redeemer, King, Creator,
> In bliss returns to reign.

A comparable assertion, not only of the responsibility of the believer but of the ultimate goal of the effort, is found in a sermon delivered in 1824 in which it was declared: "Our field is the world. Our object is to effect an entire moral revolution in the entire human race." [2] This was not felt to be an empty dream. The enthusiasm and devotion to the leaders of the movement, com-

[2] From an address by Francis Wayland to the Boston Missionary Society, later widely circulated.

bined with the optimism and confident belief in progress which
pervaded the West during this period, made the achievement
of such a goal seem quite possible. Thus, the Student Volunteer
Movement for Foreign Missions was able to take as its watchword
for the early twentieth century, "the evangelization of the world
in this generation."

In large part, the new religious understanding which lay behind
the missionary impulse had its roots in the revivals of the eighteenth and early nineteenth centuries. The portions of Protestantism in which the missionary motive was the strongest were those
which had been most affected by pietism, by the Wesleyan revival, and by the awakenings (see Ch. VI). In these, the technical
theological disputes over justification and predestination gave
way to a living experience of God's gracious forgiveness in Jesus
Christ. The rationalist reduction of religion to the following of
simple moral rules was replaced by a new sense of the all-
embracing demand of the Redeemer and of the power of liberation into a life of trust, obedience, and hope. And the absentee
God of deism was supplanted by the sovereign presence of the
Lord of history.

This renewal of the Protestant understanding was given expression in the complex of motifs which were the theological
foundation of the missionary obligation. For many, the dominant
impulse was found in the authority of the scriptures, especially
in the injunction of Jesus to preach the gospel to all the world,
and in St. Paul's declaration of God's intention: "that at the
name of Jesus every knee should bow, in heaven and on earth
and under the earth, and every tongue confess that Jesus Christ
is Lord, to the glory of God the Father" (Phil. 2:10f.); and that
through Christ God sought "to reconcile to himself all things"
(Col. 1:20). For others, the call to spread the gospel through
foreign missions was a call to be faithful to the example of the
earliest Christians. For some, a heightened sense of the nearness
of God's kingdom provided a note of special urgency. All three
of these themes had been important motifs of the Reformation.
Similarly, the Reformation doctrine of the "calling," particularly
as interpreted in the Calvinist tradition, took on renewed meaning among those who became missionaries. Many felt impelled

by a specific call of the Spirit to missionary fields. (This had been all along a characteristic feature of the Moravian communities.) Again, for some, the drive to present the gospel to all men was an attempt to make actual the universality of the church, which was already in principle universal.

In sum, the concern for missionary work came increasingly to be seen as the natural and inevitable response of faith to the revelation of God in Christ. As the reformers had revived the New Testament witness that love for one's neighbor followed naturally from one's acknowledgment of God's love for him, so out of the revivals of the eighteenth and early nineteenth centuries—and out of the growing contacts with non-European peoples—it was seen that this love must be expressed in the preaching of the gospel to all men. Whereas the former missionary societies mainly confined their interest to work in particular fields, especially the colonies, the new groups sought to lay comprehensive plans for reaching the entire world.

The new societies did not arise without considerable opposition, both from conservative elements within the churches and from commercial interests, but the movement spread rapidly. We cannot and need not here trace out the actual development in detail, but can only note a few of the hundreds of organizations and suggest some of their characteristic features.[3] A society later called the Baptist Missionary Society, was organized in 1793 as a direct result of William Carey's *Enquiry* and his subsequent efforts. Three years later the Scottish Missionary Society and the Glasgow Missionary Society were organized, and the General Assembly of the Church of Scotland adopted an official policy for missionary work in India. Just before the turn of the century, the Church Missionary Society was formed as a channel for the work of members of the Church of England, and this eventually became the greatest of all the missionary societies in the extent of its work and the amount of its resources. Already, an interdenominational group, the London Missionary Society, had been organized by those of "evangelical sentiments," for the cooperative work of various denominations and with the reso-

---

[3] An exhaustive history of the movement is to be found in K. S. Latourette, *A History of the Expansion of Christianity*, Vols. 4-7.

lution "not to send Presbyterianism or any other form of church government, but the glorious Gospel of the Blessed God." The Methodists had begun actively to support foreign missions in the late eighteenth century, and an official organ of the British Methodist Conference was established in 1817–18.

Protestant circles on the European continent also saw an awakening of the missionary spirit. A society was founded in the Netherlands in 1797, reflecting the influence of the work in Britain, and missionary interest began to develop strongly in Germany and Switzerland after 1825. The movement in France did not arise until considerably later, the Paris Evangelical Missionary Society beginning in 1882.

In America, interest in missions closely paralleled the development in England, and eventually the United States supplied the majority of the missionaries and over half the financial support for Protestant missions. Much effort had been previously directed toward the conversion of the American Indians, and an earlier mission had been sent to Africa, but it was with the founding of the American Board of Commissioners for Foreign Missions (1810) that the American churches began really to share in work outside North America. This organization was begun at the initiative of a group of students at the newly created Congregational Andover Theological Seminary. The leader of the group was Samuel J. Mills, who while at Williams College had led in the formation of a secret Society of the Brethren, in which each member pledged to devote his life to missionary service. (It is said that one of the landmarks in the formation of this group was a meeting held in the shelter of a haystack near Williams.) At Andover, the Society was joined by the later famous missionary to India and Burma, Adoniram Judson. He and Mills were perhaps the leading spirits in the early development of the missionary movement in the United States. The American Board of Commissioners was shortly followed by the Baptist Society for Propagating the Gospel in India and other Foreign Parts, the United Christian Missionary Society (for the work of Presbyterian and other Reformed churches), and other societies in every major denomination.

The development of the missionary organizations was accom-

panied by the rise of numerous Bible societies, whose aim was to
make the scriptures everywhere available and who worked closely
with the missionaries in translating the Bible into literally hundreds of native languages.

In addition to the comprehensive aims of the nineteenth-
century missionary movement, there were several other characteristics which distinguished this movement from the efforts of
the preceding centuries. 1) One was the relative lack of assistance by governments. Since the time of Constantine, when
Christianity had become the established religion of the empire,
the propagation of the faith had been actively sponsored by the
rulers of Christian countries. This had continued to be true of
the expansion in the sixteenth to eighteenth centuries, when the
work of Roman Catholic missionaries was strongly supported by
the governments of Spain and Portugal, and Orthodox missionaries by the Russian government. The former policy continued
to some extent in the nineteenth century, but for the most part,
and particularly in Protestant nations, the foreign missions received neither financial assistance from the governments, nor
(and this is equally important) the state control over missionary
activity which had often accompanied financial support. This
change in the missionary movement was a part of the broader
trend toward separation of church and state. As we saw earlier,
the idea of a religiously uniform state was being given up in
favor of a free society in which various religious groups might
exist side by side. The ideal of religious freedom gradually dominated even the nominal state-churches in Protestantism.

2) A second novel aspect of the movement, springing out of
the new evangelical zeal, was a greatly increased participation
of the rank and file of Protestant Christians. Instead of depend-
ing entirely upon the resources of a few benefactors, or of governments, or simply of the missionaries themselves, the new
missionary societies were organized on the widest possible base.
It was essentially and increasingly a popular movement. Not
only did the support come entirely from private philanthropy,
but it came from a growing minority of lay people of moderate
or small incomes. (Carey, for example, had suggested in his
Enquiry that subscriptions to the society range from a penny a

week up, and it was finally decided that membership in the society should be accorded to those who contributed 2½ pence weekly or £10 in a lump sum.)

3) A further distinctive development of nineteenth-century missions was a trend toward heightened requirements for baptism and admission to the mission churches. This was closely related to the decline of the practice of mass accessions to the faith, which had usually meant the conversion to Christianity of a particular ruler, who then made Christianity the official religion of his domain. That practice had been common in the middle ages and had made extremely difficult any substantial prebaptismal instruction. (Indeed, one of the major reasons for the medieval development of the penitential system was the necessity of providing a moral and spiritual educational program for those who had come into the church through the conversion of their sovereign.) Now, partly because of the Protestant emphasis on the position of the individual before God and the disappearance of group conversions, partly because of earlier experiences of converts' abandoning the faith after baptism, the tendency was markedly toward more strict preparation for admission to the church, toward something of the severity of discipline and testing of faith which had marked the earliest centuries of the church's life.

Sometimes, indeed, the kind of requirements imposed on converts involved a confusion of Christian ethics with Western social customs, and such incidents have given rise to the picture of the missionary as a narrow bigot or prude, chiefly concerned with putting "Mother Hubbards" on "innocent savages." But this is at best a caricature. For the missionary was often keenly aware that his goal was not to make converts to European culture but to bring the promise and demand of the gospel to men in many different social contexts. The difficulty of the missionary's work was really two-fold: on one side was the danger that the message of the gospel might not be made relevant to the moral and social problems of the new Christians; on the other side was the peril of interpreting the implications of the faith simply in terms of Western patterns. But this was a problem of which the missionaries were increasingly conscious and which became, especially in the twentieth century, the subject of intensive study.

4) Another new feature of the movement was the wide variety of non-evangelistic humanitarian activities in which the missionaries engaged—the establishment of schools, hospitals, and centers for training nurses and doctors; the reduction of many languages and dialects to writing and the translation of not only the Bible but other Western writings into these languages; the introduction of public health measures and better agricultural techniques, social work, etc. In some cases these activities were closely related to the goal of conversion, as in the case of the schools, but much of this corollary development sprang simply out of the recognition of social and physical needs which no Christian could in good conscience ignore. The missionary's call was to serve mankind in the name of Christ. Particularly in medical work, the ideal of pure service irrespective of religious influence has been prominent. (Where this was not the case, incidentally, the missionaries were frequently plagued by the problem of "rice Christians," i.e., of persons who accepted baptism not out of conviction but in order to receive food, education, medical care, etc.)

We have seen something of the origin, the causes and motivation, and the distinctive characteristics of the nineteenth-century missionary movement. Now a final word must be said about the impact and significance of the movement.

In geographical terms, the result of the missionary endeavor has been a wide dissemination of the Christian faith. While centers of Christianity had already been established by 1800 in all of the five continents, the past hundred and fifty years have seen a vigorous growth from the previously established bases and the introduction of the faith to the large majority of the peoples of the world. The work was significantly successful in the islands of the Pacific, the East Indies, Ceylon, Burma, Korea, the coastal provinces and lower Yangtze in China, Japan (mainly in the intellectual and professional classes), India (especially among the lower castes and the hill tribes), Madagascar, and South and Central Africa. Anti-clerical developments against Roman Catholicism in Latin and South America helped to open the way for

Protestant missions in those areas and numerous Protestant churches were established, mainly composed of converts from nominal Roman Catholicism.

The numerical expansion of Christianity resulting from the new missionary impulse should not, however, be exaggerated. The mission churches remain small in comparison with European and American churches, and Christians comprise a relatively small proportion of the population of the major non-Western nations. For example, though the percentage of Christians in non-Western nations has more than doubled since the turn of the present century, the proportion of the population which is Christian had reached by 1944 only 2 percent in India, 1 percent in China, .5 percent in Japan, and 5 percent to 10 percent in parts of Africa. Christianity, whether Protestant, Catholic or Orthodox, was still largely identified with the European peoples, as it had been since the fall of the Roman empire and the Moslem conquests of the early middle ages. The missionaries had least success in appealing to those from the highly developed Eastern religions and cultures, and almost no success among Moslems.

Our concern, however, is not with the history of the expansion of Christianity, or of Protestant Christianity in particular, but with the significance of the missionary movement in the life of Protestantism as such. And here the most important fact is simply that beginning with the nineteenth century the Protestant churches became thoroughly committed to an effort to communicate the gospel of Christ to all the people of the world—and that in its intensity and zeal for the dissemination of the faith this movement can be compared only with the earliest centuries of the church.

Moreover, out of the missionary endeavor, particularly as it developed in the late nineteenth and early twentieth centuries, have come at least two major influences which bear strongly upon the contemporary Protestant scene. One of these was the development of native leadership, self-support, and autonomy of control in the churches which had hitherto been largely dependent upon the paternalistic support and guidance of churches in the Western nations. This meant that in spite of the preponderance of numbers and material resources, Western Christians could no longer conceive of the Christian faith as peculiarly a religion of the "white man" or of the European.

Second, the missionary movement has called for new and profound concern for the problem of Protestant divisions, as well as of the relation of Protestantism to Orthodoxy and Roman Catholicism. In its earliest stages, the missionary enterprise (like the early nineteenth-century revivals) was marked by a spirit of common endeavor in the cause of Christ, and consequent cooperative work among the denominations. During the middle third of the last century, this spirit gave way to increasing denominational self-consciousness and competition. But denominational divisions and competition created a serious obstacle to the missionary's work. The non-Christian was not frequently attracted by the appalling variety of Protestant sects, whose divisions seemed to him largely meaningless and contrary to what Christians claimed about unity in Christ. What sense did it make for a North Chinese to be converted to the Southern Baptist Church? The recognition of this anomaly, and of the frequent duplication of effort and organization among the denominations, led, in the latter part of the century, to more cooperative and interdenominational activity, culminating in the International Missionary Council and successive international missionary conferences. Out of these, in part, has come the modern "ecumenical movement," which will be considered in a later chapter.

IX

The Formation of
Liberal Theology

The history of Christian theology is always the record of a continuous conversation, carried on within the church and between the church and the world in which it lives. Thus the development of theology is always a dual movement, an expression of the inner life of the community of faith as it acknowledges the presence of God in Jesus Christ, and at the same time a partial reflection of the contemporary world. It is the effort of this community to understand itself and to make clear the nature of its faith—in relation to the thought and life of earlier generations, in relation to new insights into the meaning of the gospel, and in relation to the perspectives of the world to which the community proclaims the gospel. The faith is thus continually restated both as a function of the church's hearing of the Word of God and as a response to the problems of a new age.

From this perspective, we can understand the vigorous debate and theological ferment of the nineteenth century. For this century was not only a period of great institutional and geographical expansion in Protestantism, but also a time of intellectual vitality and reorientation of thought. In this and the succeeding chapter we shall seek to make clear the nature of the new trends of thinking and of the forces at work in them, especially as these gave rise to the movement commonly called "liberal theology."

The problem for Protestant thought at the opening of the nineteenth century can be summarized briefly in terms of the developments of the preceding two centuries. We recall the massive theological systems of the Protestant scholastics, with their concern for precision and subtlety of thought (see Ch. IV). But these had fallen into disrepute. Their gradual encasing of the vital religious themes of the reformers in a hard shell of doctrines to be believed had meant not only the slow strangulation of the life which those themes expressed, but also the substitution of belief in correct articles of religion for faithful acknowledgment of the living God. And the seemingly endless disputes over theological minutiae had aroused feelings of boredom and disgust. Over against this scholasticism stood a non-religious rationalism which insisted on the full competence of human reason to solve all problems and to offer man effective guidance in life, and which sharply attacked the claims of religion.

Deism and natural religion (see Chs. VI & VII) sought to work out various compromises between rationalism and Christian faith by reducing religion to those "essentials" which could be "rationally" defended. The essentials were understood to be certain basic moral principles and a few "universally" held beliefs about God. All the other elements of traditional religion were merely ecclesiastical trappings and quite expendable. The Protestant scholastics, whatever their faults, had at least tried to preserve the distinctive features of the Christian message, the New Testament gospel of forgiveness and reconciliation, of incarnation, atonement and resurrection. But in seventeenth- and eighteenth-century deism and natural religion these were abandoned in the drive for simplicity and economy of belief. Deists and proponents of natural religion were quite in accord with rationalists in the rejection of orthodoxy.

The living core of the Protestant understanding was not wholly snuffed out, of course, and we recall its reappearance with vibrant power in the evangelical revivals—in pietism, in the Wesleyan movement and in the awakenings (see Ch. VI). But this resurgence of religious vitality did not remove the difficulties which had been raised for Protestant thought. These movements were almost exclusively concerned with recalling men to an immediate personal experience of the working of God in Christ, and were generally indifferent or even hostile to theological endeavors. No real attempt was made to answer the questions posed by rationalism and natural religion.

Finally, we recall the work of Immanuel Kant at the close of the eighteenth century (see Ch. VII). His "critical philosophy" not only worked a revolution in philosophy but also brought to a climax the Enlightenment attitude toward religion and symbolized the changed atmosphere in which the theologians of the nineteenth century had to work. Kant's sharp distinction between phenomena, which we know in our experience, and noumena, or things in themselves, which pure reason cannot know, was a severe blow to the traditional arguments for the existence of God, indeed to all claims to "knowledge" of God. Knowledge of the world could not lead to the knowledge of God.

Kant said that he destroyed speculative knowledge in order to make room for "faith." The affirmations of religion were to rest, not upon inference from our sensory experience (and certainly not upon revelation), but upon our apprehension of the moral law. God and immortality were to be accepted as necessary postulates of moral experience. Thus, Kant was squarely in the tradition of natural religion. Religion was still to be seen as a combination of beliefs and moral principles, only now morality was even more dominant, for religious beliefs were wholly dependent upon the dictates of the practical reason (moral experience). But at the same time Kant went quite beyond the perspective of natural religion in rejecting its view of nature as the prime datum for religious beliefs and in seeking to ground religion in another sphere of immediate experience. Both in his radical distinction between the knowledge of the world and the domain of religion and in his positive conception of religion, Kant was a source and a sign of the reordering of theology in the following century.

1. A THEOLOGY OF RELIGIOUS EXPERIENCE:
SCHLEIERMACHER

The man who, above all others, spoke to this problem was Friedrich Schleiermacher (1768–1834). His dealing with it was so significant that he has sometimes (though not altogether accurately) been called the father of modern liberal theology.[1]

Schleiermacher, like Kant, came out of a background of Moravian piety. In his early 'teens, he went to a German Moravian school and later to the theological seminary of the brotherhood. There, in spite of the opposition of his teachers, he came into contact with the thought of the Enlightenment. Subsequently, at the University of Halle, Schleiermacher made an intensive study of Kant and read widely in Greek philosophy. Both the deep and warm Moravian piety, and the critical philosophy of Kant, were major influences in Schleiermacher's constructive reorientation of theology. He later spoke of himself as "a Herrnhutter, only of a higher order" (Herrnhut was the famous Moravian community).

Perhaps the primary stimulus to Schleiermacher's new understanding of religion, however, came from a small circle of intimate friends who were caught up in the Romantic movement. The mood of Romanticism was one of reaction against the dry intellectualism of the rationalists; it pointed instead to imagination and to creative fancy, to freedom and individuality, to the spontaneity and mystery of life—i. e., particularly to those dimensions of the life of the spirit for which rationalism had no room. With the encouragement of this circle of friends, Schleiermacher wrote his first work on religion, which he called *Speeches on Religion to its Cultured Despisers*. The "cultured despisers"

[1] In Britain, it was Schleiermacher's contemporary, Samuel Taylor Coleridge, who quite independently marked the transition to the new modes of thought. Though a most unsystematic theologian, Coleridge was concerned with the same central problems—the character of religious knowledge and authority. And he effected a similar reorientation of thought, freeing the Christian understanding from Orthodox and Enlightenment molds, grounding belief in the living experience of faith, and paving the way for acceptance of biblical criticism and for a new relation to science.

Our discussion at this point is restricted to Schleiermacher for the sake of simplicity and because he was clearly the most influential figure in the total sweep of the movement.

were, of course, these same friends, and he begins by gently suggesting that despisers of religion should be sure that they know
what religion really is. But do they? He writes:

> You are doubtless acquainted with the histories of human
> follies, and have reviewed the various structures of religious
> doctrine from the senseless fables of wanton peoples to the
> most refined Deism, from the rude superstition of human
> sacrifice to the ill put-together fragments of metaphysics
> and ethics now called purified Christianity, and you have
> found them all without rhyme or reason. *I am far from
> wishing to contradict you.*[2]

Doctrines, systems of theology, notions of the origin or end of the
world, or "analyses of the nature of an incomprehensible Being,
wherein everything runs to cold argument, and the highest can
be treated in the tone of a common controversy"—these are not
the true nature of religion.

In other words, Schleiermacher is saying to his friends, if
dogmas and beliefs are what you are thinking of, then you do
not really know religion and are despising something which it is
not. Indeed, you are looking in the wrong place. The despised
systems do not come from the heroes of religion. Why not look,
therefore, at the religious life itself, at the inward emotions and
dispositions, "and first those pious exaltations of the mind in
which all other known activities are set aside or almost suppressed, and the whole soul is dissolved in the immediate feeling
of the Infinite and the Eternal? . . . He only who has studied
and truly known man in these emotions can rediscover religion
in those outward manifestations."[3]

The Romantics, Schleiermacher is suggesting, have made the
same mistake as the thinkers of the Enlightenment. They have
identified religion with a way of thinking or a set of beliefs. Or
they have confused religion with a way of acting, with ethics or
art. Or they have thought of religion as a buttress of ethics, as
necessary for maintaining the moral law. Or (as in the case of
Kant) they have made religion merely an implication of ethics.
But even those who have sought to defend religion in these ways

[2] *Speeches on Religion,* 14, (Italics ours).
[3] Ibid., 15f.

have done it a grave disservice. Religion is neither metaphysics nor ethics, nor a combination of the two. It is some deeper, unique, special thing. Only when we see this can we account for the great appeal and pervasive expression of religion.

Where, then, is the heart of religion to be found if not in man's faculty of knowing (science, metaphysics) or acting (ethics, art)? Schleiermacher's answer is that religion belongs to the realm of "feeling" (*Gefühl*) or "affection." By these terms, Schleiermacher means a kind of primal and immediate awareness, a unique element in human experience which is really more basic than either ordinary knowing or acting. In both knowing and acting, I find myself over against the world as the object of my knowledge and action. But in the religious apprehension, I am immediately aware of the deeper unity of the whole. I know God, not indirectly by inference from the world of the senses or from morality; but directly, through a realm of my experience which is quite different from knowing and acting.

Religion, more precisely, is the immediate apprehension of the Infinite in the finite, of the unity in the diversity:

> The contemplation of the pious is the immediate consciousness of the universal existence of all finite things, in and through the Infinite, and of all temporal things in and through the Eternal. Religion is to seek this and find it in all that lives and moves, in all growth and change, in all doing and suffering. It is to have life and to know life in immediate feeling, only as such an existence in the Infinite and Eternal. Where this is found religion is satisfied, where it hides itself there is for her unrest and anguish, extremity and death. Wherefore it is a life in the infinite nature of the Whole, in the One and in the All, in God, having and possessing all things in God, and God in all. In itself it is a affection, a revelation of the Infinite in the finite, God being seen in it and it in God.[4]

Religion is a sense and taste for the Infinite. It belongs to the sphere of "feeling," which is distinct from and really prior to knowing and doing.

Schleiermacher does not mean that religion is unrelated to morality and belief. Quite the contrary. Religion is the indispen-

4 Ibid., 36.

sable friend and advocate of morality, but where morality rests on the consciousness of freedom and seeks to manipulate, religion or piety begins in surrender and submission to the One. Like knowledge, religion is contemplative, but it is a contemplation (an immediate consciousness) of the Infinite and Eternal. Religious beliefs, doctrines and dogmas, come into existence as a result of reflection on this basic intuition, and are thus important. In his later work, Schleiermacher develops this point much more extensively, beginning with the proposition that "Christian doctrines are accounts of the Christian religious affections set forth in speech." [5] But here he is concerned to stress the primacy of the religious intuition. Though doctrines are unavoidable when feeling is made the subject of reflection, piety can exist without doctrines. Moreover, doctrines are not necessary for the communication of piety. In the language of a more recent time, religion is "caught," not "taught."

The gist of the reply, then, to the "despisers" of religion is that the institutions and dogmas which they criticize are only secondary manifestations of religion—reflections on religious affections which express the great variety of men's awareness of the infinite (as well as the difficulties and errors of intellectual formulation), and institutions in which men associate together seeking religion. Religion can stand on its own feet. It is an experience which is *sui generis*. It can be understood only through itself and it needs no certification from "scientific knowledge," nor any justification by moral principles. In religion, "all is immediately true."

Here we are at the crux of the matter. Much that Schleiermacher says in the *Speeches* is open to serious question—the nature of God, the relation of the religions to each other, the significance of Christ, etc.—and much of this is changed in his later works. But these are not now our concern. The important point is that in his new understanding of the essential nature of religion, Schleiermacher has not only replied to the Romantics, but also has faced the difficulties raised by Kant's critique of knowledge. Schleiermacher can readily accept the destruction of the traditional arguments for the existence of God, for he sees

[5] *The Christian Faith*, § 15.

that these are not at all the foundation of religion. Drawing on his pietist heritage, he looks rather to the living experience, the immediate awareness, out of which religious beliefs and institutions spring. Moreover, Schleiermacher's understanding of the nature of religion provides a vehicle for expressing the vital dimensions of the Christian faith which had been nearly lost sight of in Protestant scholasticism and abandoned in rationalism.

The systematic development of this latter theme is the task of Schleiermacher's greatest work, *The Christian Faith* (1821). That work begins with the same general conception of religion, but now more precisely formulated. The essence of religion, or the element which is common to *all* religion, Schleiermacher says, is the feeling (or immediate consciousness) of being absolutely dependent upon God. This awareness never appears in isolation or in pure form, but always as modified in various ways in the different religions. It is nonetheless the presupposition of all religion and, though not all persons recognize it, is an essential element of human nature.

Concrete religions can therefore be understood as centering in particular modifications of the feeling of absolute dependence. Christianity is "a monotheistic faith, belonging to the teleological [i.e., ethical] type of religion, and is essentially distinguished from other such faiths by the fact that in it everything is related to the redemption accomplished by Jesus of Nazareth".[6] Note carefully the elements of this definition. In the first place, Christianity is centered unequivocally in Christ. This assertion stands in sharp contrast to the current Rationalism, for which Jesus had been important only as a teacher of moral principles, but not as in his person the redeeming act of God. Second, the work of Christ is redemption. The Christian faith is rooted not only in the experience of dependence upon God, but also in a further duality of experience: the consciousness of sin and the consciousness of grace. Sin means our lack of God-consciousness, i.e., "God-forgetfulness," the hostility and alienation from God which is the failure to recognize our absolute dependence upon him. Redemption is the overcoming of sin, and transformation into full communion with God. This we cannot accomplish for

[6] Ibid., § 11.

(margin annotation:) Schleiermacher's definition of Christianity

ourselves. Redemption comes only by divine grace, and is communicated to us through the perfect God-consciousness of Christ.

All the Christian teachings, Schleiermacher says, are derived from reflection on this unique and complex experience. For example, the conceptions of God's eternity, omnipresence, omnipotence and omniscience, and of creation, spring from the sense of absolute dependence on God. The conceptions of original sin, and of the holiness and justice of God, are elaborations of the consciousness of sin. And the doctrines of the love of God, of Christ as the redeemer, and of justification by faith, are all developed out of the awareness of grace.

There is neither space nor need here for a statement of Schleiermacher's detailed exposition of Christian doctrines in *The Christian Faith*. But several further comments may be made. First, in tracing out the relation of the various doctrines to their roots in Christian experience, Schleiermacher finds many traditional notions which need reinterpretation and some which do not seem at all justified. For example, "original sin" is not to be understood as referring to a first sin of the first human parents, but as an expression of the fact that the whole human race is involved in sin and in need of redemption. Such doctrines as the virgin birth and the second coming, and the traditional form of the doctrine of Christ's person (two "natures," divine and human), cannot be directly derived from our experience of redemption in Christ, though some of these may arise out of our doctrine of the scriptures. Moreover, the basis of our faith in Christ is not particular events of his life, or miracles or teachings, but the total impression which he makes upon us.

Second, it is the doctrine of God which is all-determinative in Schleiermacher's understanding of the faith. This is seen not only in the emphasis upon *absolute* dependence but throughout *The Christian Faith*. Schleiermacher draws heavily upon the philosophy of Spinoza in working out his conception of God (especially in his identification of the "divine causality" with the total causal order of nature), but he stands equally in the tradition of the radical theocentricity of Luther and Calvin. Through the interpretation of religious experience, Schleiermacher was

able to reassert the Reformed doctrine of God and to relate it
to his audience.

Third, the religious life is essentially a social life. For the
Enlightenment thinkers, and often for the pietists, religion was
primarily an individual matter. But for Schleiermacher (as for
the New Testament and Christianity in general) to be a Christian is to share in an organic life which derives from Christ. As
we are bound together in sin, so we are redeemed in a community. Finally, Schleiermacher ignores the differences between
Protestant branches of Christianity. There is, he feels, an important difference between Protestant and Roman Catholic
piety: in Protestantism an individual's relation to the church
depends upon his relation to Christ; in Roman Catholicism the
individual's relation to Christ depends upon his relation to the
church. But no such differences exist between, e.g., the Reformed
and Lutheran traditions. They do not represent different types
of piety, and their moral teachings and practice are not really
different; hence, there is no finally valid reason for different
theologies or even for continued separate existence of these
Protestant denominations.

Enough has now been said to enable us to see the crucial place
of Schleiermacher in the development of Protestant thought.
Though Kant had anticipated the turn to a realm of subjective
experience as the beginning-point for theology, Schleiermacher
first made explicit the understanding that the teachings of the
church are really explanations or explications of Christian experience. By this means, the criticisms of the rationalists and
of the Romantics were held to be essentially beside the point.
The affirmations of faith are not dependent upon the construc-
tions of natural theology or ethics, nor are they simply deduced
from an infallible scripture or creed. The Bible and the creeds
are important, but as records and interpretations of the experience of Christians. The Christian does not have faith in Christ
because of the Bible; rather the Bible gains its authority from
the believer's faith in Christ. The heart of Christianity, Schleiermacher had learned from the Moravians, is not doctrine or ethic,
but a new life in Christ.

It was this new approach to the work of theology, and to the nature of the scriptures and of doctrines, which more than anything else earned Schleiermacher the title of "father of modern theology." That view, and many of the implications which Schleiermacher drew from it, became central in Protestant "liberal theology" (sometimes also called "empirical theology," or the "theology of religious experience"). Much of Schleiermacher's understanding of the Christian affirmations, and indeed his whole approach, were later subjected to the severest kind of criticism (see Ch. XII). But even his sharpest critics are one with Schleiermacher in the recognition that God and faith belong together. We cannot speak significantly about God from a neutral corner. We know him only as we meet him in a venture of trust and obedience, i.e., as we respond in faith to his forgiving and liberating work in Christ. This was genuinely a renewal of the Reformation understanding of the gospel.

2. BIBLICAL CRITICISM

At the same time that Schleiermacher was completing his work, there appeared another important movement which was to exert a powerful influence in the development of Protestantism —viz., the elaboration and growing acceptance of the methods of "biblical criticism," or "historical criticism" of the Bible.

The term *biblical criticism* must be properly understood, for confusion as to the meaning of the word "criticism" has often led to wholly misguided opposition to "critical" views of the Bible. In popular English usage, "to criticize" usually means "to find fault" or "to attack." But this is not at all the intent of the biblical scholars. They are critics simply in the sense of the Greek *kritikos,* which means "literary expert." In general, biblical criticism can be described as the application to the Bible of the same kind of analysis that is applied to the works of Homer, Virgil, Shakespeare and other forms of literature.

A somewhat different kind of critical study of the Bible had long been accepted in the church—viz., "textual criticism," or what was frequently called in the nineteenth century "lower criticism." This was a study of all available ancient manuscripts of the Bible for the purpose of determining, as nearly as possible, the original text of the biblical writings, thereby eliminating errors which had crept into the text in its transmission (e.g., through faulty copying). Such criticism had been given strong impetus by the Reformation, which challenged the authority of the Latin Vulgate (the official version in the Roman Church) and stimulated the study of Hebrew and Greek texts. Thus, Luther used a Greek edition of the New Testament published in 1516 by the great Renaissance scholar Erasmus. Textual criticism also played an important part in the King James translation of the Bible (1611), in which a number of errors in the Vulgate version were corrected; and textual studies have continued to have a central role in subsequent translations, especially with the discovery of previously unknown and very early manuscripts.

The new criticism of the nineteenth century went far beyond the attempt to ascertain the original text of the scriptures. Leaving aside, for the purposes of their study, traditional notions about the authorship or inspiration of the scriptures, the critics now sought to answer afresh such questions as the following: what is the relation of the biblical books to each other? how were they written? by whom? when? what did the writers intend to say? were there historical causes which might account for the recorded developments in the scriptures? what is the relation of the biblical record to other records of ancient times?

For the most part, answers to these questions were sought in an intensive study of the scriptures themselves, using tools of analysis which were being developed in other literary study (though it should be noted that biblical scholars have contributed perhaps more than any other group to the origin and refinement of this kind of literary criticism). An example of such analysis is the work of the Italian Lorenzo Valla, who in 1440 had proved that the "Donation of Constantine" was a forgery (see Ch. I). The Donation was supposedly a decree of the Emperor Constantine, granting to the Pope temporal rule over the central states of Italy. Valla showed that the document referred to several events which had occurred centuries after the death of Constantine, and that therefore it must have been composed at a later time and attributed to the emperor.

Historical criticism of the Bible did not originate in the nineteenth century. It had been employed even in ancient times by some opponents of the church and by a small minority of Christian scholars. Moreover, developments in the Reformation and the Renaissance turned the study of the Bible increasingly in this direction. The reformers, especially Luther and Tyndale, had insisted on interpretation of the Bible according to the "plain meaning" of the text. This was in contrast to "allegorical interpretation", i.e., the search for hidden or "spiritual" meanings, which had been a favorite method of dealing with apparent contradictions within the Bible. The reformers themselves did not altogether relinquish the method, but their stated opposition to allegory made it increasingly difficult to adopt this means of explaining the difficult passages. This insistence, together with the Protestant emphasis on the centrality of the Bible, helped to prepare the way for historical criticism.

Yet biblical studies in the church had continued to be largely insulated from literary criticism or defensive in reaction against it. There were important works of critics outside orthodox circles, such as Spinoza's study of the miracles and Old Testament sources (in the *Tractatus theologico-politicus,* 1670) and Thomas Hobbes' outline of methods for critical study of the Old Testament (in the *Leviathan,* 1651). But these began to receive sympathetic attention from Protestant scholars only in the late eighteenth century, in such men as Ernesti and Semler (see Ch. VII). Then in the nineteenth century, as theological leadership passed to the freer atmosphere of the German universities, historical criticism began to gain wide acceptance in the church and the methods of study were developed further. The goal of biblical study came to be historical objectivity: the task was to be purely factual and descriptive.

The method and significance of historical criticism can best be illustrated by some of the problems with which the scholars were concerned. One was the relation of the Synoptic Gospels (Matthew, Mark, Luke) to the Gospel of John. There are certain striking differences between the Synoptics and John which have to be accounted for in some way. The chronology of the life of Jesus is different. To cite only one example: according to John, Jesus twice celebrated the Passover in Jerusalem, the first being the occasion of the cleansing of the temple and early in Jesus' ministry (Jn 2:13ff.), the second at the time of the crucifixion (Jn 11:55ff.). The Synoptics record only one trip to Jerusalem for the Passover, at the end of Jesus' ministry, and the cleansing of the temple is placed there (see Mk 11:15ff.). Equally important is the remarkable difference between the Synoptics and John as to the form of Jesus' teaching. In the Synoptics we find Jesus speaking usually in short, pointed sayings or parables; in John we find him speaking in long, involved discourses. In the Synoptics, Jesus says very little about himself; in John he talks at length about his own person and his relation to the Father. Moreover, the latter gospel often seems confused about the geography of Palestine.

On the basis of these and many other considerations, the biblical critics concluded that the gospel of John was a less reliable source than the synoptics for accurate information about the events of Jesus' life or his actual teachings. It was rather a later theological interpretation, which sought to set forth the meaning of the events, without primary regard for historical accuracy, and which ascribed to Jesus much that he did not actually say (though the speeches recorded might be the author's expansion of certain of Jesus' sayings).

What then of the relation of the first three gospels to each other? A careful comparison of these gospels showed that nearly all of Mark, the shortest gospel, is included in Matthew and Luke —not only that the events and the sayings in Mark are related in the other gospels in the same way and order, but also that the language of the accounts is frequently identical. This was not a new discovery, but now a new interpretation was placed on the evidence. It was suggested, contrary to the tradition that Matthew was the earliest gospel, that in fact Mark was written first and the writers of Matthew and Luke had drawn on Mark for their portraits of Jesus. This was the simplest explanation and the one which would be given for any other three documents which were similarly parallel.

When this relation of the first three gospels was accepted, a further question arose from the fact there are substantial portions (about 250 verses) of Matthew and Luke which are the same, and practically identical in language, but which do not appear in Mark. These parallels consist entirely of sayings of Jesus. The logical conclusion is that in addition to Mark, the writers of Matthew and Luke had another common source of information which each one incorporated into his gospel, together with the material from Mark and information which each had secured from other sources. As to what lay behind these written sources, subsequent analysis led to substantial agreement with a suggestion of Schleiermacher, that the gospels ultimately consist of a large number of fragments, more or less artificially connected.

Another closely related result of historical criticism was the conclusion that the various parts of the New Testament reveal distinctive "points of view," and that these show the particular background and interest of the writers and also indicate the existence in New Testament times of different and sometimes antagonistic wings or parties in the church. Thus the gospel of Matthew emphasizes the continuity of Christianity with Judaism (Jesus as the fulfillment of the law) and this gospel is seen as a product of a Jewish Christian community. Luke, however, stresses the abrogation of the Jewish law, in line with Paul's view of Christ as superseding and making unnecessary obedience to the Jewish law; this was a gospel directed to the Gentiles.

So far, we have been speaking only of the study of the New Testament. Historical criticism had been applied even earlier to the Old Testament, and here there were some even more acute difficulties. If it was true that the gospels were composite writings, i.e., that they were not simply the products of individual writers but were compilations from various sources, this was even more true of the Old Testament. One important example is the book of Isaiah. By a thorough analysis of references in the book to the social and political environment, and to the religious situation of the Hebrews, it was concluded that the prophecies attributed to Isaiah were the work of at least two men, who lived centuries apart. Most of chapters 1 to 39 came from a man who prophesied in the kingdom of Judah between 740 and 700 B.C. Chapters 40ff. were largely the work of a prophet during the exile in Babylonia, specifically about 540 B.C. Moreover, Old Testament prophecy in general could no longer be understood as specific prediction of details in the life of Christ, but only as expressions of the general hope of the Hebrews for a Messiah, and thus perhaps as a general preparation for the revelation in Christ.

The most revolutionary conclusion of Old Testament criticism had to do with the composite character of the Pentateuch (the first five books of the Old Testament), which even before the time of Christ had been considered the work of Moses. (This in spite of the fact that in one of these books, Deuteronomy, Ch. 34, the death and burial of Moses are described and it is stated that "no one knows the place of his burial to this day." The phrase "to this day" clearly suggests that it was written at a later time.) Close analysis of the style of the writing, of the use of different names for God, of the duplication of narratives (e.g., two stories of creation and two interwoven accounts of the flood), the variation in religious conceptions, etc., led to the theory that these five books of the Bible were the product of at least four different writers or schools of writers. The final form of the Pentateuch was held to be work of a group of "editors" who, probably after 550 B.C., combined: 1) two ancient traditions about the origins of the world and of the Hebrew people—these were commonly called "J" and "E" writers, because they used the names Jahweh and Elohim, respectively, for God; 2) a law code, now comprising most of the book of Deuteronomy; 3) some other early snatches of poetry and legend; and 4) their own interpretative pattern and amplification of the laws. A similar composite character was discovered in other historical books of the Old Testament.

These illustrations make clear the crucial problems which biblical criticism introduced for Christian thought. The reliability of the Old Testament record was seriously questioned, not only as regards the stories of creation but even with respect to the history of the Hebrews. In some cases the traditional view of Israel's development was exactly reversed: the great law codes did not come before but after the prophets. Moses was not the author of the laws; indeed it was not clear that much of anything could be known for certain about Moses. In the case of the New Testament a similar embarrassment concerned the gospel records. Considering that the earliest was written a generation after Jesus' death, considering their uncertain authorship and the points of view or "biases" evident in the writings, could one be at all sure of their accuracy in reporting the life and teaching of Jesus?

In spite of these questions, scholars at the end of the century could speak of "the assured results of biblical criticism." Many of the more extreme negative theories had been thoroughly discredited (such as the notion that Jesus never lived). The critics were confident that while many traditional conceptions of the Bible had to be given up, it was now possible to know truly the Jesus of history, to distinguish the words and character of Jesus from the interpretations which the church had later placed upon him and his work. It should be noted, however, that the confidence of the nineteenth-century scholars in the assured results of their work was due for some rude shocks (see Ch. XII). Later study exposed serious deficiencies in their interpretations and showed that in some cases their conclusions were dictated more by "scientific" assumptions or by theological and philosophical presuppositions than by "objective analysis." Thus, the miracle stories were often rejected as unauthentic simply because "miracles can't happen," and Jesus' teaching about the kingdom of God was frequently either rejected as a later addition or construed more in terms of nineteenth-century thought than in the thought-forms of the first century. Nonetheless, in principle, biblical criticism was firmly and irrevocably established.

The decisive issue was not the specific interpretations of historical criticism, but lay at a deeper level—viz., at the level of the *significance* and *authority* of the Bible as a whole, i.e., precisely in the giving up of traditional conceptions of biblical revelation. The acceptance of biblical criticism meant the abandonment of the belief that the Bible is an infallible record of divine revelation to men. There might be much in the Bible which is inspired, much that is divine, but there is also much that is human and even in error. The Bible is not a book delivered to men from on high and preserved from all error, so that men might trust it absolutely. It is instead a very human book, including widely differing understandings of God and of his will for man, and including not only valuable historical documents, contemporary with the events they recorded, but also legends and even fiction, which often contradict each other and known historical facts.

In short, it was all up with the dogma of the inerrancy of scripture. This was perhaps the most important development in nineteenth-century Protestant thought, even more far reaching in its implications than the influence of the new scientific theories. The result of the new understanding of the Bible was a revolution in thought comparable to the Reformation itself. The reformers had challenged the absolute authority of the church and tradition and had insisted that final authority rested in the scriptures alone. True, Luther had stoutly insisted that Christ is supreme over the scriptures and could label some of the biblical writings as of lesser value then others; and by no means all of Protestantism had been committed to the rigid view of biblical inerrancy developed in Protestant scholasticism. The destruction of the notion that the Bible is from cover to cover a recording of divinely revealed truths was in part a return to the classical Protestant view. But none of the reformers had envisaged so radical a questioning of biblical authority as this.

It has often been said that biblical criticism was far more disturbing to Protestantism than to Roman Catholicism, because the former had relied exclusively on the scriptures. This is true in the sense that biblical criticism came to be generally accepted in Protestantism and led to basic reorientations of thought. In Roman Catholicism, on the other hand, the authority of church and tradition were appealed to in defense of the infallibiblity of scripture, and the church steadfastly set its face against the new views, notably during the pontificate of Pius X.[7]

The differing reactions of Protestantism and Roman Catholicism to biblical criticism are indicative of the basic differences between the two communions. The Roman Church, by its very nature, requires the existence of a visible, earthly, absolute authority, located in scripture, in tradition, and ultimately in the teaching authority of the church, centering in the Pope. Protestantism, however, is not only hospitable but ultimately committed to the view that God alone is absolute authority, and that only relative

---

[7] Thus in 1906 the Vatican Biblical Commission declared that the arguments against Moses' authorship of the Pentateuch were worthless, and later affirmed that the Gospel of John was equally reliable with the synoptics as an historical source. Pius X specifically forbade Roman Catholic scholars to use the methods of "secular" historical analysis on the Bible.

The effect of the proscription against the use of such critical methods has been moderated in recent years, but the conclusions of Roman Catholic biblical students regarding such matters as the authorship and historical accuracy of the Fourth Gospel, the priority of Matthew over Mark, and the Mosaic authorship of the Pentateuch, are still bound by the decisions of the Biblical Commission as noted above.

For a full discussion of the official Roman response to historical criticism of the Bible, see Alec Vidler, *The Modernist Movement in the Catholic Church.*

authority can be attributed to any other, whether creed, church, tradition or scripture.

We have spoken thus far of biblical criticism as posing certain problems for Christian thought. This does not mean, however, that the new conception of the Bible which came to characterize Protestant liberalism originated simply as a reaction to the discoveries of historical criticism. In fact, the situation was more nearly the reverse. It was new conceptions of religious authority and of the meaning of revelation which made possible the development of biblical criticism. One of these was the religious philosophy of Hegel (d. 1831), which influenced several of the leading biblical critics of the first half of the century. According to this philosophy, the essence of Christianity lay in the great ideas which were enshrined in such doctrines as the Trinity and the Incarnation. The truth of these was not dependent upon the historical accuracy of the Bible, therefore the findings of the critics did not at all compromise the truth of the faith. The Hegelian interpretation was, however, relatively shortlived except in certain types of the philosophy of religion. It was quickly seen that Christian faith cannot be indifferent to the historical facts of its origin.

A far more important reinterpretation of religious authority had been suggested by Friedrich Schleiermacher—and it was along this line that there developed the characteristic view of liberal Protestantism which made possible a ready acceptance of historical criticism. Schleiermacher had insisted, we recall, that at its root religion is neither belief nor obedience to a moral code, but an immediately experienced relation to God. All Christian doctrines, creeds and confessions are human interpretations of the experience of redemption through Jesus Christ. Not any external authority, Bible or creed or church, is finally normative, but only the living experience of Christians.

This insight led to a new understanding of the authority of the Bible—not the authority of a purely objective and external revelation, delivered by God for acceptance by men, but rather the authority of a record of religious experience. As a product of the overwhelming experience of the earliest Christians, the New Testament has immense significance and authority for all subsequent understandings of the Christian gospel, and it serves to communicate the experience to later generations. But interpretations in the New Testament as to the meaning of Christ do not have to be taken as infallible divine deliverances. The central fact to which the New Testament points, the presence of God in Christ, is of all-embracing import, but differences in interpretation and in the reporting of events are to be expected. No longer is it necessary tortuously to explain away discrepancies in the accounts, or differences in point of view. The Bible is a human and fallible, albeit inspired and inspiring, record of the response of men to the revealing work of God. Biblical criticism does not destroy the religious value of the Bible; it enhances that value. In the New Testament it enables us to penetrate behind the documents to the central facts of the life of Christ. In the Old Testament, through the distinguishing of the various layers of tradition and their dates, it reveals to us the gradual development of Hebrew religion into the ethical monotheism of the great prophets.

Such was the general understanding of the Bible which emerged from the re-interpretation by Schleiermacher and from the new biblical research. Theological leadership was centered in Germany throughout the nineteenth century, but the movements which began there spread rapidly to France, Britain and America, so that by the end of the century the new patterns of thought were rapidly becoming dominant throughout Protestantism.

3. A THEOLOGY OF MORAL VALUES: RITSCHL

Before turning to a third major feature in the rise of Protestant liberalism, the changing attitudes toward science, we must look briefly at a German theologian of the latter half of the nineteenth century who also contributed much to the development of liberal theology.

Albrecht Ritschl (1822–1889) marked the confluence of several of the trends already described. He was an astute biblical critic, and his motto was "Back to the New Testament by way of the Reformation." He meant also "by way of the tools of biblical criticism," for these enable us to see clearly the historical facts and the original gospel at the heart of Christian faith. Above all else, Ritschl sought to restore the historical Jesus to the center of theology. Christ was the *punctum stans* for all Christian thinking. Thus Ritschl stood in the tradition of Schleiermacher, emphasizing the absolute centrality of Christ and seeking to ground all faith affirmations in Christian experience (though for Ritschl, religious experience was essentially *moral* in nature).

Moreover, Ritschl was deeply influenced by the critical philosophy of Kant. This is evident in two ways. First, Ritschl thoroughly agreed with Kant's limitation of theoretical "knowledge" of God. For Ritschl, this was a healthy step, for religion is not at all concerned with abstract and speculative assertions about God, but only with judgments made on the basis of living experience of Christ's work for and in us, i.e., with affirmations which spring from an appreciation of Christ's significance or value for us. Second, Ritschl accepted Kant's close identification of religion and morality. Religion is essentially a practical affair. It is concerned with winning the victory of spirit over nature in human life. Similarly, the judgments of faith are judgments of value or worth. We call Christ divine because he has the value of God for us, i.e., he does for us what only God can do.

Ritschl described the gospel as an ellipse with two foci: 1) Justification and Reconciliation, and 2) the kingdom of God. Justification and Reconciliation describe the redemptive work of Christ, which is mediated to the Christian through the church. This is the deliverance of man from bondage to nature, so that the Christian enjoys dominion over the world, victory over sin. Christ, as the historical founder of Christianity, initiates this victory by his perfect identity of moral and religious purpose with the purpose of the Father. But the purpose of God is the establishment of a fellowship of redeemed persons, thus we are led to the second focus of the ellipse: the kingdom of God. Reconciliation is for the sake of the kingdom, "the organization of humanity through action inspired by love."

Viewed in retrospect, Ritschl's conception of the kingdom of God is subject to serious attack. He misunderstood the New Testament view of the kingdom (see Ch. XII), and he too readily identified the ethical goals of Christianity with the cultural ideals of his time. The latter tendency led to the development of what the Germans call *Kulturprotestantismus,* i.e., the

confusion of Protestantism with cultural faith and goals. At the
same time, Ritschl's rediscovery of the central place of the idea
of the kingdom of God in the New Testament, gave powerful
impetus to the development of the "social gospel" in Protestantism
(see Ch. XI). Also, his stress on the practical nature of religion
helped in the formation of the characteristic liberal concern for
morality. Christianity, he insisted, is an absolutely ethical religion.

Closely related to the emphasis on ethics were two other aspects
of Ritschl's teaching which became central in liberal theology.
First, his insistence that God is love—not simply that love is one
of the attributes of God, along with justice, power, etc., but that
God *is* love. This is his inmost nature, his very being. Thus the
notion of God's holiness and justice was suppressed (and the idea
of God's wrath was denied). This teaching resulted in the practical abandonment of the traditional doctrines of punishment of
the damned. Second, and connected with the former, was a
qualification of classical doctrines of sin. Partly because of his
notion of the religious problem as one of spirit versus nature,
partly because of the prevailing mood of the late nineteenth century, partly because of his opposition to "theoretical" doctrines,
Ritschl rejected the idea of "original sin." He was much more
optimistic about the possibility of overcoming sin than either
traditional Protestantism or Protestant thought since the First
World War.

4. RELIGION AND SCIENCE

Along with the historical criticism of the Bible and the
theological reconstruction led by Schleiermacher and Ritschl, a
third central feature in the rise of Protestant liberalism was the
opening of a new phase in the relations of science and religion. At
least since the time of the discoveries of Galileo and Kepler,
which destroyed traditional conceptions of an earth-centered
universe, the problem of the relation between the biblical conception of the world and the scientific conception of the world
had been acute. But until the nineteenth century, the religious
response to the problem had generally taken one of three directions. Protestant scholasticism had made its peace with the new
astronomy, but with little effect upon its interpretation of the

traditional religious views. The natural religion of the eighteenth century was the product of a rationalism which abandoned the tradition in favor of a thoroughly "scientific" world-view—in this case, the machine-like world of Newtonian physics, in which all events were to be explained as parts of a network of natural causes. Thus rationalism logically led to the superannuated deity of deism, whose function it was merely to start the machine, to guarantee the validity of moral laws, and to insure the rewards of heaven for the righteous. The pietist and evangelical revivals, suspicious of rationalism and scholasticism alike, had simply by-passed the question.

Now in the nineteenth century, the whole discussion took a significantly new turn. The new attitude was a result both of the rapid advance and expansion of science and of the religious developments already described in this chapter. If there was any single scientific event which brought the matter to a focus, it was the publication in 1859 of Charles Darwin's *Origin of Species*. Certainly this book, and the theory which it presented, evoked more intense discussion of the problem of religion and science than any other book in modern times. (It should also be noted that Darwin's theory provoked some sharp opposition in scientific circles.)

The idea of "evolution" was certainly not originated by Darwin. It had been suggested by early Greek philosophers, and it had been championed (in various forms) by Hegel and Comte earlier in the nineteenth century. The significance of Darwin's work was three-fold. 1) He supplied a vast amount of data to show that at least within certain areas of the biological world, there had been gradual evolution from simpler to more complex organisms. That is, he proved the notion of organic evolution to be true in so far as any scientific hypothesis is capable of such proof. 2) He offered a plausible suggestion as to how the development from simpler to more complex forms took place, viz., by "natural selection," by the survival of the best adapted forms in the struggle for existence. Among the multitude of variations which appeared in the production of offspring, those strains persisted which were best suited for the struggle against the environment—these were "superior" strains which could successfully compete for existence with similar organisms. The gradual accumulation of such variations resulted in the appearance of new species. 3) Darwin used this theory to account for the origin of the human race.

It is easy to see why the intensified discussion of religion and science should have centered on Darwinism (rather than, e.g., on the discoveries of geology). This theory seemed in direct conflict with Christian faith, and at a peculiarly vital spot. The assertion that man had gradually evolved from lower forms of life appeared to contradict the biblical story of man's origin. It detracted from the dignity of man as the "special creation" of God, (this was what gave such emotional force to the debates over "man or monkey"). And by setting back the date of the origin of the human race by countless thousands of years, it led to doubts as to the traditional view concerning the central place of Hebrew-Christian history in the history of mankind. Both by this and by its apparent conflict with the Genesis accounts of creation and the Fall of man, the theory of evolution seemed to strike a vital blow at the whole Christian conception of redemption.

Moreover, to some there now seemed to be no room for the working of a beneficent purpose in nature or in the development of man. For the eighteenth century, the worlds of nature and of man obeyed the same inexorable laws, prescribed by a just and all-wise God. Now the natural law and the moral law were no longer in perfect harmony, but in harsh contradiction. Nature, "red in tooth and claw," dominated by the struggle for existence, was anything but moral. Here, then, was a vast magnification of the problem of evil: how to reconcile the terrible struggle and waste of the evolutionary process with the existence of a good and all-powerful Creator. (This was much less of a problem, of course, for the Calvinistic tradition, which acknowledged the inscrutability of God's ways and the radical corruption of the world.)

The initial reaction of the Christian community was mixed. There was bitter denunciation of Darwinism by many, especially in the English-speaking countries, who judged traditional Christianity and the theory of evolution to be irreconcilable. Others were prepared to wait and see what the theory would come to. Some Christians from the first saw the compatibility of evolution and Christianity, and it was in this direction that the central stream of Protestant thought was to move, toward a genuine partnership of science and religion, in which neither the essential witness of Christian faith nor the integrity of scientific investigation would be given up.

This movement was made possible by the developments which were already taking place in nineteenth-century Protestant thought. Biblical studies had shown that the Genesis stories of creation and the Fall could no longer be uncritically accepted as God's own description of the origins of man but had to be understood rather as ancient Hebrew traditions. The theology of religious experience had taught that the doctrines of the church, including even the biblical statements, were not infallible revealed truths, but human interpretations of religious experience. All doctrinal formulations were thus subject to continual restatement. Moreover, the temper of the newer theological understanding was one of friendliness rather than hostility toward the scientific enterprise. Theologians and scientists alike were concerned to discern the truth, whether of the structure of the natural world or the verities of religious experience. Biblical criticism, after all, was intended to be scientific both in spirit and in method.

Thus the way was already opened for the acceptance of at least a modified Darwinism. There were, to be sure, certain types of evolutionary *theory* which could not be accepted without abandoning essential Christian affirmations. For example, the notion that the processes of natural selection provided a *complete* explanation of the origins of mankind, without any reference whatsoever to external or internal working of God, did stand in contradiction to the belief in creation. But the evidence did not, and in the nature of the case could not, compel the acceptance of this interpretation; for all purely "naturalistic" or "materialistic" explanations of the evolutionary process involved certain philosophical assumptions which were not necessitated by the evidence itself.

It was equally possible to view evolution as a process by which the creative activity of God was expressed. While the discovery that man had come into being as the result of a very long process of development from lower forms of life required a drastic alteration of the traditional views as to "how" God created the world and man, it did not affect at all the conviction "that" God is the creator (nor did it say anything as to the purpose, the "why" of creation).

Along this line, the new conception of the relation of religion and science developed. It is the province of science to tell us the *structure* of the physical universe and to describe the processes by which it has come to be what it is. But religion is concerned with more ultimate questions of origin and meaning, and from religious experience we know that God is the creator and sustainer of the universe and that he is continually at work in it, in the natural processes which science describes and in the lives of men, working out his eternal purposes. The Bible is not a book of science, but a book of religion. The "science" of the Bible is the science of those who wrote it, and we should not expect that the biblical authors should have any more insight into the processes of nature than did their contemporaries. Indeed, the Bible itself shows no interest in natural processes for their own sake. It affirms that nature as well as history is ordered by the purpose of God, but its primary concern is with the redeeming work of God in human history. Modern men cannot be satisfied with as simple a view of the physical universe as men of former times, and this means that the task of relating the insights of faith to the "secular" knowledge of the world becomes increasingly complex, but the witness of faith remains in substance the same.

It can hardly be said that the whole-hearted acceptance of the work of science won immediate and universal acclaim among religious interpreters. The victory in Protestantism came only after prolonged and frequently bitter controversy. And there were two groups of Protestants who did not finally accept the kind of adjustment which characterized Protestant liberalism: one, the ultra-conservative wing, vigorously continued to defend the cosmology of the Bible against the "atheistic" attacks of science; the other, an extreme "liberal" or "modernist" wing, abandoned much of the Christian tradition in favor of a "scientific" worldview. These groups will be described more fully in the next chapter. It is important to note here only that fundamentally they agreed on the incompatibility of science with the central affirmations of Christian faith. The main body of Protestant thought went in the other direction. Even in the United States, where the shift of opinion came somewhat more slowly, the tide had definitely turned by the beginning of the First World War. In some of the major denominations the ghost of opposition to evolution was not effectively laid until the 1920's, but generally speaking, it was only the sporadic outcries of a minority of extreme conservatives and the gross ignorance among some journalists and part of the public concerning what was being taught in the churches, that made evolution seem any longer a live religious issue.

The most important influence of evolutionary theory on religious thought came from the application of the idea in fields other than biology, and especially in interpreting the development of religion. In the critical study of the Old Testament, for example, the concept provided a fruitful pattern for interpreting the great variety of religious insights there recorded. The history of Israel could be understood as the gradual evolving of the Hebrew religious consciousness, from the simple and crude conceptions of the earliest writings to the exalted ethical monotheism of the prophets. As God had brought man into existence through a long evolutionary process, so he had progressively revealed himself to man, with the climax being reached in Christ. A similar pattern of explanation was widely adopted in the study of the history of religions (or "comparative religions"), which came into prominence about the beginning of the twentieth century. Both in the interpretation of Christianity and in this general study of religions, increased emphasis was laid upon the influence of cultural environment in the development of religious thought and practice.

A comparable result of the adoption of evolutionary categories in religious thinking, was the strong reinforcement of at least three trends in Protestant thought which may properly be associated with liberal theology. One was an increased emphasis on the "immanence" of God, that is, on the working of God *within* natural processes rather than by miraculous interruptions of the natural order. As one writer put it in a very influential book, *Lux Mundi,* published in England in 1889:

The one absolutely impossible conception of God in the present day is that which represents him as an occasional visitor. Science had pushed the Deists' God farther and farther away, and at the moment when it seemed as if he would be thrust out altogether, Darwinism appeared and under the guise of a foe did the work of a friend. It has conferred upon philosophy and religion an inestimable benefit by showing us that we must choose between two alternatives. Either God is everywhere present in nature, or he is nowhere. He cannot be here and not there. . . . It seems as if in the providence of God the mission of modern science was to bring home to our un-metaphysical ways of thinking the great truth of the divine immanence in creation, which is not less essential to the Christian idea of God than to a philosophical view of nature.[8]

This trend of thought had been given earlier impetus by Spinoza, by the Romantics, by Schleiermacher and Hegel, and by the nineteenth-century poets, but it was intensified by the acceptance of evolution.

The use of evolutionary patterns of thought also hastened the reinterpretation of traditional conceptions of sin and redemption. The view that man had been created in a condition of perfect innocence and had then fallen into sinfulness from which he had to be redeemed, was exchanged for a view which put the golden age of man in the future. That man needs to be redeemed from sin was not denied, but redemption was likened more to a process of gradual education from the state of the brute to a condition of obedient sonship to God. Thus, in the "social gospel" movement (see Ch. XI) the pattern of evolutionary development in religion was extended to the expectation that the work of redemption initiated in Christ would soon culminate in the achievement of a truly Christian civilization.

Finally, the relation of Christianity to non-Christian religions was increasingly understood in evolutionary terms. The relation is not one of white and black, entire truth and utter falsity. Rather, the religions of mankind represent stages in the development of religious insight, Christianity being the highest and fullest revelation of God and of his will for man.

[8] p. 82.

X

Patterns of Liberal Theology

In the preceding chapter we described some of the principal forces at work in nineteenth-century religious thought. These forces converged in what is commonly called "liberalism" or "liberal theology," a movement which reached its zenith in the early decades of the twentieth century. Despite recent reaction against many of its tendencies, theological liberalism has left a permanent mark on the mood of Protestant thinking and on the interpretation of many central Christian affirmations. A more careful and systematic statement of its main features is therefore needed. There is no single definition that can be applied equally well to all who would call themselves "liberal" Protestants. But certain principles and motifs stand out as widely characteristic of the movement as it developed in Britain and America and on the Continent, and from these we can gain a relatively clear picture of what can properly be called the central stream of liberal Protestant theology.

It will be helpful to begin by looking at a small book which has often been hailed as one of the classical expressions of liberal Protestantism. This will be a "case study" in liberalism. Then we may broaden the scope of the description by setting forth some of the basic *principles* of liberalism. To this will be added an analysis of some of the more specific theological reinterpretations which have been typical of liberalism. Finally, we shall take account of two significant movements in Protestant thought which diverged (in opposite directions) from the main line of development: "modernism" or unitarian liberalism, and fundamentalism.

1. WHAT IS CHRISTIANITY?

What is Christianity? is the English title of a book by the Berlin professor, Adolph Harnack, often acknowledged as the greatest Protestant historian of the late nineteenth century. This book, called in German *Das Wesen des Christentums* (literally "The Essence of Christianity"), is a transcript of extemporaneous lectures delivered in the winter of 1899–1900 to a class of six-hundred students from all parts of the university. The views Harnack expresses represent a relatively extreme form of liberal theology, but just this fact makes the book useful as an illustration of tendencies of thought which appeared in varying form elsewhere.

As the title of the work indicates, Harnack proposes to delineate what is truly essential in Christianity—to get behind the externals, to strip off the husks and lay bare the kernel. The gospel, he says, "contains something which, under differing historical forms, is of permanent validity." Behind the metamorphoses of Christianity, the changing formulations and expectations, the altering ways of feeling, behind even the form of the New Testament witness, there is that which is "really classical and valid for all time." Moreover, this "Gospel in the Gospel is something so simple, something that speaks to us with so much power, that it cannot easily be mistaken."

Where shall we look for this permanent and essentially simple gospel? Not in the dogmatic statements of a later time, nor in the ecclesiastical organization, nor in the ascetic morality of medieval Christendom. Not even in the formulas of the apostle Paul, for while it was his great work to free the original gospel from the bonds of a parochial Judaism, he also began that process whereby foreign and speculative ideas about the person of Christ came to obscure and even pervert the majesty and simplicity of the gospel. We must look, Harnack says, rather to the founder of Christianity himself, as he is known to us through the synoptic gospels. Those three gospels "offer us a plain picture of Jesus' teaching, in regard both to its main features and to its individual application;

in the second place, they tell us how his life issued in the service of his vocation; and in the third place, they describe to us the impression which he made upon his disciples, and which they transmitted."

These facts are known to us through the critical understanding of the gospels. Harnack warns that we must not stumble over such matters as miracles, or belief in demons, or the apocalyptic element (i.e., the belief that the catastrophic end of the world was near). These are only part of the framework in which the gospel is presented; they are not essentially connected with it but merely belong to the age in which the gospels were written. We know that miracles do not happen, that there are no demons, and that the end of the world is not near; but the essential gospel is quite independent of these things.

The core of Christianity is to be found in the personality of Jesus and in his teaching. "He spoke like a prophet, and yet not like a prophet," for he impressed his followers as one having authority. "His words breathe peace, joy and certainty. . . . He lived in the continual consciousness of God's presence. His food and drink was to do God's will. But . . . he did not speak like an heroic penitent, or like an ascetic who has turned his back upon the world. His eyes rested kindly upon the whole world, . . . He ennobled it in his parables . . . and he recognized everywhere the hand of the living God."

The teaching of Jesus, Harnack says, can be summarized under three heads:

> Firstly, the kingdom of God and its coming.
> Secondly, God the Father and the infinite value of the human soul.
> Thirdly, the higher righteousness and the commandment of love.

The simplicity of Jesus' message is found in the fact that each of these leading thoughts expresses, in a different way, the whole of the gospel; at the same time the message is so rich that each of these seems inexhaustible in meaning.

Jesus' teaching about the kingdom, according to Harnack, referred to the coming of the rule of God in the hearts of individuals. In the gospels, this thought of the kingdom is paralleled

by an expectation of a dramatic, external, cataclysmic overthrow
of the kingdom of the devil and the establishment of God's rule
over the world. But that view of the kingdom, with its implicit
Jewish nationalism, was part of the framework of ideas into which
Jesus came, and though he did not dispute this idea, it was not
his own. His concern was exclusively with the kingdom within,
with the rule of God that is already present in the hearts of men,
with the presence of God himself in his power. This is the element
which has permanent validity.

The second heading places Christ's message in the clearest light.
Here is indeed the essence of religion: "God as the Father, and
the human soul so ennobled that it can and does unite with him."
God's fatherly providence, his loving care, extends to the whole
world and is particularly directed to men as his children. Every
human soul is of infinite value to him. Thus, the recognition of
the Fatherhood of God leads to reverence for humanity. This is
the religion which Jesus himself believed and taught. He did not
desire men to worship him, but only the Father; "he desired no
other belief in his person and no other attachment to it than is
contained in the keeping of his commandments."

So we are led to the third inclusive summary of the gospel: the
higher righteousness and the commandment of love. The gospel is
uncompromisingly an ethical message, one which distinguishes
the ethical from the ritualistic and which goes straight to the
root of morality, to inner intention and disposition. This is the
higher righteousness, the law of *love*. It is the practical proof of
religion; without neighborly love and mercy, religion is but a vain
pretense.

These three statements, then, which really coalesce with one
another, comprise the heart of Jesus' teaching, and find expression in everything that he said. This is the gospel, and Jesus
himself stands behind it, in perfect embodiment of his teaching.
It was Harnack's belief that this gospel had again and again
been lost sight of or distorted in the later development of the
church and its dogmas. The Reformation was a recall to the
essential gospel in its protest against all external authority in religion, whether of council, priest or tradition. But Protestantism,
too, has had its tendencies toward Catholicism: therefore, it is

continually necessary to seek out the pure gospel, as found in the teachings of Jesus, and let it show its true authority.

It would not be fair to Protestant liberalism to say that Harnack was fully typical of the movement. Not only later interpreters, but most liberal thinkers of his own day saw that this was too simple a rendering even of the teaching of Jesus, and that Harnack had eliminated much that is essential to the Christian gospel. A more careful look at the fundamental principles and trends of liberal theology will give us a better perspective on both the virtues and defects of the movement.

2. FORMATIVE PRINCIPLES OF LIBERALISM [1]

The distinguishing features of liberal Protestantism can best be understood when we recognize that it rested on a duality of interest. On the one hand, this liberalism was open to all the prevailing thought-currents of the nineteenth century. It was part of a broader development which affected not only religious but also scientific, philosophical, economic and political thought as well. Liberalism in theology was thus a response and adjustment to nineteenth-century trends in all of these areas. On the other hand, liberal theology was the product of a resurgence of religious vitality which expressed itself in other ways as well, most prominently in the missionary movement (see Ch. VIII) and in the application of Christianity to social problems (see Ch. XI). It grew out of a renewed and deepened insight into the Christian faith itself. It may be said, then, that the central principles of liberalism were drawn from two sources: the general intellectual outlook of the nineteenth century, and the Christian experience out of which faith arises.

Central among the presuppositions, or informing principles, of liberal Protestantism was *the liberal spirit*—the spirit of open-mindedness, of tolerance and humility, of devotion to truth wherever it might be found. This spirit can hardly be traced simply to the intellectual perspective of the nineteenth century. For such an attitude had from the beginning been present in Christian thinking (though, of course, in widely varying degree).

[1] This summary of principles is adapted in part from a statement by H. P. Van Dusen, in the volume *The Vitality of the Christian Tradition* (ed. by G. F. Thomas, Harper, 1945), pp. 169–174.

It was represented in whole-hearted commitment to the unity of truth, in the conviction that God is the source of all truth and that nothing that can be known by science or philosophy can ever finally be in contradiction to faith in him. The same respect for truth and honest inquiry is required of theologian and of non-believer. The prevailing mood of the Enlightenment and the nine-teenth century, however, powerfully reinforced this tendency in Christian thinking, leading to markedly greater freedom in deal-ing with the historic affirmations and to new conceptions of the similarity of the search for truth in religion, philosophy and science.

A classic expression of the liberal temper is found in Frederick D. Maurice, the most influential British theologian of the mid-nineteenth century. A biographer writes that "his whole sym-pathies lay with the scientific men when they were asserting what they had humbly, patiently investigated and found to be true. He was never tired of quoting the spirit of Mr. Darwin's investi-gations as a lesson and model for Churchmen." [2] The liberal spirit was neither that of defensiveness nor that of compromise. For the Christian faith, if true, did not need either to be com-promised or to be preserved from attack. Thus Maurice replied to the claim that biblical criticism was dangerous by insisting that the true danger—and impiety!—was in attempting to prevent criticism of the Bible. Opposition to biblical criticism implies "either that the Word of God is not really speaking to men in all ages as the Bible affirms; or else that the Bible is the one book in the world, which God does not care about, which is not safe under His protection, which we must patronize and watch over and keep from injuries. Priests and doctors in all ages . . . have looked upon the Bible as a feeble and tender plant, which was committed to their nursing, which they were not to let the winds of heaven visit too roughly." [3] But this is to make mockery of God and to doubt the truth of his word declared to us in Christ.

The spirit of liberalism meant not only open-mindedness to-ward new modes of thought; it meant mutual sympathy and

[2] *The Life of Frederick Denison Maurice,* edited by his son, Frederick Maurice, London: Macmillan, 1884, Vol. II, 608.
[3] From Maurice's *The Claims of the Bible and Science,* cited in W. L. Knox and Alec Vidler, *The Development of Modern Catholicism,* Milwaukee: Morehouse, 1933, 55.

tolerance within the Christian community. This is one of the reasons why denominational differences became less important in nineteenth- and twentieth-century Protestant theology. Often, where the liberal spirit was combined with suspicion of theology in general, it was held that theological differences were insignificant. But even where this was not the case, the liberal temper induced a new attitude toward the discussion of differences— these were not to be grounds for mutual recrimination and excommunication, but occasions for mutual conversation in humility and in love, for the sake of deepened understanding of the fullness of the gospel.

Four other themes of liberal Protestantism were more definitely derivative from the nineteenth-century intellectual milieu. These were in part specific developments of the liberal spirit, but were also partly independent tendencies which gave to nineteenth-century theological thinking its distinctive character.

1) *Respect for science and the scientific method.* This was by no means a wholly new characteristic of religious thought, for the history of the church has been marked by recurrent endeavors to take account of the science of the time. But it is certainly true that in the nineteenth century the wealth of scientific discovery and the increasingly successful application of science to the practical mastery of nature, led to new and overwhelming confidence in the scientific method as a means to truth. In liberal theology this meant not only the whole-hearted acceptance of scientific study of the material world, but also the application of scientific methods of research in biblical criticism and the history of religion.

2) *Tentativeness or scepticism as to the possibility of achieving certain knowledge of ultimate reality.* This uncertainty about metaphysical judgments, which stemmed primarily from the critical philosophy of Kant, was often paralleled by a suspicion of theological formulations in general. Both of these tendencies were strongly reinforced by Schleiermacher's sharp distinction between "knowledge" and "religious affection," according to which faith is essentially independent of all theoretical judgments.

3) *Emphasis upon the principle of continuity* (i.e., concern for similarity and likeness rather than difference and opposition).

This was due, among other things, to belief in the unity of all truth, to the liberal spirit of tolerance, and especially to the evolutionary principle. Thus liberalism accepted the continuity of man with the rest of the natural world. It emphasized the common features of Christianity and non-Christian religions. In particular, it sought to bridge the gap between the natural and the supernatural, between man and God, stressing the immanence rather than the transcendence of God. It questioned the traditional doctrines of Christ's person, which seemed to rest upon a too sharp disjunction of divinity and humanity. And it emphasized the similarity and even unity of all means of attaining truth: scientific research, artistic perception, the accumulated wisdom of experience, religious intuition, revelation—these being but varying aspects of the common quest for knowledge and understanding.

4) *Confidence in man and his future.* This is one of the points at which liberalism was most obviously under the spell of the late nineteenth-century outlook. The whole course of Western history seemed to conspire to promote a spirit of optimism. the relative peace of the century; rapid industrialization and growth of trade; a rising standard of living; political liberalism and steps toward more democratic structures of government; economic theories of a "harmony of interests"; the Romantic movement; the use of the idea of evolution in the interpretation of the course of history; and the new-found confidence in the scientific method. Man's age-long struggle against nature seemed almost ended. The final victory was not yet here, but the means for achieving it were, and the time when men could live in harmony and free from physical want was just around the corner. The achievements of man still left much to be desired, but the possibilities seemed unlimited. If man was not yet perfectly good, he was perfectible.

The optimism of the late nineteenth century appears strange and unreal to one who looks back through the agony of two World Wars and a world depression, but at that time it seemed wholly justified. In religious thought, it nurtured the conviction that a truly Christian society could be achieved. (In Ch. XI, this hope will be discussed at length.)

These are some of the major elements of the nineteenth-

century spirit which went into the formation of the liberal movement in Protestant thought. We shall see in the next section how
such presuppositions affected the understanding of particular
Christian doctrines. But it should be noted in passing that these
factors varied greatly in the permanence of their influence on
Protestant thinking. The liberal spirit and the respect for science
and scientific method became established features of Protestant
thought. The tentativeness regarding metaphysical certainty and
the emphasis on continuity persisted, but in modified form, in
that liberalism which continues to play an important role in
Protestant theology. The overwhelming optimism of the nineteenth century soon passed from the scene.

Together with these aspects of liberalism may be put four
principles which were derived from its rooting in Christian tradition.

1) The first of these has already been noted: *the authority of
Christian experience*. In place of the infallible Bible and the
pronouncements of the church in its dogma, liberalism put the
living witness of the religious life. This we saw was the new
understanding of religion which made possible the acceptance of
biblical criticism, of the new sciences, and of philosophical criticism of the traditional arguments for the existence of God. It
was given expression in Schleiermacher's appeal to the religious
consciousness and in Ritschl's stress on the experience of reconciliation through Christ. It provided a new understanding of the
significance of Bible, creed and church, and of the development
of Christian thought. A leading American liberal thus sounded
the theme, asking:

> Are the doctrines which form the subject matter of the-
> ology, dogmas to be received on authority, irrespective of
> their contents; or are they living convictions, born of ex-
> perience, and maintaining themselves in spite of all oppo-
> sition because of the response which they wake in the hearts
> and consciences of men? [4]

2) *The centrality of Jesus Christ*. In spite of all the questions
which had later to be raised about the adequacy of the liberal's
interpretation of Christ, it was the person of Christ which stood

[4] W. A. Brown, in his inaugural address as Professor of Systematic
Theology in Union Theological Seminary, 1898.

at the heart of the religious experience to which liberalism
pointed. Here liberalism was true to its roots in the evangelical
revivals. In Christ, Christians know the forgiveness of God and
his will for men. By reference to him and to his teaching all the
doctrines of the church are to be judged, doctrines of God, of
creation, of providence, of redemption. As Harnack put it, the
essence of Christianity is nothing else than Jesus Christ and his
gospel. The historical facts of his life and work are the touchstone
from which all Christian faith springs. The goal of the "new
theology," according to W. A. Brown, was in fact "the old cry,
'Back to Christ.' Let no theology call itself Christian which has
not its center and source in Him."

3) *Criticism of the tradition from within.* This liberal Protestantism was consciously a movement within the Christian
church. Its criticisms of the old orthodoxies were offered within
the community of those who shared a common experience and
a common loyalty to Christ and his church. At this point, and
in the stress on the person and teaching of Jesus, we see the
crucial divergence between this liberalism and the more extreme
patterns of "modernism" and Unitarianism (see below, section
4). However sharp might be the criticisms of orthodoxy, however
much a break with tradition and a new start was demanded, this
liberal Protestantism intended that its views should be expressions
of the same truths which were encompassed by the orthodox statements. Much that earlier generations of Christians had affirmed
was now thought to be not essential to the faith, much had to
be adjusted and accommodated to new knowledge and new ways
of thought, but the essentials remained the same—and this could
be affirmed especially because the essentials were not external
forms of dogma, but the religious experiences which lay behind
the dogmas. The classic expression of this view is found in the
phrase of Harry Emerson Fosdick, "abiding experiences in
changing categories."

4) *Social idealism.* The new social idealism of the late nineteenth century will be dealt with at length in the next chapter.
It may simply be said here that this movement was closely interrelated with theological liberalism and grew in part from liberal
emphases: renewed appreciation of the social or corporate nature
of the Christian life (emphasized, e.g., by Schleiermacher), of

the uncompromisingly ethical character of the gospel, and of the importance of the kingdom of God in Jesus' teaching (as, e.g., in Ritschl and Harnack). These combined with a new sensitivity to the needs and injustices of industrial society to produce a profound sense of the church's responsibility for the righting of social wrongs and for bringing the social structure itself into harmony with the ideal of the kingdom of God on earth.

3. SOME SPECIFIC REINTERPRETATIONS

Liberal Protestantism has now been described as a complex of principles or motifs of thought. But this liberalism was more than this. It was also a movement characterized by certain quite definite trends in the reinterpretation of specific Christian doctrines. The term *liberalism* refers to a theological position (or a pattern of doctrinal interpretation) as well as to a theological outlook. Of course, the very nature of liberalism makes generalization difficult at this point, but it is possible at least to mark out some basic lines of interpretation which were widely represented in liberal theology, and to indicate how these are related to the background and formative principles of liberalism. For convenience, these conceptions may be grouped under the headings of God, Christ, man, and religious authority.

1) *The doctrine of God.* One major tenet of the liberal view of God, perhaps the most important, has already been suggested: the immanence of God. The Romantic stress on the inner divine spirit, Schleiermacher's conception of the identity of the working of God with the laws of nature, Hegel's philosophy of history and nature as the manifestation of the life of the universal Spirit, the theory of evolution—all these served to focus attention on the presence and working of God *within* the world rather than upon it. This was not a novel idea: early Christian thought had strongly emphasized the universal presence of the divine Word in the world process, and the doctrine of God's omnipresence had been consistently affirmed by Christian interpreters. But the older conceptions had almost uniformly taken for granted a radical distinction between the infinite, perfect and immutable God and the finite and corruptible world. This distinction was now being severely modified. The new interpretations began, not with radical discontinuity, but with the assumption of a basic continuity,

or even unity, of God with the world. Liberalism was more conscious of the nearness and "availability" of God than of the transcendence and holiness of God. This did not mean that God and the world are identical, but it did mean that God is somehow, in varying degrees, present everywhere *in* creation as well as active upon it.

The meaning of the doctrine of immanence can be seen most clearly in the understanding of the way in which God works in the world. God is not one who, existing wholly apart from the world, acts only occasionally, or interrupts the natural order in effecting his will. His providence is the guidance of the whole process by his presence within all the processes of nature. "If God appears periodically, he disappears periodically. If he comes upon the scene at special crises he is absent from the scene in the intervals. Whether is all-God or occasional-God the nobler theory? Positively, the idea of an immanent God, which is the God of evolution, is infinitely grander than the occasional wonder-worker who is the God of an old theology." [5] The notion of a God who must break into the world process in order to act is not only discredited by science, but it is a less worthy conception than one which sees the whole natural order as the working of God.

In effect, the liberal doctrine of immanence involved the breaching of the traditional distinction between natural and supernatural. And this meant a profound change in the attitude toward miracles. Since the divine is present in all nature, there are no miracles in the sense of divine intrusions into the natural order. In another sense, everything can be said to be a miracle. As Schleiermacher had put it in his *Speeches*:

> Miracle is only the religious name for event. Every event, even the most natural and common, is a miracle if it lends itself to a controllingly religious interpretation. To me all is miracle.[6]

Thus, it is both futile and erroneous to appeal to miracles as proofs of God's activity, or of the divinity of Christ, or of the truth of Christianity. One does not believe in Christ because of "miracles" (as Protestant Orthodoxy had supposed). It is the

---

[5] Henry Drummond, *Ascent of Man* (1894), 334.
[6] F. Schleiermacher, *On Religion*, 88.

other way around. One sees events as miraculous because he apprehends God working there, whether in ordinary and well-known natural processes or in strange and inexplicable events.

The emphasis on the immanence of God affected conceptions of revelation in a similar way. As God is present in all, so he is known in all. Thus, Elizabeth Barrett Browning expresses a favorite theme of liberalism:

> Earth's crammed with heaven,
> And every common bush afire with God,
> But only he who sees takes off his shoes.

This does not mean that God is equally revealed everywhere, for he is more clearly known in the insights of religious men, and supremely seen in the life and teaching of Jesus Christ. But these are the "highest" points, the "fullest" revelations of a universal manifestation of God. God is most truly known in Christ, but this revelation is not different *in kind* from other knowledge of God. Moreover, because God is immanent, revelation comes from within; it is to be sought in the religious experience of men, in mind and conscience, rather than in some special voice from without.

Finally, the liberal doctrine of divine immanence influenced the conceptions of Christ, of man, and of the Church. The traditional doctrine of Christ's person had been formulated at the Council of Chalcedon in 451 A.D. It asserted that the one person, Jesus Christ, possessed two distinct "natures," divine and human, which were somehow united, but without destroying or altering either of the two. The theology of immanence seemed to provide a solution to the difficulties inherent in the traditional formula, for now it was not necessary to think of the divine and human natures as essentially opposed to each other. The perfection of humanity *is* the fullest embodiment of deity. The divine and the human in Christ are not alien to each other, but are one. Thus the notion of immanence also led to more optimistic conceptions of human nature. Man is not God, but the divine spark is present in man—in human reason and conscience. Man is essentially capable of conforming to the will of God. Similarly, the church as the sphere of divine redemptive activity came to be defined in more universal terms. The contrast between the church and the "world" became less sharp, and less importance was attached to the church as an ecclesiastical institution.

Two other characteristic elements in the liberal doctrine of God may be mentioned briefly. First, human personality is the best clue to the nature of God. God is a personal being, infinitely greater than human persons, but to be known by analogy from human personality. God's dealings with men are "like" relationships among men; God does not treat us as "things," mechanically, but as persons, respecting human freedom and responsibility. Second, God is "Christlike." He is essentially loving, kind, merciful. He is just, i.e., he upholds the moral order, but never in a cruel or arbitrary way. He is the divine Father, who ever seeks the good of his children. His punishment is always corrective in purpose, never vengeful or retributive. He is not the kind of God who would condemn men to an eternity of punishment; he desires that eventually all men shall be brought into full and perfect fellowship with himself. Moreover, he does not impose his will arbitrarily upon men. He seeks the salvation of men, but he does not deny their freedom to resist his will. The doctrines of predestination and irresistible grace must be given up as "immoral," for they violate human personality and contradict our highest insight into the character of God.

2) *The humanity of Christ.* We have already noted the influence of the idea of immanence on the understanding of Christ's nature. Related to this was another major development in liberal Protestantism: the rediscovery of the *humanity* of Christ. The traditional conceptions of Christ, according to liberalism, had almost invariably tended toward "docetism," that is, they had so interpreted the divinity of Christ as to deny his real humanity. In appearance he was a man, but essentially he was God, all-knowing and all-powerful, having really none of the limitations of manhood. Biblical criticism, however, had shown unmistakably that the figure described in the gospels was most assuredly human—not just having a human body, but limited in knowledge, sharing the intellectual outlook of his contemporaries (including, e.g., the mistaken belief that Moses was the author of the Pentateuch), knowing real temptation, despair and even frustration. Whatever else Jesus was, he was man. The "orthodox" interpretations, which had infected Roman Catholicism and

Protestantism alike, contradicted not only the New Testament but also the formula of Chalcedon.

By the rediscovery of the humanity of Christ, liberalism rendered a profound and lasting service to Christian thought. But the movement which accomplished this went further, and in directions of less permanent value. For having focused on the humanity of Christ, liberalism found it hard to say that Christ was anything more than a man—a man in whom God was supremely immanent, whose character and teaching was divine (or at any rate God-like), but this was only humanity raised to the highest power. Jesus was interpreted as teacher, leader, brother, source of power, morally unique, the fulfillment of the divine indwelling. It could be said that we see him as God, or that he shows us God, or has the value of God for us, but beyond this it was felt better not to go.

Moreover, liberalism drove a wedge between the "Jesus of history" and the "Christ of the creeds." It looked almost entirely to the "historical facts" which the synoptic gospels disclosed about the life and teachings of Jesus, and discounted as of secondary importance all theological interpretations. A sharp distinction was seen even in the New Testament, between the gospel of Jesus and the gospel of Paul, the "religion *of* Jesus" and the "religion *about* Jesus." Few would go as far as Harnack's assertion that "Jesus asks of us no belief in him other than obedience to his teachings"; but many agreed that there was a real cleavage between Jesus' message and the conceptions of Paul and the later church.

This distinction was thought to be the result of biblical criticism. Actually, however, it was as much the result of the grinding of theological axes. So also was the overly simple conception of the message of Jesus, which often overlooked or reinterpreted elements of his teaching which were out of harmony with fundamental tenets of liberalism. There is real point, though exaggerated in its reference to liberalism as such, in the comment of a critic of Harnack: "The Christ that Harnack sees, looking back through nineteen centuries of Catholic darkness, is only the reflection of a liberal Protestant face seen at the bottom of a deep well."

Concern for the humanity of Jesus, together with emphasis on man's freedom, also led to altered interpretations of Christ's work of redemption. The influence of Jesus was seen in the power of his example, or the "potency of his God-consciousness" (Schleiermacher), or the identity of his moral and religious purpose with the purpose of God (Ritschl). Through these, men are inspired to realize in their own lives that which Jesus embodied. This is his work of atonement (or "at-one-ment"), not some external or "magical" act whereby God is appeased and man made righteous.

3) *The dignity of man.* The dominant tendencies of the liberal conception of man are apparent from what has been said earlier. Liberalism emphasized the created dignity of man rather than his degradation, the ideal man rather than the actual, the possibilities of human achievement rather than the present failures. This trend was fostered by the doctrine of divine immanence and had its strong roots in the Romantic humanitarianism of the preceding century. It was also a reaction against the deprecation of man which seemed implied in the world-view of nineteenth-century science, not only in the idea of evolutionary origins, but in the general tendency to reduce human existence to the interplay of brute natural forces. Thus Ritschl interpreted the religious goal as the victory of spirit over nature, and Henry Drummond proclaimed the "ascent of man." Personality was hailed as the supreme value.

The doctrines of the Fall and of an inherited guilt for original sin were rejected in favor of an appreciation of the natural goodness of man. The reality of sin was not denied, but its existence was often attributed to impulses of man's animal nature, and traditional conceptions of the depth and extent of human sin were greatly modified. Emphasis was laid on the freedom and ability of man to respond to the commandments and proffered forgiveness of God, and on the cooperation of the human will with the divine will in the process of redemption, rather than on the radical perversion and corruption of human nature which had been stressed especially in traditional Protestant thought. The life after death became a relatively less central emphasis, attention being focused on the fulfillment of life here and now, and the future life was increasingly interpreted as "immortality of the spirit" rather than as "resurrection of the body."

The view of man is summed up in such phrases, repeated countless times by liberal thinkers, as "the sacredness of personality" and the "infinite value" of human personality; and the conception typified by these phrases influenced the whole range of liberalism's interpretation of Christian doctrines. It can be argued with cogency that the heart of liberalism was its estimate of man.

4) *The nature of religious authority*. In the preceding chapter and in a previous section of this chapter, we examined the liberal appeal to religious experience as the ultimate authority. In one sense, this was an appeal, genuinely in the tradition of the Reformation, from all finite authorities (Bible, church, tradition) to the sole authority of God himself; and the Reformation perspective was reflected in the view that the Bible remained a unique record of the experience of the Hebrew-Christian community. But at the same time, the emphasis upon the inward (and individual) experience was often such as to make religious authority wholly subjective. Thus, the final court of appeal becomes one's own reason, conscience and intuition; the witness of the scriptures, of the creeds and traditions of the church, and of the existing Christian community, becomes subordinate to one's individual religious insight. Insofar as liberalism insisted that no religious claim can be finally valid for anyone until it has spoken directly and compellingly to him, liberalism was true to the Protestant understanding. But the tendency was to go much further, rejecting the claim of any objective witness (e.g., Bible or creed) to be an authoritative or indispensable bearer of the word of truth. At this point, certainly, liberalism was primarily concerned with man and his dignity.

It is in doctrinal interpretations such as this that we see why liberalism was due for severe chastening at the hands of a later religious generation (see Ch. XII). Liberalism did represent, according to one of Protestantism's most perceptive interpreters, the renewal of "a dynamic element in religious life; it was a revolt against the fatalism into which the faith in divine sovereignty had been congealed, against the biblicism which made the Scriptures a book of laws for science and morals, against the revivalism which reduced regeneration to a method for drumming up church members, and against the otherworldliness which had made heaven and hell a reward and a punishment." [7] But, as the same writer goes on to show, liberalism also reflected a loss of the religious heritage—a dimming of the sense of divine sovereignty, a greater concern for religion than for God, an identification of human values with divine, a weakened sense of the estrangement from God and a corresponding view of the ease with which Jesus the teacher might bring about the full development of the spiritual capacities of mankind. In extreme form, liberalism taught that "a God without wrath brought men without sin into a kingdom without judgment through the ministrations of a Christ without a cross." [8]

At the same time, the themes which liberalism stressed (and overstressed) were often those which had been traditionally neglected and were now brought clearly into focus. Moreover, liberalism meant the appearance of certain new features of Protestant thought—e.g., the liberal spirit, biblical criticism and the accompanying abandonment of the inerrancy of the Bible, a new social concern, and full recognition of the humanity of Jesus—which persist and have had a permanent effect on Protestant thinking.

4. TWO DIVERGENT TRENDS

The dominant movement in the development of nineteenth-century Protestant thinking was the emergence of liberalism. Roughly parallel to the main stream of thought, however, were two theological trends which diverged from liberalism in radically opposite directions.

a. An Inversion of Liberalism: Unitarianism

One extreme trend was most vividly illustrated by Unitarianism, led in the United States by William Ellery Channing (1780–1842) and in Britain by James Martineau (1805–1900). Unitarianism first appeared as a protest against objectionable features of the early nineteenth-century orthodoxies, particularly as found in the Calvinistic churches. One central item of dispute was, of course, the doctrine of the Trinity, which the Unitarians thought incompatible with the unity of God (and certainly many

---

[7] H. R. Niebuhr, *The Kingdom of God in America*, 185.
[8] *Ibid.*, 193.

current interpretations of the Trinity were guilty on this count, portraying the Father and the Son as separate personal beings, different even in character—the Father stern and forbidding, the Son merciful and pleading for the deliverance of mankind). But the Unitarians were equally concerned to protest against such doctrines as original sin, total depravity, infant damnation, the wrath of God, predestination, and traditional notions of the atonement. Such doctrines, they felt, made God immoral, violating conscience and every rational standard of morality, and were contrary to New Testament teaching. Christian doctrine ought instead to emphasize the moral perfection, the goodness and mercy of God, the work of Christ in leading men to a righteous life, the goodness of man, and the demand for true holiness of Christian living.

In the specific reinterpretations of orthodoxy which Unitarianism demanded, there were many points of agreement with the main body of liberal thought, and in many ways Unitarianism could be called an extreme form of liberalism. But a crucial difference lay in the principle behind the respective reinterpretations. Liberalism was essentially an attempt to recover the truth of the gospel as it spoke to the hearts of men and to present it in the thought forms of the modern world. It was a vital, existential, experiential recreation of theology which was not primarily concerned with creed or orthodoxy but with the living reality which lay behind these. This was also the spirit of Channing, but even in him we find a strong intellectualistic and rationalistic strain, which became dominant in later Unitarianism. Orthodoxy was to be rejected primarily because it seemed incompatible with the dictates of reason and rational morality—this had been the theme of seventeenth- and eighteenth-century rationalism, and Unitarianism typified the continuation of this view in the nineteenth century. Thus, later Unitarianism came to be less and less concerned with the distinctively Christian witness and increasingly interested in general religious affirmations which would be wholly consistent with a "scientific world-view" and with a profound ethical concern. More recently Unitarianism has tended to split into two wings—one seeking to maintain essential connection with Christianity, the other abandoning any specifically Christian orientation in favor of an ethical humanism or some "general" religious view which serves as the basis for devotion to morality in individual and society.

The spirit which came to characterize Unitarianism, notably its rationalism and its attitude toward science, was not restricted to this particular religious group. Unitarianism rather symbolized a more general perspective which we may call "modernist" rather than "liberal." Exact lines of distinction between "liberals" and "modernists" are difficult to draw, for these terms have been used in various senses and often interchangeably. But whatever terms we use, we can see a clear difference in intention and emphasis between the two perspectives. In the "modernist" view, the central and over-riding consideration was the relation of science and religion, and the validity of the scientific method was accepted as the starting point for all human investigation. That is, modernism took its stand first of all with the presuppositions of science and the new thought, and *then* sought to reclaim what it could of the traditional faith. Liberalism, however, though equally concerned to relate Christianity to science and the new intellectual movements, was committed first and ultimately to the Christian tradition, and from that vantage point attempted effective adjustment to science and the changing world scene. Throughout the century (and in the first quarter of the twentieth century), these two perspectives were in constant tension and struggle. But it was the latter view which was dominant in liberal Protestantism and which made permanent contribution to the Protestant understanding.[9]

b. A Rejection of Liberalism: Fundamentalism

At the other extreme from Unitarianism and "modernism" was a movement which in its American variety has commonly been called fundamentalism. In one respect at least, fundamentalism strangely resembles modernism, for both assume that traditional Christianity is essentially incompatible with modern thought. Modernism, however, chooses to give up the tradition,

[9] There was also a "modernist" movement in the Roman Catholic Church at the beginning of the twentieth century. This should not be confused with either "liberal" or "modernist" Protestantism, though it has affinities with both. Modernism in the Roman Church was condemned by Pope Pius X and after 1910 ceased to be a live issue. See Alec Vidler, *The Modernist Movement in the Catholic Church.*

while fundamentalism seeks to preserve Christian doctrine intact from all the attacks of science and modern thought. It sets itself consciously and rigidly against the spirit of compromise and adjustment which prevailed in liberal theology.

In this respect, the fundamentalist attitude needs to be sharply distinguished from that of other conservative Protestants. For there were many Protestants of the nineteenth and twentieth centuries who were not basically affected by the liberal theological formulations but who had no fear of the liberal spirit or of science and modern thought generally. This we might call the conservatism of the common people (the non-theologians), which was only very gradually influenced by the spread of liberalism. In terms of sheer numbers, this was probably the most important nineteenth-century Protestant viewpoint, but it was not a self-conscious theological movement. There were also major conservative theologians (e.g., Martin Kähler in Germany and Peter T. Forsyth in Great Britain) who protested strongly against such elements of liberalism as the weakening of the classical notions of divine transcendence and of man's radical plight and need of redemption—though these men shared liberalism's openness to biblical criticism and to science and the spirit of "critical" appreciation and restatement of the tradition. These critically conservative voices were largely lost in the chorus of late nineteenth-century liberalism but served as an important point of contact for more recent criticism of liberalism (see Ch. XII).

Fundamentalism is to be distinguished from these other forms of conservatism by its self-conscious and inflexible resistance to the entire liberal development. It took its stand on certain specific doctrinal formulations (and on a legalistic view of Christian ethics), insisting that without these Christianity could not be true to the Bible or to the historic faith. The name *fundamentalism* is taken from a series of tracts published in 1912–14, called *The Fundamentals*, which sought to state these fundamental truths, essential to Christianity.

At the center of the fundamentalist opposition to liberalism was the question of the authority and inspiration of the Bible. For the fundamentalist, Christianity is irrevocably committed to the inerrancy of the Bible. Of course, it may be allowed that there have been certain minor errors in the process of transmission of the scriptures, but no such concession can be made regarding the "original autographs." The writers of the Bible were inspired by God in such manner that they were preserved from any distortion or error whatsoever in recording his Word for man. Therefore the Bible is in detail an absolutely reliable and authoritative source of knowledge of God and his activity. To admit even the slightest amount of "higher criticism" is to cast doubt on everything in the Bible. (To say that we can have only a little bit of criticism, which will leave intact the essentials, would be to the fundamentalist mind like saying that a woman can be "just a wee bit pregnant.") As soon as we have questioned the authenticity of any of the recorded sayings of Jesus, or the validity of Paul's theology; as soon as we have said that the Bible is in part a result of the natural working of the human mind, without the full inspiration of the Holy Spirit; then we have left the solid rock of truth and embarked upon a hopeless sea of uncertainty. Either the words of the Bible are infallibly the words of God or we have no basis for our faith. It is all or none.

Moreover, the fundamentalist sees in biblical criticism a denial of the uniqueness of Christianity, for the indisputable proof of Christianity lies in the miracles and the fulfillment of prophecy as recorded in the Bible. To deny that the prophets foretold in detail the coming of Christ, or to deny the historicity of the biblical miracles, is to reject the signs by which God's activity is recognized. If these be not accepted, then Christianity has no claim to final truth.

This line of argument reveals a basic cleavage between the fundamentalist and the liberal conception of divine activity. For the liberal, God works primarily through natural processes; for the fundamentalist, he acts by supernatural intervention in nature. This is most vividly seen in another of the "fundamentals," the virgin birth of Christ. To deny the virgin birth, or to say that it is unimportant, is, according to the fundamentalist, to deny the incarnation and the deity of Christ. The virgin birth (no less than Christ's miracles and his resurrection) is the necessary proof that Christ was the Son of God.

At least two other fundamentals were of primary importance: the "deity" of Christ, and the atonement for man's sin by his crucifixion. By the deity of Christ was meant his divine (i.e., complete and infallible) knowledge and his divine power as shown in the miracles (as well as, of course, his moral perfection). With this was associated an insistence upon the physical resurrection and the ultimate return of Christ in the flesh to judge the world. The doctrine of atonement, as understood by fundamentalism, meant Christ's offering of himself on the cross as a sacrifice in place of sinners, substituting for men in receiving punishment for sin, thereby making it possible for God to forgive men without compromising his justice (which demands that sin be punished).

Together with the assertion of these "essentials" of Christianity, fundamentalism has been characterized by vigorous opposition to the theory of evolution because of its conflict with the Genesis story of the creation of man. It was the questions of evolution, biblical criticism, and the deity of Christ which occupied the center of the conflict between liberals and fundamentalists. This debate, which was particularly vigorous in the United States, was carried on mainly in the early twentieth century. Properly speaking, fundamentalism as a definite and self-conscious movement appeared first in the last quarter of the nineteenth century. During the early years of the present century, fundamentalist groups in each of the major denominations made determined efforts to stop the tide of liberalism in their respective churches, either by securing positions of administrative leadership, or by the elimination of "liberal" professors from the seminaries, or by the adoption of doctrinal tests for ministers. By about 1925, however, the height of the controversy had passed in most of the denominations, and thereafter the influence of the fundamentalist wing declined markedly.

We are not suggesting that fundamentalism is dead. Far from it. On the European continent, some Protestant churches have recently seen a resurgence of uncritical biblicism and "orthodoxy" which has much in common with American fundamentalism. In this country, fundamentalists are currently waging a vigorous campaign. Some of the most rapidly growing (though still quite small) American sects are fundamentalist. In these groups, characteristic fundamentalist tenets are often bound up with the expectation of the imminent return of Christ (the "premillennial" sects) or with the insistence on radical and overt signs of the working of the Holy Spirit, especially in conversion (the "Pente-costal" sects). Even within the "liberal" denominations, signifi-cant minorities are still fundamentalist in outlook. The cleavage between liberalism and fundamentalism (with a correlative divi-sion between social liberalism and social conservatism) is still in numerical terms the basic division in Protestant thinking in America, though such judgments must be qualified by recognition of the large numbers of "conservatives" who ought not to be considered fundamentalist.

The strength of the fundamentalist refusal to compromise with liberalism was not simply a resistance to change. It lay also in a valid apprehension of the difficulties which the liberal views created (and at this point fundamentalism had much in common with more moderate conservatism). For it was certainly true that liberalism involved fundamental alterations in the form at least of traditional Christian doctrines, and it was a valid question whether it had not also violated the intention of the classical affirmations. Even more important, by giving up the infallibility of the Bible, liberalism did seem to abandon all except the most subjective claims to religious certainty; nothing was absolute, all dogmas, all scripture, and even the gospel itself were made relative. No sure, objective ground for faith seemed left. And liberalism was indeed to lead to other vigorous reaction (which, however, took quite different lines from fundamentalism—see Ch. XII).

But at the same time, fundamentalism was from the beginning a lost cause, theologically speaking. It was an intellectual rear-guard action. It was not simply an attempt to be faithful to the Christian tradition; it was an effort, in the face of the perplexities and shifting currents of a changing world, to fix Christianity in the mold of a particular doctrinal complex and world view. The doctrinal complex to which fundamentalism clung so tenaciously was not that of the ancient church, nor of the Reformation, nor of the Protestant development in general. It was essentially akin to the hardened framework of Lutheran and especially Calvinistic scholasticism of the seventeenth and eighteenth centuries (see Ch. IV). Only in that scholasticism had the doctrine of the inerrancy of scripture been carried to such extremes; and in such doctrines as the atonement and the deity of Christ, fundamental-ism (often unconsciously) assumed that the Protestant scholastics spoke for the entire tradition. Moreover, in its insistence that doctrine is irreformable, fundamentalism shared the scholastic equation of "faith" with "correct articles of belief." And espe-cially in its notion of "miracle," fundamentalism took over the seventeenth-century view of the relation of Christian faith to science and philosophy. In its own day that view represented a significant attempt to bring religious, philosophical and scientific thought into harmony; but the effort to perpetuate that adjust-ment in the world of the nineteenth and twentieth centuries was not only hopeless but violated the intent of scholasticism itself.

At root, fundamentalism has been seeking to preserve a kind of certainty in a world of apparent confusion and flux—a kind of certainty which was simply no longer possible. The movement was part of a general resistance to social change. This was par-ticularly evident in fundamentalism's commitment to legalistic views of personal morality (mostly of the nineteenth-century pat-tern) and its hostility to the "social gospel." The fundamentalists' bitter opposition to the Federal Council of Churches (and sub-sequently to the National Council of Churches) has been focused as much on the social as on the theological liberalism of those organizations. And the extreme social conservatism was often paralleled by a suspicion of modern education because of its "scientific, sceptical and secular influences." Here, too, was an attempt to hold on to the familiar, the simple and safe patterns, in the face of new and bewildering problems which the old pat-terns were not designed to meet.

Insofar as fundamentalism has been committed to this sort of program, it is hard to see how the movement can claim the allegiance of thoughtful persons. There are some signs at the present time, however, that the fundamentalist position is being modified—by less hostility to evolution (and science in general), by reinterpretation of the meaning of miracle (i.e., of the relation of the supernatural and the natural), and by a more liberal social outlook. If this trend continues, fundamentalism in the former sense will cease to exist and will have merged with other con-servative patterns of Protestant thought.

XI

The Christian Criticism
of Society

The internal vigor which gave rise to the missionary movement and to liberal theology in nineteenth-century Protestantism,
was expressed in yet another major direction, viz., in a movement
dedicated to the reconstruction of society in accord with the ideal
of the kingdom of God. In its peculiarly American form, which
will be our primary concern, the movement was called the "social
gospel"; but this was but one manifestation of an impulse which
appeared also with great intensity in Great Britain and on the
continent of Europe. The tenor of the movement is revealed in
a declaration by one of the early leaders of the social gospel,
Richard T. Ely: "Christianity is primarily concerned with this
world, and it is the mission of Christianity to bring to pass here
a kingdom of righteousness and to rescue from the evil one and
redeem all our social relations." It marked a profound alteration
in the understanding of the relation of Protestantism to its envi-
roning social structure, and in particular to the economic order.

1. RELIGION AND CULTURE

In order to set the social gospel and its parallels in perspective, several aspects of the relation of Protestantism to society in
the preceding centuries may be called briefly to mind.

1) The first is a shift in attitude toward "the world" which
became prominent in Protestant thinking roughly during the
period of the Enlightenment. This change has been described in
very general terms as "the acceptance of a positive attitude

toward political and economic and cultural achievements for their own sake." [1]

The center of attention in the medieval church and largely also in the Reformation, had often been the "other world" rather than "this world." Men's minds were directed primarily above and beyond the satisfactions of earthly life. In popular conception, this usually meant that religious interest was focused on the "hereafter." This world was conceived as a place of preparation, a place of pilgrimage in which one journeyed for a time but always, if he be a Christian, with his whole gaze directed toward the world to come (*Pilgrim's Progress*, by John Bunyan, is a vivid portrayal of this view of the world). The institutions of this world were important and necessary—they were ordained by God—but only as they could be used to further the religious life. Thus, the frequent hostility toward the arts and the theater, for which the Puritans are so well known, is to be understood as a rejection of things which did not seem to contribute directly to the main purpose of human life.

The roots of the new attitude may be found partly in the spirit of the Renaissance. Here was a "humanism" which called attention to the glories of humanity and its achievements without much reference to the supernatural destiny of man. It was confident of the goodness of the natural man and prized his culture for its own sake. At the same time, the more positive Christian attitude toward the world reflected a recalling of the biblical sense of creation. The world, though distorted by evil, was nonetheless created good and intended to be the proper sphere of man's service to God. This biblical view found expression especially in the more activistic and "this-worldly" side of Calvinism (see below; also Ch. V), and in the natural religion of the Enlightenment.

Such factors as these, together with the development of science and the growth of commerce, converged to bring about in religious thinking a greater emphasis on the achievement of happiness in this present life and a growing optimism regarding man and his accomplishments.

2) The changing Protestant attitude toward the world may

[1] James H. Nichols, *Primer for Protestants,* 79.

also be seen in the light of the post-Reformation development of the idea of the "calling" or "vocation" which symbolized the role of the Christian in the "secular" world. The primary import of this Reformation doctrine was its rejection of the superiority of "religious" or priestly vocations over lay or secular vocations. The distinction between priest and farmer was one of function only, not of significance; priest and farmer were equally charged with the responsibility of serving God in their respective ways.

In the thought of Luther, the new understanding of vocation was expressed in the view that a man is called to serve God in whatever situation he finds himself. In Calvinism, however, the idea was given a slightly different, more "activist" turn. The all-controlling purpose and duty of the elect man is to glorify God. Every aspect of individual and social life must be brought into line with this aim. Conversely, every aspect of a man's life can be the means of exhibiting the glory of God. And the elect man will glorify God in his daily work precisely by his honesty, diligence, moderation, sobriety, and thrift.

It was in this latter application that Calvin's doctrine of the calling is important for our present purpose. For coupled with the demand for actively glorifying God in one's daily occupation, was a new openness toward the world of commerce and finance. The medieval feudal economy was rapidly giving way to embryonic capitalistic forms of economic organization, particularly in the areas in which Calvinism appeared. Calvin's sympathy with the new forces was indicated by his willingness to permit, with strict qualifications, the charging of interest (a practice uniformly prohibited, though also widely practiced, by the medieval church; it was also frowned upon by Luther). This concession, and the attitude which it symbolized, meant that commercial enterprise was no longer to be suspected as inherently evil, but was properly a field for the fulfillment of one's religious duty.

The studies of Max Weber and R. H. Tawney have suggested a close correlation between Calvinism and the growth of capitalism. It was precisely in the Protestant (and especially Calvinist) countries that capitalism developed most strongly. This does not mean that Calvinism was the cause of capitalism. But Calvin was at least less opposed to the incipient capitalism of his day than other religious leaders, and the virtues which the Calvinists preached provided a powerful impetus for the growing spirit of economic enterprise. "What in Calvin had been a qualified concession to practical exigencies appeared in some of his later followers as a frank idealization of the life of the trader, as the service of God and the training-ground of the soul." [2] In the process, religious ideas were both active and acted upon.

In the time of Calvin, when the city of Geneva was rigidly organized as a society in every particular directed to the glorification of God, the economic activities of the individual had been subjected to sharp control by the community. But this iron collectivism could not be exported, whereas the "economic virtues" of industry, sobriety and thrift as means of glorifying God went everywhere that Calvinism spread. Thus later, particularly in English Puritanism of the seventeenth century and following, a further development of the ethic occurred, in which collective restraints upon the economic activity of the individual were given up. This did not yet mean the abandonment of morality in economic life, but the individual alone, under God, was to be the judge of the justice of his business dealings. We must not underestimate the effect which the sense of responsibility to God had in moderating some of the more flagrant abuses of emerging capitalism. But the responsible employment of time and energy in one's work was a religious duty second only to worship, and in such a view, if duty seemed to be profitable, then perhaps profit-making was a duty. There seemed to be a remarkable coincidence between the service of God and the pursuit of private economic interest. In this situation, the strain upon conscience is evident. Appetite for gain might readily be transformed into resplendent virtue. Duty to oneself and to God could merge, the world being so ordered that one might, after all, serve two masters, being paid by one while working for the other.

From this point on, it became increasingly difficult to maintain effectively the sense of direct religious responsibility and moral restraint upon economic activity, particularly in the face of purely secular versions of economic "ethics." The Calvinistic ideal of a total society oriented toward the glorification of God

[2] R. H. Tawney, *Religion and the Rise of Capitalism*, 199.

had been dimmed to the point of invisibility. In its place appeared a sharp distinction between the specifically "religious" and the secular. Religion is concerned with a man's private relation to his Creator and is publicly expressed in the worship of the church. The world of economic activity is left to its own immutable laws, and in this world the law for individual action is the pursuit of self-interest. The way is open, then, to economic individualism and self-aggrandizement pure and undiluted. But not undisguised! For the semblance of morality was given to the pursuit of self-interest by the theory of the harmony of interests. By this theory, which was at the root of free enterprise economics (given classical expression in Adam Smith's *Wealth of Nations*, 1776), the laws of the economic world were given divine sanction. The laws of society and the laws of nature alike were held to be unchanging expressions of the will of God, the divine ordering of the world in the best interest of the whole. Therefore, if a man pursue his own economic interest, it will be for the good of all.

This is roughly the situation which obtained in the late eighteenth and early nineteenth centuries. The Protestant ethos had been gradually accommodated to the demands of the prevailing economic trends. In the area of politics, the Reformed and Free Church influence had been an important factor in the development of democratic structures of government (see Chs. V, VII), and perhaps here there persisted more of a sense of religious judgment upon social activities. But certainly in the economic realm, the capitulation had gone far.

We may speak of this process as a partial abandonment of the religious claim to govern the "secular" life, when economic activity for the sake of the glory of God becomes simply the good of production for its own sake. Or we may speak of the process as the synthesis of Christianity and civilization, based on a faith in the harmony of interests, and issuing in the identification of Christian goals for society with free enterprise, democracy, and patriotism (as in the case of the pervasive "American faith"). In either case the result was the implicit and often explicit sanctioning by Protestantism of the social, political and (particularly) economic status quo.

3) It would be grossly unjust to suggest that the Protestant ethic had simply ceased to involve any restraints upon economic activity. What we have said is that there was no effective re-thinking of fundamental economic relationships in the light of the gospel. The growth of commerce and the beginnings of the indus-trial revolution presented problems for which the religious com-munity was as yet unprepared. Still the ethical dimension of faith could find expression in various ways. Within those relationships (debtor-creditor, employer-employee, buyer-seller, getting and spending), Christians did feel and exercise responsibilities as Christians.

One of the ways of exercising Christian responsibility was through individual "stewardship." It was hardly possible to take literally Jesus' extreme condemnation of wealth. But Jesus had also spoken of the faithful steward, the man who had used wisely—and profitably—the money entrusted to him. Here was an appropriate ideal for the growing Protestant middle class! The Christian was to be bound by moral principles in the acquiring of wealth and was to use well that which providence had given him. Stewardship was crowned by philanthropy. The prosperous man could express his love for his neighbor by giving of his wealth to the less fortunate (though poverty was like as not the result of sloth or bad management). This might not help to improve the fundamental economic position of the poor, but it could make their lot more bearable.

Also, the ethical demand could and did find expression in noble attempts at the correction of abuses in the working of the system. From the seventeenth-century Quakers through the nineteenth century, profound Christian concern for the welfare of men led to many important reforms. One might refer to the work of Elizabeth Fry and John Howard in prison reform, John Woolman and William Wilberforce in the abolition of the slave trade, or Lord Shaftesbury in the improvement of factory conditions and the fight against child labor.

These reforms had great significance, and their leaders were devoted and sincere. But this being accepted, it is still noteworthy that such reforms were conceived largely within the context of the prevailing economic patterns. It was not the system which

had to be changed; it was specific abuses which needed alleviation.[3] And "social reform" was to be accomplished by the action
of individuals as part of their stewardship.

Moreover, the concern for the reform of abuses was for the
most part still associated with belief in the overwhelming priority
of the life to come and the relative unimportance of the in-
equalities and hardships of the present world. The purpose of
religion was to make less intolerable the burdens of economic and
social inequality. Thus, even Wilberforce, in his *Practical View
of the System of Christianity*, could explain that Christianity
makes social inequality less galling to the lower classes. It counsels
for them a life of diligence, humility and patience. It explains

> that their more lowly path has been allotted to them by the
> hand of God; that it is their part faithfully to discharge its
> duties, and contentedly to bear its inconveniences; that the
> present state of things is very short; that the objects about
> which worldly men conflict so eagerly are not worth the
> contest; that the peace of mind which Religion offers indis-
> criminately to all ranks, affords more true satisfaction than
> all the expensive pleasures which are beyond the poor man's
> reach; that in this view the poor have the advantage; that,
> if their superiors enjoy more abundant comforts, they are
> also exposed to many temptations from which the inferior
> classes are happily exempted; that, "having food and rai-
> ment, they should be therewith content," since their situation
> in life, with all its evils, is better than they have deserved
> at the hand of God; finally, that all human distinctions will
> soon be done away, and the true followers of Christ will all,
> as children of the same Father, be alike admitted to the
> possession of the same heavenly inheritance.[4]

In sum, the Reformation doctrine of vocation had given a new
dignity to common labor, and the spirit of the seventeeth and
eighteenth centuries had made for a more positive acceptance of
cultural, political and economic achievements for their own sake,
thus also greater concern for happiness in this life. At the same
time, in the face of a new economic situation, the more activist

[3]. There were important exceptions to this generalization: e.g., in the
opposition to slavery (as in Woolman, Wilberforce, and Samuel Hopkins),
and in Woolman's views on property.

[4] Quoted in J. W. and B. Hammond, *The Town Labourer*, 231–2.

form of the doctrine of vocation had been transmuted into a glorification of economic enterprise and a merging of Christian ideals for civilization with the prevailing patterns of the economic and political order. With the sanction of religion thus placed upon the existing order, even the programs for reform were palliative, and apart from these the effective role of religion was limited to the privacy of a man's relation to God and to concern for the "spiritual" rather than the "secular" life. It was this kind of uncritical acceptance of the social order as a whole (particularly the economic order) which was to call forth most vigorous criticism in the nineteenth century. The objection came from two quite different directions, one outside the church, the other within.

2. THE CHALLENGE OF MARXISM

The most trenchant external attack on the church's position came from Marxist socialism, notably as expressed in the *Communist Manifesto* (1848) and Marx's *Das Kapital* (1867). According to Marx, history moves irresistibly along a path dictated by economic forces and marked by continual class conflict. All human institutions and ideas are to be understood as direct or indirect products of the economic struggle.

The historical pattern which Marx saw developing in his own day was this: capitalism by its nature required continual expansion, concentration and centralization, and was predicated upon the exploitation of the workers for the sake of owners. Thus, capital and labor, whose interests were in principle contradictory, grew steadily further apart and all society was being sharply divided into the exploiting capitalist class versus the exploited proletariat. The conflict between the two groups could only grow in intensity, and the resolution of the conflict would come through revolution by the working classes, leading to the establishment of a communistic society in which every man would produce according to his ability and share in the goods of society according to his needs.

What is the significance of religion, according to this understanding of history? Religion is a product of economic forces. It is an instrument whereby the dominant capitalist class is able

to maintain its power to exploit the workers. Religion is the
"opiate of the people." [5] It anaesthetizes the sensitivity of the
oppressed by holding before them the prospect of reward in the
hereafter.

This was not an empty charge. Much evidence can be adduced
to support the assertion of a recent interpreter that "no slave or
servile class was ever more brutally exploited than the industrial
proletariat" during the Industrial Revolution in England in the
latter eighteenth century, and "in no age perhaps was the use
of Christianity as an antidote to social unrest more blatant" than
during this period.[6] Marx's accusation can be matched by only
slightly less extreme statements by defenders of religion. The
comments of Wilberforce, cited above, are one example. Another
writer urged in 1798 that concrete steps be taken to bring the
"lower classes" into the churches, in order that they may "learn
the doctrines of that truly excellent religion which exhorts to
content and to submission to the higher powers." And critics
before Marx had insisted that "what the millions should generally know is this: that no rich man believes in religion of any
sort except as a political engine to keep the useful classes in sub-
jection to the rich." [7]

The full impact of the Marxist critique of Christianity did not
come until the twentieth century. Moreover, Marxism had relatively little appeal to the disinherited in Protestant countries except in Lutheran Germany. Neverthless, the appearance of Marxism in the mid-nineteenth century was of the greatest importance
as a symbol in at least two respects. First, Marxism represented
the judgment which Christianity had not effectively pronounced
upon the injustice and exploitation of the Industrial Revolution.
It was a voice of protest against a system which seemed inevitably to lead to enslavement. But this was a word hardly heard
from within the churches for the clamor of "the harmony of

    [5] Marx was not the first to use this language. Charles Kingsley, novelist
and Anglican priest, had earlier used a similar phrase in confessing the
failures of the church. (See below)
    [6] W. D. Morris, *The Christian Origins of Social Revolt*, London:
Allen & Unwin, 1949, 153.
    [7] Bronterre O'Brien, in the *Poor Man's Guardian*, Dec. 12, 1835.

interests" and the loud enthusiasm for middle-class culture. Therefore, it appeared as judgment upon the churches.[8]

Second, the Marxist vision of a perfect society corresponded to (and had roots in) the Christian hope for the kingdom of God on earth. In this respect particularly, Marxism has often been called a "Christian heresy." Like the idea of progress, the Marxist view of history as moving toward the final climax of judgment and fulfillment was ultimately derived from the Christian theology of history. In Marxism, this hope was stripped of its religious foundation, historical necessity was substituted for the will of God, and judgment and fulfillment were translated into economic terms. But even this secularized version of the hope for the kingdom symbolized clarity in the recognition of social evil, confidence that the movement of history was toward the establishment of justice, and a prophetic denunciation of the idols of free enterprise. This in a time when the churches, to put it mildly, were confused and hesitant.

The Marxist dream was far more, of course, than a symbol of hope and prophetic criticism. It was also an utter disregard of the Christian view of the worth of persons, and it was to have terrible historical consequences as developed in modern Russia. These horrors are perhaps also partly a judgment upon failures to deal adequately with the problems of industrial society.

3. THE SOCIAL GOSPEL

At the time that Marxism appeared, however, there were already stirrings within the church of a powerful movement to overthrow the uncritical identification of Christianity with the existing order. Moreover, while the philanthropists and reformers of the early nineteenth century had not often envisaged radical transformation of society as such, their concern for the correction of social abuses did affect profoundly the tone of industrial society and paved a way both for the more incisive and trenchant criticism which was to follow, and for more radical proposals for reform.

[8] There had been earlier Christian parallels to the Marxist critique (e.g., the writings of Gerrard Winstanley), but these had been largely ineffective.

One major sign of the changing attitude of Protestantism may be seen in the Christian Socialist movement in Britain, led by F. D. Maurice (theologian), Charles Kingsley (pastor and novelist), and J. M. Ludlow (lawyer). The movement began in 1848, the year in which the *Communist Manifesto* appeared and popular insurrections swept over continental Europe, and was explicitly an effort to provide a Christian method of social reform as an alternative to class struggle. The Christian Socialists recognized the failings of the churches. "We have," wrote Kingsley, "used the Bible as if it were a mere special constable's handbook, an opium dose for keeping beasts of burden patient while they are being overloaded." They sought to improve working-class conditions through religious regeneration, the formation of producers' cooperatives in which men might be their own employers, the encouragement of trade unions which would work peacefully for better conditions of their members, and the promotion of popular education.

The Christian Socialists still shared much of the attitude of a condescending, though genuinely benevolent, philanthropy. But, while they deplored suggestions of class militancy, they were far more realistic in assessing the depths of the evils of industrial society. Their influence, while relatively slight in their own day, was immense in the later development of social concern in England. They marked a definite recognition of the church's duty to work for the creation of a just social order. And they saw that this might require more than stewardship, philanthropy, and the regulation of abuses. The spirit of Maurice and his associates permeated both the Anglican Church and the various non-conformist churches.[9] This spirit was partly responsible for preventing the opposition between organized labor and the church which appeared almost everywhere on the European continent, and its influence was felt through the Free Churches in the profound religious animation of later British socialism and the Labor party.

On the Continent, Protestant concern for the reconstruction of society appeared strongly in those influenced by Ritschl (see Chs. IX, X) and in the Swiss religious socialism of the first decades

---

[9] For a recent statement representing the Anglican view, see *Christianity and the Social Order,* by Archbishop William Temple.

of the twentieth century. And in the Roman Catholic Church, Popes Leo XIII (1878–1903) and Pius XI (1922–1939) gave official approval and active encouragement to religious activities for social reform.

The most distinctive expression of the Protestant "social conscience" in the nineteenth and early twentieth centuries is to be found in the American movement known as the "social gospel," which came into being in the last quarter of the nineteenth century and reached its height in the optimistic years just prior to the First World War. Here more than anywhere else was sounded the theme that the thoroughgoing reconstruction of society is both imperative and possible. Here, too, was clearly expressed the primary difference between the new social concern and the older humanitarianism, viz., the conviction that the well-being of men required the transformation of the social environment as well as the changing of individuals.

The social gospel had unique roots in the American heritage. The dream of a kingdom of God on earth had long been a part of the American ethos (though the goal of the kingdom was often confused with the more immediate achievements of society). The Puritans had come in hope of the creation of "a new Heaven, and a new Earth in new Churches, and a new Common-wealth together." The hope of the kingdom had blended with the democratic ideal in the foundation of the republic and its later equalitarian aspirations. That hope was nourished in the evangelical revivals and accounted in no small measure for the fervor devoted to missions and against slavery (thus Edward Beecher wrote: "Now that God has smitten slavery to death, he has opened the way for the redemption and sanctification of our whole social system"). Moreover, the United States, with its rapid growth in size, population, industry and wealth, was notably receptive to the spirit of progress and indefinite perfectibility of society which was current in eighteenth-century literature.

The birth of the social gospel was also assisted by a variety of distinctively nineteenth-century forces. One was the challenge of socialism and the rising labor unions. The American labor leader, Samuel Gompers, wrote in 1898, explaining the absence of workers from the church: "My associates have come to look upon the church and the ministry as the apologists and defenders of the wrong committed against the interests of the people, simply because the perpetrators are possessors of wealth . . . whose real God is the almighty dollar, and who contribute a few of their idols to suborn the intellect and eloquence of the divines. . . ."

A second force was liberal theology. The moral idealism of liberalism, and its insistence on practical fruits of religion, intensified the sense of Christian responsibility for doing something about the evils of society. Liberalism's view of the sacredness of human personality and its optimism about human virtue were primary assumptions of the new social emphasis. Conceptions of the immanence of God and of evolutionary progress in history buttressed the faith that the transformation of society was possible.

Liberalism also contributed by helping to break down the extreme individualism which had entered Protestant understanding of sin and redemption. Horace Bushnell (1802–1876), who did more than any one else to further the liberalization of American theology, had emphasized the overwhelming importance of social environment in the development of character. Men are indeed united in sin, he asserted, not in some formal legal sense or through biological inheritance, but through their common involvement in the social texture in which personality is formed. And if sin is social, so is virtue. Men cannot be redeemed in isolation from society but only in and with it. There is social solidarity both in sin and in salvation.

Moreover, the liberal approach to the Bible was instrumental 1) in the renewed appreciation of the demand for social justice by the Hebrew prophets (notably Amos and Micah); 2) in the application of the teachings of Jesus regarding wealth, the family, the state, and non-resistance, to problems of the industrial and political orders; and especially 3) in the rediscovery of the centrality of the kingdom of God in Jesus' message and the interpretation of the kingdom as a real ideal for the present world.

A third major nineteenth-century force which helped to call forth the social gospel was the intensity of the social problems themselves. By 1880, the United States was rapidly becoming a closely knit industrial society, and it was the problems of this society that the social gospel sought to meet. The new economic interdependence, the maladjustments attendant upon the growth of industry and the cities, the disruptions of social and family life, the failure of the new technology to fulfil the promise of plenty for all, mass unemployment and unprecedented poverty, growing labor discontent, the exaggerated individualism of the capitalist, the disregard of human rights—all these showed clearly that the neighbor could not be served in isolation. The social gospel was a new application of the Christian ethic in response to the demands of a new historical situation. Conscience had to become "social conscience."

From its birth (about 1870) the social gospel was marked by a two-fold emphasis: a broader conception of the church's function, and a nascent critique of the patterns and ideology of the existing order. Penetrating criticism was directed against the theory of the harmony of interests, especially against the supposition that private gain always makes for public good. On such a view, it was suggested, the greatest public benevolence would be the most unrestrained, comprehensive self-seeking! Examination of the facts showed that unrestricted competition was leading directly to the most inhuman treatment of men, in arrogant denial of Christian ethics and of the dignity of human personality. The good of all did *not* come simply as a by-product of the pursuit of self-interest.

Moreover, the early proponents of the social gospel saw (quite correctly, as later experience showed) that the crux of industrial maladjustment lay in the conflict between capital and labor. They insisted that the relations of capital and labor constitute a moral issue. It is, they said, not only inadequate but perverse to relegate these matters to the class of purely "economic" problems. The Christian law of love must be considered as well as the law of supply and demand. Thus Washington Gladden, often called the "father of the social gospel," wrote in 1876:

> Now that slavery is out of the way, the questions that concern our free laborers are coming forward; and no intelligent man needs to be admonished of their urgency. They are not only questions of economy, they are in a large sense moral questions; nay, they touch the very marrow of that

religion of good-will of which Christ was the founder. It is plain that the pulpit must have something to say about them.[10]

Such a view required an enlarged conception of the church's function. It must speak not only of "honesty" in acquiring wealth, and "generosity" once it is acquired, it must speak also of "justice" to those who labor in the production of wealth. It must be concerned with the *patterns* of economic enterprise. There must be "new applications of the truth and the adoption of methods unknown to former times." The church can, if she will, provide these! So wrote Josiah Strong: "The world in this sociological age needs a new social ideal to direct the progress of civilization. Let the church fully accept her mission and she will furnish this needed ideal, viz., her Master's conception of the kingdom of God come upon earth." The church is to be the source of self-giving love to take the place of selfish competition.

The demand that the church assume an active role in the establishment of social justice, and that Christian ethics be applied to every aspect of social life, was voiced not only by individuals but by dozens of new journals and organizations. The social gospel was celebrated in popular hymns, such as Frank Mason North's "Where Cross the Crowded Ways of Life," Washington Gladden's "O Master, Let Me Walk with Thee," Clifford Box's "Turn Back, O Man," and Ernest Shurtleff's "Lead on, O King Eternal." The most distinctive literary production of the movement was the social gospel novel, which dramatized the possibilities of reforming society through the application of Christian principles in business and politics. The best known of these novels, a story by Charles M. Sheldon called *In His Steps: What Would Jesus Do?*, probably did more than any other medium to make people aware of the claims of the social gospel. In the generation after its publication (1896), this book sold an estimated 23,000,000 copies in English and had been translated into twenty-one other languages. As a social tract, *In His Steps* ranks with such other American classics as *Uncle Tom's Cabin* and *Ten Nights in a Bar Room*. In spite of the fact that *In His Steps* is still relatively

[10] Cited in H. Hopkins, *The Rise of the Social Gospel*, 24.

individualistic in its conception of methods of social reform, a comparison of this book with *Pilgrim's Progress* shows vividly how far Protestant thinking had changed in two centuries in its view of the role of the Christian in society.

4. THE SOCIAL GOSPEL'S GREATEST PROPHET: RAUSCHENBUSCH

In 1917 Walter Rauschenbusch, professor of church history in Rochester Theological Seminary (New York), could say:

> "The social gospel . . . is no longer a prophetic and occasional note. It is a novelty only in backward social or religious communities. The social gospel has become orthodox. It is not only preached. It has set new problems for local church work, and has turned the pastoral and organizing work of the ministry into new and constructive directions. It has imparted a wider vision and a more statesmanlike grasp to the foreign mission enterprise . . . Conservative denominations have formally committed themselves to the fundamental ideas of the social gospel and their practical application. The plans of great interdenominational organizations are inspired by it. It has become a constructive force in American politics." [11]

This assertion may suggest a wider popular acceptance of the social gospel than a more sober judgment would allow, either for Protestantism in 1917 or a generation later. But certainly no one person was more responsible for gaining popular response and official recognition for the social gospel than Rauschenbusch himself.

The son of a German Baptist pastor and professor, Rauschenbusch served for eleven years a congregation of German immigrant workers in "Hell's Kitchen," the tough West End of New York City. There he found problems of human misery and economic maladjustment to which the inherited forms of his faith seemed to have little to say. A re-examination of the faith and of the Bible led to new convictions which were expressed first in a periodical *For The Right*, published (1889ff.) with the help of several friends for the discussion of the "interests of the working class." Shortly afterward, Rauschenbusch and a few

[11] *A Theology for the Social Gospel,* 2f.

other young pastors formed the Brotherhood of the Kingdom, meeting for a week every summer until 1914, to examine and to promote "the ethical and spiritual principles of Jesus, both in their individual and their social aspects." Rauschenbusch became the acknowledged leader of the social gospel movement with the publication of *Christianity and the Social Crisis* (1907). His writings gave mature expression to the purpose and program of the movement, as well as to some of the assumptions which a later generation was to find of dubious significance (see Ch. XII).

In a summary statement of the meaning of the social gospel, Rauschenbusch makes explicit the self-understanding which had characterized the movement from its beginning: the social gospel is new in its emphasis and broader in its scope, but it springs from the old evangelical faith.

> The social gospel is the old message of salvation, but enlarged and intensified. The individualistic gospel has taught us to see the sinfulness of every human heart and has inspired us with faith in the willingness and power of God to save every soul that comes to him. But it has not given us an adequate understanding of the sinfulness of the social order and its share in the sins of all individuals within it. It has not evoked faith in the will and power to God to redeem the permanent institutions of human society from their inherited guilt of oppression and extortion. Both our sense of sin and our faith in salvation have fallen short of the realities under its teaching. The social gospel seeks to bring men under repentance for their collective sins and to create a more sensitive and more modern conscience. It calls on us for the faith of the old prophets who believed in the salvation of nations.[12]

The underlying principle of this new understanding of the gospel was the explicit and consistent recognition of the social nature of personal existence. Society was seen as an organism rather than as a mere collection of individual units, and human inter-relationships as "vital" and "solidaristic." This theme had been sounded vigorously by Bushnell and had been instrumental in the creation of the social gospel. With the full elaboration of

[12] *Ibid.*, 5f.

the new gospel, as seen in Rauschenbusch's thought, that crucial insight was carried further in several directions: 1) in relation to the idea of the kingdom of God, 2) in a more thorough-going demand for reorganization of the economic *system*, 3) in a more scientific approach to the study of social problems, and 4) in an attempt to restate Christian theology so as to take fuller account of the social gospel.

1) The concept of the kingdom of God was for Rauschenbusch the focus of the original gospel and ought always therefore to be the center of the Christian message. Study of the New Testament was showing with increasing definiteness that the heart of Jesus' teaching was his proclamation of the coming kingdom. The social gospel, therefore, meant to Rauschenbusch and his associates the re-establishment of the ideal of the kingdom of God in the place it occupied in the message of Jesus. They (quite rightly) insisted upon the intimate connection between the ethical teachings of Jesus and his preaching of the kingdom. Moreover, though here they wrongly interpreted Jesus' teaching, they believed that the kingdom was to grow out of the existing institutions of society. The kingdom would come not with the destruction of the present social order, but with the redemption of the "permanent institutions of human society." The kingdom is not an other-worldly hope, but a goal for this world, the end toward which all the divine activity is leading, viz., the organization of humanity according to the will of God.

Rauschenbusch never supposed, as some of his lesser followers seem to have done, that the kingdom could be established simply or even primarily by human effort. For him, it is *God's* kingdom:

> "The Kingdom of God is divine in its origin, progress, and consummation. It was initiated by Jesus Christ, in whom the prophetic spirit came to consummation, it is sustained by the Holy Spirit, and it will be brought to its fulfillment by the power of God in his own time. . . . The Kingdom of God, therefore, is miraculous all the way. . . ."[13]

Nor did Rauschenbusch suppose that the kingdom could come without great struggle against the kingdom of evil (i.e., organized sin, evil which has become entrenched in the patterns of society).

[13] *A Theology for the Social Gospel*, 139.

Nevertheless, the kingdom is in part already present and comes by slow growth; it is possible for men to help it along. "Every human life is so placed that it can share with God in the creation of the Kingdom, or can resist and retard its progress. The Kingdom is for each of us the supreme task and the supreme gift of God." [14] It is not to be expected that society will ever fully achieve perfection; but it is possible and a duty to move along the path of approximation to a perfect social order. "The Kingdom of God is always but coming," but it is also true that the kingdom of God is always coming.

2) In some respects, Rauschenbusch and others felt Western society was relatively far along on the way toward the kingdom— e.g., in education and in democratic government. These agencies, then, could be means for promotion of the kingdom in that area in which least progress had been made, viz., in the economic order. From the first, the social gospel had been particularly concerned with problems of economic justice; nowhere was the power of organized sin more apparent than in the cruelties of industrial society. The beginning of the twentieth century, however, revealed a trend toward a more radical approach to economic problems and their solution. Appeals to individual regeneration, and to love as the means to establishing industrial harmony, were definitely recognized as quite inadequate apart from social reorganization.

As early as 1890, this tendency appeared in a greater friendliness toward socialism, particularly in the demand of the latter for fundamental social reorganization. For the most part, however, those who sought to make common cause with socialism refused to identify the Christian social ideal with any specific "socialist" programs, and socialism was approved as a means to a social and religious end rather than as an end in itself. It was at the point of the *criticism* of the competitive and predatory features of unregulated capitalism that Christian ethics and the socialist critique seemed to have the most in common.

3) The scientific note was prominent in multiplied efforts to accumulate accurate and complete information regarding social problems and to incorporate this into programs of religious edu-

[14] *Ibid.*, 141.

cation. More objective studies were made of the function of religion in society. The role of the church was reconceived as in part that of a social service agency, and such institutional organizations as the religious social settlement and the "labor church" were accepted as essential elements in the church's ministry. The study of sociology and social problems became an integral part of the curriculum of theological seminaries. A correlative form of the emphasis on social science was the entrance of numerous Protestant ministers into professional social service work and into research and teaching in sociology.

4) A final direction of the developed thought of the social gospel was the attempt to restate Christian doctrine in terms of the new social vision. The classic expression of this effort was a series of lectures delivered by Rauschenbusch at Yale University in 1917, published under the title *A Theology for the Social Gospel*. In these lectures, Rauschenbusch explicitly undertook to formulate "a systematic theology large enough to match (the social gospel) and vital enough to back it," to show "how some of the most important sections of doctrinal theology may be expanded and readjusted to make room for the religious convictions summed up in 'the social gospel' " [15]

Rauschenbusch's own theological perspective was largely free from the sentimental optimism of much of the social gospel thought of his day and of the 1920's; and many of his deepest convictions ran counter to the prevailing liberal theology. Yet Rauschenbusch's concern to emphasize the distinction between the old theology and the theology for the social gospel made it inevitable that primary attention should be given to those aspects of his reinterpretation which seemed most in accord with liberalism. His keen sense of the kingdom of God as judgment, and of the deepening of the burden of guilt through the recognition of social sin; the new validity which he found in the doctrine of original sin through the recognition of the social transmission of sin; the sense of crisis in individual and social life, and the demand for repentance and rebirth; and the desperateness of the struggle against the "kingdom of evil" (the super-individual forces of evil infecting the whole social organism)—these ele-

[15] *Ibid.*, I.

ments of Rauschenbusch's theology were less influential than those which reinforced the characteristic liberal tenets.

With the liberals, Rauschenbusch defined sin as selfishness. The conception of God was to be freed of all despotic and monarchial elements, and "democratized" by reappropriation of Jesus' teaching of the Fatherhood of God: "the worst thing that could happen to God would be to remain an autocrat while the world is moving toward democracy." The immanence of God should be recognized as the basis of social solidarity: "the all-pervading life of God is the ground of the spiritual oneness of the race and of our hope for its closer fellowship." Conceptions of revelation and inspiration were to receive new meaning, and the spirit of prophecy (in its vision of the kingdom) would once more become central in the work of redemption. The redeeming work of Christ's life was seen as the battle against religious bigotry, graft and political power, corruption of justice, mob spirit and mob action, militarism, and class contempt—i.e., precisely those universal social sins which conspired to kill him. His death supremely revealed the power of sin and of the love of God, and strengthened "the power of prophetic religion and therewith the redemptive forces of the Kingdom of God."

5. ACCEPTANCE AND MODIFICATION OF THE SOCIAL GOSPEL

Rauschenbusch's declaration that "the social gospel has become orthodox," if it implied full popular acceptance, was an exaggeration. But during the first decade of the twentieth century, the Presbyterian, Protestant Episcopal, Congregational, Methodist, and Northern Baptist Churches had begun the establishment of official agencies for study and recommendation in the area of social problems; and by 1912 eleven other denominations had pledged themselves to carry out social service programs through existing church agencies. The official recognition of the social gospel was symbolized by the organization in 1908 of the Federal Council of the Churches of Christ in America (now merged into the National Council of the Churches of Christ in the U.S.A.). The Council was formed partly for the specific purpose of providing a centralized organ for the expression of Protestant concern in every area of social problems, and after a difficult struggle against elements both within and without the churches, it became a prominent force in the American scene. It has continued to provide an effective framework for Protestant social action.

In similar fashion, the acknowledgment of the church's social responsibility has been a prime factor in the movement for interdenominational cooperation on a world-wide scale (see Ch. XIII). This concern was focused in the "ecumenical" conferences at Stockholm (1925) and Oxford (1937) and in the Universal Christian Council for Life and Work (formed in 1929). The Life and Work movement became in turn a part of the program of the World Council of Churches. The World Council took as the theme for its first meeting (Amsterdam, 1948) "Man's Disorder and God's Design," dealing specifically with the problem of the church's relation to social and international disorders. Among the fruits of this study was the much-publicized criticism by the Council of both communism and laissez-faire capitalism.[16]

Since the middle 1930's, the Christian social movement has undergone important reorientation. As liberal theology has come under severe criticism in the light of a renewed appreciation of many classical Christian insights, the social concern of the church has been increasingly freed from dependence on the theological patterns of liberalism. The buoyant and often sentimental optimism of the "social gospel," in spite of Rauschenbusch's warnings, had continued unabated through the 1920's in such leaders as Shailer Mathews and Francis J. McConnell. But this

[16] This appeared in the report of Section III, on "The Church and the Disorder of Society." The relevant paragraph reads as follows: "The Christian churches should reject the ideologies of both communism and laissez-faire capitalism, and should seek to draw men away from the false assumption that these extremes are the only alternatives. Each has made promises which it could not redeem. Communist ideology puts the emphasis upon economic justice, and promises that freedom will come automatically after the completion of the revolution. Capitalism puts the emphasis upon freedom, and promises that justice will follow as a by-product of free enterprise; that, too, is an ideology which has been proved false. It is the responsibility of Christians to seek new, creative solutions which never allow either justice or freedom to destroy the other."
The study papers prepared for the Amsterdam meeting, and the official reports of the four sections, have been published in *The Amsterdam Assembly Series*, "Man's Disorder and God's Design," 4 vols.

has given way to soberer views of human virtue and a more radical understanding of the divine judgment upon human society and schemes for its redemption. The concern for peace, prominent even before World War I, had led in the 1920's to the channelling of much of the enthusiasm for the social gospel into uncritical pacifist positions. Recent thought has taken more positive account of the necessity of restraint of evil, even through war. (Perhaps the best expression in America of this changing perspective is to be found in the report of the commission chaired by Robert L. Calhoun on "The Relation of the Church to the War in the Light of the Christian Faith," 1944.) The frequent tendency of many social gospel proponents to rely simply on church pronouncements has been counter-balanced by more serious study of the processes of social change, of the role of the church in relation to legislative processes, and of the technical problems of the economic and political orders. The hope of "bringing in the kingdom" has been replaced by more concrete attempts to find proximate and viable solutions to social problems which continually recur in new forms.

Nonetheless, the ethical imperative of the social gospel, the emphasis on Christian social responsibility, the sharp criticism of any Christian ethics which deals only with "individual morality," the primary concern for the welfare of oppressed classes and races—these remain from the social gospel as an integral part of the Protestant witness, and this in spite of recent (often violent) criticism from ultra-conservative groups. Most important, the social gospel both symbolized and popularized an apparently permanent shift in the Christian attitude toward social institutions in relation to man's salvation. Earlier it had been assumed that the patterns of the social orders were fixed, and that the quality of the spiritual life was essentially separable from the quality of social life. Now, however, social institutions themselves were seen to be malleable, and both redemptive and restrictive in relation to the spiritual life. Thus, where prior to the social gospel, the influence of Christianity on social structures had been largely indirect and unconscious, now it became conscious and explicit. Now men felt required, as part of their Christian witness, to conceive of the transformation of social structures as such, and of the creation of new patterns.

XII

Directions in Recent
Protestant Thought

The pattern of Protestant theological development has been one of recurrent reinterpretation of Christian faith in response to new needs and situations—of reaction and revival in the midst of fundamental continuity. This was true of the origin of Protestantism. The reformers were in revolt against serious perversions of the gospel which had come to dominate the medieval church, and they sought to recall the church to its task of proclaiming the gospel of God's graciousness in Jesus Christ, as that gospel was set forth in the New Testament and as it spoke to the religious situation of the sixteenth century. At the same time, the reformers were speaking to the church from within, and the understanding of the gospel which they revived had never been wholly lost. A similar pattern was evident in the evangelical revivals and in the growth of the free church tradition. Liberalism, too, was marked by a breaking down of false and dated idols of creed and confession and a reappropriation of crucial facets of the Christian witness which had been abused, neglected or forgotten.

The latest in this series of renewed apprehensions and interpretations of the gospel may be said to begin with the publication in 1918 of a commentary on Paul's Epistle to the Romans, by Karl Barth, a Swiss pastor. This was a book of violent protest against the fundamental premises of "liberal" theology, and it called for a radical re-examination of the basis of Christian thinking.

Barth had himself been trained in the liberal tradition of Ritschl and Harnack. But as he sought to work out the implications of their views, and especially as a young pastor, faced Sunday after Sunday with the task of declaring the Christian message to his congregation, Barth felt with growing keenness that liberalism had really no *gospel* to offer at all, but only an attempted sharing of private religious experiences. Thus he reported later the "joyful sense of discovery" with which he found, through renewed study of the Bible and especially of St. Paul, a radically different perspective for Christian faith.

It was this new insight which Barth sought to develop in the commentary on Romans. The biblical message, he affirmed, is not concerned with man's discovery of God, or "religious experience," but with *God's Word* to man. This is a Word which comes to man in judgment on all his pretensions, including his religious pretensions. It is a Word about God's faithfulness, which reveals man's utter faithlessness and rebellion. The divine Yea comes to man as an uncompromising No. It reveals, not a fundamental continuity between human and divine, but distance and estrangement. "God is in heaven and thou art on earth." The confidence of faith can, therefore, never rest in human religiousness or claim to goodness or social progress. Faith can only refer to the strange and unexpected Word from above. In a later essay, Barth wrote of the new perspective as the discovery of a "strange new world within the Bible":

> It is not the right human thoughts about God which form the content of the Bible, but the right divine thoughts about men. The Bible tells us not how we should talk with God but what he says to us; not how we find the way to him, but he has sought and found the way to us; not the right relation in which we must place ourselves to him, but the covenant which he has made with all who are Abraham's spiritual children and which he has sealed once and for all in Jesus Christ. . . . We have found in the Bible a new world, God, God's sovereignty, God's glory, God's incomprehensible love. Not the history of man but the history of God! Not the virtues of men but the virtues of him who

hath called us out of the darkness into his marvelous light! Not human standpoints but the standpoint of God![1]

The reception with which Barth's commentary was greeted was one for which he was quite unprepared. He compared his experience to that of a man climbing in a church steeple in the middle of the night, who reaching out for support discovers to his dismay that he has seized the bell rope and awakened the whole town. Barth immediately became the center of a storm of discussion and he has continued for a quarter of a century to be the leading and most controversial prophet of contemporary Protestantism. Protestant and Catholic thinkers both have had to take account of his work.

We should not suppose, of course, that a new mood and direction in religious thought is ever simply the result of one man's work. Rather, Barth's dramatic protest and polemic was the focus of a widely felt need for a new look at the gospel and all theological formulations. Powerful forces were already at work, both within the church's understanding of its message and within the world to which the church sought to speak, which necessitated theological reconstruction. The time was ripe for a thorough reassessment of both liberal and traditional forms for the understanding of the gospel. Karl Barth's work gives a key to the direction which such a movement was to take, but development has proceeded along numerous and often independent lines. In the United States it was Reinhold Niebuhr who became the chief spokesman for the new theological perspective. His *Moral Man and Immoral Society* (1933) had the same sort of "shock-value" for America which Barth's *Romans* had for Germany. And Niebuhr was led to a similar recovery of the Reformation doctrine of justification by faith (and also the Augustinian-Lutheran analysis of sin) by the pressure of social and economic issues. It was the abysmal problems of human nature, which Niebuhr began to see in the intensive industrialization of Detroit during the years of his pastorate there (1915–1928), that required the rejection of the liberal dogmas. The doctrines of justification by faith and original sin had to be reasserted as indispensable for

[1] From *The Word of God and the Word of Man,* by Karl Barth. Copyright, The Pilgrim Press. Used by permission. 43, 45.

the interpretation of human history (and therefore just as relevant for sociology and the philosophy of history as for theology).

The purpose of this chapter is to sketch the broad outlines of the theological tendencies of which Barth and Niebuhr have been important (and often extreme) representatives. This is not intended as an all-inclusive survey of the contemporary Protestant scene. Such a survey would have to include the "ecumenical movement," which has had profound influence on recent theology (see Ch. XIII). It would also have to recognize the persistence of both liberal and fundamentalist thought. At the same time, the patterns of thought described below are not limited to any single theological "school" or "type." They represent a mood or direction in theology which has become increasingly characteristic of Protestant thinking in the past three decades.

1. THE NEW THEOLOGICAL SITUATION

One patent characteristic of the new mood in Protestant thinking has been the reaction against liberal theology. It has demanded re-examination of the fundamental premises of liberalism in the light of the Christian tradition, and the place of honor has been given to some elements of the tradition with which liberalism was most sharply at odds. Yet the new theology (unlike fundamentalism, which sought to by-pass the liberal challenge, see Ch. X) is unquestionably a "post-liberal" theology. It has come out of the midst of liberalism and its perspective has been shaped by the problems with which liberalism had to deal. The revolt against liberalism is the revolt of a child against its father, a conflict required by the new situation in which the child must live, by the deficiencies which new experience and reflection reveal in the outlook of the parent, and by the desire to be loyal to the entire tradition of which the immediate parent is but one representative.

At its center, then, the new theology is an attempt to exhibit anew the realities which Christian faith attests, in relevance to the situation of twentieth-century man. Contemporary Protestant thinking involves both a continuation of liberal developments and a hammering out of new insights in opposition to many liberal tendencies. The new patterns show both a reappropriation and a reinterpretation of classical Christian doctrines. They have sprung both from renewed insight into the Christian witness and from the necessity of newly interpreting that gospel to a contemporary world.

1) One aspect of the new situation, certainly the most obvious one, which called for renewed appraisal of the Protestant understanding of the gospel, was the dramatic alteration in the world scene. In the nineteenth century it was possible to speak of a harmony of interests, based on faith in a good Creator and the order of the universe, because there did seem to be a rough sort of harmony among the various activities of men. It was possible to believe in the progressive realization of a world of justice and plenty, because the relative peace and prosperity of the nineteenth century seemed amply to justify such a hope. But after a world war, the fatuous and irresponsible 1920's, and a great depression, this kind of outlook was simply out of the question. The problem was no longer one of a Christian understanding of the gradual perfecting of man and society. It became instead a problem of understanding human misery, tragedy and bestiality. The word of the gospel had to be interpreted to a world of disorder and conflict, in which the whole fabric of society appeared to be rotting away, a world in which hope had been swallowed up by despair and a sense of futility. The Second World War accentuated this attitude and brought with it the fear of imminent and ultimate doom for all human achievements. The optimism of liberalism seemed naive and superficial, and the question had to be asked whether Christian insight really warranted liberalism's supreme confidence in man's response to reason and ideals. Thus, Reinhold Niebuhr could write in 1934:

> The liberal culture of modernity is defective in both religious profundity and political sagacity. . . . (It) understands neither the heights to which life may rise nor the depths to which it may sink. . . . It is quite unable to give guidance and direction to a confused generation which faces the disintegration of a social system and the task of building a new one.[2]

2) A second feature of the new situation was the further de-

[2] Reinhold Niebuhr, *Reflections on the End of an Era*, 14, ix.

velopment of biblical criticism. At the end of the nineteenth century some scholars were speaking of the "assured results" of
criticism and were quite confident that the "historical Jesus"
could be distinguished from the layers of "later" theological
interpretation which were present in the New Testament record.
It was thought that the "permanently valid" elements of Jesus'
teaching and example could be lifted directly out of their context and presented as a universal claim upon men. But this assurance was quickly and rudely shaken by further New Testament study. For one thing, largely as a result of the writings of
Albert Schweitzer, who was later to become the most famous
missionary of the twentieth century, it now appeared that the
expectation of an imminent, catastrophic establishment of the
kingdom of God on earth was central to Jesus' teaching. Jesus
believed that the kingdom would come soon, perhaps even in his
own lifetime and certainly within his generation; his own mission
was to call men to be prepared for its advent. Thus, it was not
possible for modern interpreters to say that Jesus' followers had
misunderstood him and had transformed his message of an inner
spiritual kingdom into the hope of the overthrow of the external
social order. Nor was it possible to say (with Harnack) that the
external elements in the hope of the kingdom were merely the
Jewish framework in which Jesus cast his message and were not
really significant for his teaching. It was also impossible simply to
separate Jesus' teaching about the Fatherhood of God or his
ethical demands from the belief in the kingdom. All of Jesus'
teaching had to be re-examined.

This new understanding of the nature and importance of Jesus'
teaching about the kingdom therefore raised new questions about
the permanent validity of Jesus' teaching. It was not simply a
question whether Jesus was mistaken about the time of the
coming of the kingdom, for liberalism had long since recognized
that the gospels portrayed a truly human person, sharing in the
limitations of finite existence. The problem was now deepened
and broadened by new understanding of the extent to which even
the most central elements of Jesus' teaching were bound up with
the perspectives of his time. It was no longer possible to separate
the "historical Jesus" from his social environment and to make
of him a "modern" teacher. Few interpreters have accepted

Schweitzer's judgment that Jesus viewed the kingdom as purely a future event, or that the ethical demands referred only to the brief "interim" between Jesus' preaching and the coming of the kingdom. But Schweitzer's summary (in 1906) of the results of biblical criticism remains a classic expression of the kind of problem which now appeared:

> The study of the Life of Jesus has had a curious history. It set out in quest of the historical Jesus, believing that when it had found Him it could bring Him straight into our time as a Teacher and Savior. It loosed the bands by which He had been riveted for centuries to the stony rocks of ecclesiastical doctrine, and rejoiced to see the life and movement coming into the figure once more, and the historical Jesus advancing, as it seemed, to meet it. But He does not stay; He passes by our time and returns to His own. What surprised and dismayed the theology of the last forty years was that, despite all forced and arbitrary interpretations, it could not keep Him in our time, but had to let Him go.[3]

On the one side, then, it was discovered that the historical Jesus could not be sundered from the world of first-century Judaism. But on the other side, it was seen that he could not be separated from the early Christian community and its faith. A better understanding of the process by which the gospels came into existence revealed that none of them could be considered "biographies" in the modern sense. They were documents written from the point of view of faith. This does not mean that the gospels were fictional creations, though there are clearly elements of legend in them; but rather that the writers of the gospels were not concerned simply with recording "facts" about the life of Jesus. They were interested in these facts because of their conviction that in this man God had wrought a mighty work of redemption. The Passion was the focus of the story. Jesus' deeds and sayings were significant only because of his death and resurrection, which disclosed him to be the Christ, the Son of the living God. Thus, the gospels are just that: "gospels," the good news of the work of God in Christ. They are from beginning to end colored by the faith of the church, and any attempt *finally* to distinguish the "facts" of the life of Jesus from the inter-

[3] Albert Schweitzer *The Quest of the Historical Jesus,* 397. New York: The Macmillan Company, 1948. Used by permission of the publisher.

pretations of the early believers is foredoomed to failure. Not only the gospel of John, but also the synoptics are *interpretations* of Jesus, though the synoptics are relatively more accurate in their historical detail.[4]

Further, the recognition that liberalism had erred in stripping away from the picture of the "historical Jesus" those elements which seemed foreign to the modern mind, and the new appreciation of the character of the gospels, has led to emphasis on the unity of the New Testament witness. It is no longer possible to say that Paul distorted the simplicity of the original gospel of Jesus by the interjection of "theological" interpretations foreign to it. The gospel of Jesus was in fact not so simple. The Jesus of history is no less distant from modern man (and no less relevant to him!) than the faith of Paul. Moreover, the faith in Jesus as the Christ is so integral to the entirety of the New Testament witness that whether or not Jesus declared himself to be the Messiah or the Son of God, none of his teaching (whether about God, the kingdom, or the ethical demand) can be lifted out of the context of the faith in his person. The New Testament has to be considered as a whole, and the point from which Christian thinking begins is the Jesus Christ whose life, death, resurrection and redemptive power the whole of the New Testament attests.

3) This further development of biblical interpretation was closely related to a wider appreciation of the extent to which all human knowing is colored by the point of view, the location in time and space, of the knower. All institutions and ideas—political, economic, scientific, moral and religious—are influenced by their particular historical and social environments. All visions of truth are the apprehensions of men in definite historical situations and are in part shaped by the perspectives of those situations.

One aspect of this problem we saw in the failure of the liberal attempt to portray Jesus in the categories of the nineteenth century, for liberalism had overlooked the significance of the vast difference of perspective between a Jew of the first century and

---

[4] It should be noted that this was not a problem peculiar to biblical study, but that historians generally were coming to recognize that no history can be simply a recital of facts, but always involves the selection and interpretation of data in accordance with insight into the meaning of events.

a Western European of the nineteenth. Jesus' teachings could not simply be abstracted from their context, for to understand the content of his message one had to see it from the standpoint of his own time, to think in the same historically conditioned terms in which he thought. Similarly, the creeds of the church could be understood only in the terms of their historical backgrounds and contexts. So also, the religious intuitions of nineteenth- and twentieth-century Christians could not be taken as complete and finally valid interpretations of Christian truth, but rather as the views of men whose understanding was determined in part by the outlook of their contemporary Western civilization.

Thus, the question of authority and finality in Christian faith had to be re-examined at every level. On one level, this concerned the claim of Christianity to be the final or highest religion. Liberalism had destroyed the appeal to miracles and to prophecy as "proofs" of the truth of Christianity, but had found the superiority of Christianity in its higher ethical ideals and the nobility of its conception of God. Now, however, it had to be recognized that even these ethical criteria were peculiarly part of a Western tradition strongly influenced by Christian contexts.

At the level of the statement of the Christian faith itself, however, the problem was no less acute, particularly with respect to liberalism's appeal to religious experience as the ultimate authority. In turning to the "Christian consciousness" or "value judgments" or "abiding experiences" as the norm of religious truth, liberalism had tended to lose the sense of an objectively "given" Christian message. And what liberalism placed at the center of attention and tried to make the foundation of Christian thought was precisely the subjective element which is most obviously conditioned by its cultural context. "Religious experience" could have even less claim to objectivity and permanence than Bible or creed.

Yet the church lives in the conviction that it has indeed a gospel, a word to men which is not simply the voice of their own consciences or the consciences and beliefs of past ages, but a word of truth and deliverance from One who transcends the relativities of time and space. The question then is: What is it that the church has to preach which is not simply bound to particular historical and social perspectives of past and present times? If the gospel cannot be identified with Bible or creed or religious experience, what is it? And if all human conceptions and experience are historically conditioned, how can Christians of one generation share in the convictions and experiences of those of an earlier generation? How can the gospel be communicated from one social context to another? Clearly, the problem of stating and transmitting the gospel has become infinitely more complex and requires a more profound understanding of the meaning of revelation.

4) A fourth feature of the new theological situation has been the renewed study of the Protestant Reformation. This was stimulated especially by the German (and later Scandinavian) "Luther-research" of the early twentieth century. Luther had commonly been interpreted through the eyes of the later Lutheran scholasticism (see Ch. IV), but now it was seen that Luther was a far more lively and diverse thinker than his Lutheran commentators, and at many points they had gravely distorted his teaching. Central in the reinterpretation of Luther has been the recognition of his utter theocentricity (God-centeredness), of his conception of faith as free communion with God rather than a religious quality of the believer, and of his appreciation that evil originates at a deeper level than the psychological or sociological. These aspects of Luther's thought have been particularly important in revealing the profound relevance of the classical Protestant understanding of the gospel to the religious situation of the twentieth century. Thus, the study of Luther directed attention also to the whole of the Reformation and to the distinctive character of the Protestant witness.

5) Similarly, the contemporary theological situation has been affected by a more vivid awareness of the numerous voices in the nineteenth century which had spoken out against the prevailing trends of the time. There were those conservative strains of thought which, while they did not go the way of American fundamentalism, were yet severely critical of liberalism. This was particularly important in Germany and Scandinavia, where parallel to the liberal trend there was a less obvious but nevertheless active resurgence of biblical and pietistic Protestantism. In this move-

ment there was a vigorous protest against the "subjectivism" and optimism of liberal theology, together with an insistence upon the essential unity of the New Testament witness, upon the validity of classical Christian affirmations, and upon the objective reality of a revelation and redemption which came to sinful men from the transcendent, holy and merciful God. When the structure of liberalism began to totter, this conservative line of thought helped to provide the basis for a more sober reappraisal of the Christian tradition.

There were also throughout the nineteenth century occasional prophetic voices which anticipated (and influenced) the later critique of liberalism. The Danish writer Soren Kierkegaard (d. 1855), for example, protested vehemently against the identification of Christianity with "Christendom," against the easy assumptions that a culture could become Christian or that an individual could become a Christian simply by growing up in a "Christian" culture, against the reduction of Christian truth to "rational" systems, and against the philosophies of immanence. Christianity, he insisted, teaches an "infinite qualitative distinction between time and eternity," a paradoxical gospel of divine love and incarnation before which the human mind can only confess its utter inadequacy; a radical, even impossible demand for love of the neighbor; the utter precariousness of the human situation, which inevitably leads to anxiety over one's life and destiny and thence to self-centered rebellion against God; the absolute necessity for radical decision in the transition (the "leap") from sin and unfaith to faith; and the paradoxical nature of faith as a wholly God-given "comforted despair." (The recovery of Kierkegaard's thought has also been a stimulus to "existentialist" philosophies, see below.)

A vivid sense of tragedy and estrangement in life was reflected also in the novels of the Russian Fyodor Dostoyevsky. In contrast to the dominant nineteenth-century appeal to the indefinite perfectibility of man, he pointed graphically to the actual and patent cruelty, torment and pathos of life, to the suffering and humiliation as well as the exaltation of the human spirit. Both Dostoyevsky and Kierkegaard wrote as Christians. Friedrich Nietzsche, though wholly antagonistic to Christianity, whose ethic he condemned as a morality of weakness and pity, and whose influence he thought to be degrading, nonetheless saw more clearly than the liberal theologians the extreme character of the Christian ethic. As against the easy compromise of liberalism with the ethos of the nineteenth century, he emphasized the stark contrast between the Christian demand for compassion and self-sacrificing love, and the ethic of self-affirmation and will to power which he thought to be both appropriate to the ennobling of man and the proper outcome of an evolutionary outlook. And while he opposed it utterly, he showed the entire "transvaluation" of values which Christianity had effected in ancient modes of thought.

6) Finally, the contemporary theological situation has been influenced by recent trends in philosophy and psychology. These have been important both in shaping the categories of theological expression and in the understanding of the world to which faith speaks.

Varieties of "existentialism," especially as these have been stimulated by the thought of Soren Kierkegaard, have focused attention on the nature of personal existence as the prime philosophical question. Here the question of truth is a question of the meaning of life. It is a religious and ethical question, a question of freedom and destiny. Every man is concerned with truth that makes a difference to him. He cannot be a neutral, uncommitted spectator. He thinks as an "existing individual," who is directly and immediately involved in the question. And this kind of thinking always involves decision, a choosing in the face of all the possibilities which the future continually presents. Thinking and acting are inseparable. The individual must decide what is true for him; his own destiny is at stake, for by his choosing he makes himself what he is. Thus the question of "time" takes on a special significance. Each moment is fraught with significance, as the point of decision. At every moment one is confronted by the question of his own being, of his relation to others, of future possibilities and of the eternal. These "existentialist" themes have been particularly important in contemporary theological reflection on the meaning of faith, on the nature of man, and on eschatology.[5]

[5] See especially the writings of Paul Tillich and Rudolf Bultmann.

The philosophy of process has stemmed most directly from the writings of Henri Bergson and Alfred North Whitehead. This philosophy draws heavily on the biological category of "organism" for its patterns of interpretation (rather than on notions of a machine-like world). Its dominant theme is the conception of the world in terms of "events" occurring in space-time rather than in terms of inert substances or "things." Process philosophy understands ultimate reality as dynamic rather than static. It sees change and movement as integral to the existence of all things, and not as the result simply of the application of external force to static objects. It is a philosophy of "becoming" or "being-in-becoming" rather than a philosophy of "being." To some religious interpreters, such a conception of ultimate reality seems to provide a philosophical doctrine much more in accord with the biblical and Christian understanding of the living and acting God than the ancient and medieval philosophies of being.[6] Others, however, feel that the process philosophy tends to make God simply a factor in process and that the traditional philosophy of being better expresses the Christian view of the sovereignty and majesty of God; but these interpreters have also emphasized the dynamic nature of ultimate being in contrast to notions of static or inert substance.

Another philosophical trend important for theology has been the growing interest in the analysis of language and symbol. In some of its forms (e.g., logical positivism) this has meant the denial of any valid theology whatever. All true and meaningful statements are held to be either (a) verifiable by the scientific method, or (b) tautological (e.g., a dog is a dog). Metaphysical statements (statements about ultimate reality) are not only impossible of verification but meaningless. More recent forms of this philosophical "analysis" have been less extreme in their claims for the exclusive validity of the scientific method. It is affirmed that logical propositions based on scientific verification cannot involve metaphysical assertions, but the way is left open for other kinds of affirmations and meanings. Thus, this way of thinking makes contact with the broader interest in the symbolical character of

[6] See especially the work of Daniel D. Williams, Charles Hartshorne, and Nels F. S. Ferré.

all thought forms (whether scientific generalization or primitive myth). Different realms of experience may involve different kinds of meaning and ways of communication, i.e., different symbols. (This has special importance for the interpretation of Christian affirmations regarding creation, the "fall," the "last judgment," etc.) [7]

Developments in psychiatry and "depth-psychology" have also been of particular significance for theological reconstruction. New psychological insights into the subrational levels of human motives and desires, and new appreciation of the depths of personal disintegration and disruption, have helped to give new meaning to traditional Christian affirmations about human nature and sin. And new understandings of psychotherapy have been important in reflection on the meaning of redemption and salvation for the reintegration of personal existence. [8]

The relation of these philosophical and psychological trends to recent theological patterns has been less widespread and definite than the developments we noted previously. These movements have been of widely varying importance in different schools of Protestant thought and in relation to particular theological problems. But taken together they have special significance as concrete ways of expressing the central Protestant concern always to relate the gospel to the contemporary world.

2. THEOLOGICAL RECONSTRUCTION

The mood of recent Protestant thought is one of renewed appreciation of traditional Christian modes of thought. It is a mood of increased sympathy with the biblical point of view, with the creeds and doctrines of the church, and with the principles of the reformers. Thus, in one sense the newer theological emphases can be described as a return to the past, a reaction against liberal interpretations and a revival of "classical" patterns of thought. So such terms as "neo-orthodoxy" and "neo-Protestantism" have been used to refer to the new theology. But the spirit of the new

[7] See, e.g., Paul Tillich and Richard Kroner; and on the problem of symbol in general, Ernst Cassirer and Suzanne Langer.
[8] See, e.g., the work of David E. Roberts, Albert C. Outler, Seward Hiltner and Rollo May.

movements is not simply a study of the past for its own sake, nor is it a kind of conservatism which seeks to preserve the stable and "secure" patterns of the past in the flux of the present. It is a revolutionary movement which recalls the past because it finds there, often precisely in those elements of the tradition which were nearly forgotten by liberalism, principles which are relevant to the problems of the present. The new theology returns to Paul, Augustine, Luther and Calvin because it finds in them means to renewed understanding and appropriation of the gospel.

In a summary, then, of the directions of contemporary Protestant thought, it will be convenient to focus on certain distinctive motifs which represent reactions to liberal tendencies and the reappropriation of classical Christian categories. But it must be kept in mind that the purpose of contemporary rethinking of Christian faith is neither that of simple attack on liberalism nor of a return to traditional views, but rather of renewed understanding of the relevance of the Christian message to the situation in which we live. Thus, the revival of traditional doctrines has meant also their reinterpretation, and to this process the insights of liberalism have contributed much.

a. The Sovereignty of God

If the divine immanence was a primary concern of the liberal conception of God, recent Protestant thought has emphasized the transcendence, the otherness, the sovereignty of God. The nineteenth-century doctrine of immanence emphasized the presence of God "in us," the identification of God with the goodness of the world, and of the divine activity with the progressive realization of human goals. But such a view was possible only in the context of the nineteenth-century outlook, and with the sobering realization of the falsity of the nineteenth century's optimism and confidence in man, renewed validity was seen in the traditional conceptions of God's transcendence over and judgment upon all finite existence. The limitations of all human perspectives and ideals were brought sharply into view (see pp. 262 f., above). The liberal doctrine of immanence was seen to be, not simply a recognition of the divine working in the world process, but also a subtle self-worship through the identification of human ideals and plans with God's good.

The rejection of "immanentism" did not mean the denial of God's active and continuous relation to the world. On the contrary, it has been emphasized even more strongly that God's activity enters into the determination of all existence, life and action. He acts not simply as one inward working power among others, but as One who is the Lord of history and nature, the source and ground of all that is. But he is eternally what he is— radically distinct from all creaturely existence, the free and living Lord. This means that his goodness cannot be known simply by inspection of human goodness. His goodness is always judgment upon finite goodness. Though there is no moment of history in which God is not active, his being and action are never exhausted in history. He transcends the whole of history. He is known but he is also hidden. Moreover, God's "immanence" is given concrete meaning by reference to Jesus Christ. *He* is the immanence of God. Christian thought begins, not with some vague general presence of God in all things, but with his concrete presence in Christ. Theology is "incarnational" rather than "immanentist." From the standpoint of this concrete immanence it is understood that God freely acts in and upon the world as transcendent power and goodness.

The liberal view, in other words, had tended to bind God's activity to his immanent working in the orderly processes of history and nature. It had enclosed him in the "one-story" world of natural law which modern science had created. The ancient "three-story" universe, in which the world of man and nature were encompassed by heaven and hell, and thus controlled by forces from above and below, had been contracted by a scientific picture which explained the entire universe as ordered by a single pattern of natural process. Liberalism had sought to find room for God simply within this flattened world and had lost the dimensions both of height and of depth. But the God of Christian faith could not be contained in such a perspective. Liberalism had been right in denying that God works only in the gaps of natural process, or only occasionally, but it had failed to give due recognition to the transcendence and freedom of the Creator in acting in and upon his creation. Thus, recent thought has insisted upon the radical freedom of his eternal self-determination, the freedom of his relation to created existence.

The problem may be put in a different way by reference to the appeal to religious experience. For liberalism, God became essentially the counterpart of religious experience, and revelation tended to become identical with history (Ritschl) or religious experience (Schleiermacher). The primary reality, the one directly known, was religious experience. Of course, religious experience involved an objective ground or source of the subjective experience, viz., God. But God then is defined simply as the source of religious experience, and the reality of God is logically dependent upon the reality of religion. The existence of God is argued from the existence of religion, and the nature of God is discovered from the nature of religious experience.

The point of this is that, as it seems to more recent thought, a terrible inversion had taken place. Religion had been substituted for God. The process was similar to the later development of Lutheranism, in which the doctrine of justification by faith in God had been subtly transformed into faith in faith itself, i.e., into a confidence in the saving power of faith rather than of the God of faith. Now liberalism had fallen before the same temptation by putting the emphasis on religion rather than on God. A leading Protestant interpreter writes,

> "Religion became . . . the enhancer of life, the creator of spiritual and social energy, the redeemer of man from evil, the builder of the beloved community, the integrator of the great spiritual values; the God of religion, however, came to be a necessary auxiliary, though it could be questioned whether a real God was necessary to religion or only a vivid idea of God. The term 'religionist' which has been invented in modern times applies aptly to those who follow the tendency inaugurated in part by Schleiermacher, for religion is the object of concern and the source of strength for them rather than the God whom an active faith regards as alone worthy of supreme devotion." [9]

[9] H. R. Niebuhr, *The Meaning of Revelation*, 28. New York: The Macmillan Company, 1941. Used by permission of the publisher.

(The accuracy of this statement can be tested by anyone who will note how frequently "religion" or "faith" is appealed to as the way out of our present crises, not only by ministers, but by countless "religiously minded" journalists and even politicians.)

Here, then, is the aim of the emphasis on the sovereignty of God. It is to be true to the Christian witness to the absolute primacy of God, to rebut again the perennial tendency to the "inversion of faith whereby man puts himself into the center, constructs an anthropocentric universe and makes confidence in his own value rather than faith in God his beginning." [10] Christian faith does not point primarily to Christianity, it points to God. At the center is not faith or religious experience (or church or creed) but only the God of Jesus Christ. And it is impossible to speak of God simply by speaking of man in a very loud voice.

From this perspective, the function of the church is clarified. The church exists for the purpose of bearing single-minded witness to the God of Christian faith. It is neither an association for the cultivation of pious feelings nor a society for the promotion of culture. Indeed, in directing attention to the God of faith, Christian faith declares the falsity of all idolatry, which would put anything other than God at the center, whether faith, or religious institution, or nation or culture. It points to the finitude and relativity of human insights and ideals, and to the estrangement of man from God which is sin, but first and finally to God.

The sovereignty of God means the claim of God to total lordship over all human endeavor; and under God, the "religious" life has no priority over the political, economic, or scientific life—nor have the latter any exemption from the sovereignty of God. It must be emphasized again that it is not religion or theology which is sovereign, but *God*. Therefore a theology which recognizes the sovereignty of God is not concerned about attacks on religion, e.g., that of logical positivism. It sees that science, too, is relative, and "scientific philosophies" even more so. But more important, its certainty is of *God*, not of religion or theology. Recognizing its own finitude, such a theology does not seek immunity from conflict with rival views; it demands only that there

[10] *Ibid.*, 31.

be absolute humility in all branches of study. It is not concerned about the charge that religion is being outworn by culture, for it knows that it is really culture which is continually being outworn by the God to whose reality theology seeks to point.

This stress on the primacy of God over all religion and culture is in no small measure a reappropriation of the radical theocentricity of Luther and Calvin. It also involves a deeper appreciation of the biblical perspective. Thus Karl Barth could speak of the discovery of a "strange new world within the Bible," the world of God (see above, pp. 256f.). The biblical perspective is also evident in a recognition that Christian faith must speak of God's wrath and judgment as well as mercy and love—not in the sense of capricious or vengeful judgment, but the inevitable judgment of love itself upon the denials of love which haunt all human achievements. It is a judgment upon pretension and pride, upon all efforts to make absolutes out of the finite and relative, i.e., upon the modern idolatries of self and society. Therefore, God's love is seen, as the reformers also understood it, as paradoxical and strange to ordinary standards, given to man quite without regard for "merit," given freely not because of what man is but in spite of what he is.

b. Revelation

The emphasis on the sovereignty of God is intimately related in the Protestant thinking of today with a profound concern for *revelation* as the source of the knowledge of God and as the basis for all Christian thinking. This may be approached by way of what is frequently called the "I-Thou" relationship, which means simply that the relation of God and man is one of personal confrontation. The God of Christian faith is exclusively personal, a Thou. He is not a neuter, an It, an object about which men may speak in the third person as if his presence or absence were a matter of indifference. He is not known by argument about an ultimate cause, but as the eternally present Thou who meets man as a personal subject. God "confronts" man, comes to man as One who is over-against him, and lays claim upon him. He meets man with the demand for acceptance or rejection, the demand for faith. And faith is *decision*. In the personal encounter with

God, a decision must be made—for or against, obedience or rebellion, faith or unfaith.

So far, the emphasis of recent thought is not unlike that of the liberal stress on religious experience. Liberalism, and before it pietism and the Reformation, had seen that God and faith belong together, that God is known only as men respond to him in faith, and that he is wholly personal. But the connotation of this view is quite different from that of liberalism. For here the emphasis is not on the human discovery of the divine, but on God's self-manifestation to man; not on the continuity of man and God, which makes easy the ascent to God, but on the distance and the estrangement of man from God, which makes God's coming to man in revelation and reconciliation a radical and paradoxical event. *God* reveals himself to faith. His Word to man stands in judgment on all human words and conceptions. The final court of appeal is not rational norms, or conscience or experience, but the self-revelation of God, and there is a "given-ness" in revelation which makes it always "over-against" man.

It is revelation, then, which is the ground of all Christian affirmations. But in this assertion, modern thought does not return to the view that God has revealed certain truths or propositions which could be called "revealed truth" and identified with the words of the Bible or the creeds. The work of historical criticism cannot be undone. The fundamentalist notion of an inerrant Bible is not only untenable; it is a form of idolatry, a kind of perversion which exalts the finite and the fallible to a place of authority belonging to God alone. In contrast, the modern view understands that the content of revelation is *God himself*, not scripture or creed or tradition. This is the heart of the matter. Revelation means, simply, God personally present. It is God's coming to man, his disclosure of himself. It is identical with his creating, redeeming, judging and sanctifying work.

One way of expressing this concept of revelation is the assertion that God reveals himself "in act" or deed, rather than in the form of propositions or truths. God makes himself known as he works in historical events, being present to men in judgment and redemption; all statements or propositions are statements *about* God's activity and are human, fallible assertions which can never be adequate to express the reality to which they point. Revelation is thus an event, though it is only *in faith* that God is known in the event. There is revelation in Jesus Christ as men are enabled to see in him "God reconciling the world to himself." The facts about his teaching and life are inseparable from faith's witness to incarnation and resurrection, to atonement and reconciliation, i.e., faith's witness to the activity of God of which the words and deeds of Jesus are a part.

Such a view of revelation recognizes the absolute centrality of Jesus Christ. He is, uniquely, the revelation. In him God was fully present, and all Christian thought of revelation finds its starting point and norm in him. He is the decisive event. Christian faith is unequivocally faith in him, for in him God is personally present as Lord, confronting men with the demand for decision.

Thus, recent emphasis on revelation gives a far more important place to the Bible than was characteristic of liberalism and involves at least a partial return to the classical Protestant norm *sola scriptura.* For liberal theology, the Bible was important as a record of developing religious experience, and especially as a record of the experience of the earliest Christians—but in the last analysis the Bible had always to be judged by modern religious experience. The final test of religious truth was always the reason, conscience and experience of the individual believer. Recent theology has tended to reverse this order of priority. As one writer has put it, the conceptions of the Bible are to be taken at least as seriously as our own conceptions. For the Bible is related to the revelation of God in a unique and authoritative way.

It needs repeating that this does not mean the Bible is to be considered as an inerrant collection of religious truths. Throughout, the Bible must be understood as conditioned by the relative historical situations of those whose words appear in it. Nevertheless, the witness of the Bible is crucial and indispensable; it is authoritative for Christian life and thought, For one thing, it speaks uniquely of the utter priority of God, as we noted above. More particularly, it is the indispensable testimony of the revelation of God in Jesus Christ—and not only to the events of his life, death and resurrection, but also to the dealings of God with man

in the history of the Hebrews in anticipation of the coming of
the Messiah, to the fulfillment of reconciliation and revelation in
the community of faith, and to the final fulfillment of history.
The revelation of God is Jesus Christ, but that revelation is
mediated to men through the scriptures. At this point, recent
thought is influenced by Luther's view that the Bible is the cradle
in which Christ is laid. It is through the biblical record that Jesus
Christ is presented to men, and the biblical word *becomes* the
Word of God as it speaks to the heart of the believer.

Moreover, the Bible is not simply the record of revelation; it is
itself part of the event of revelation, both as a human response
to the divine act in Christ and as a medium of communication
of revelation. The act of revelation is complete only as it is received by men. "The Bible is both original event and original
document; it witnesses to that of which it is a part." [11] While the
Bible cannot be accepted as *absolute* authority (this belongs only
to God), it does have *relative* authority over the preaching of the
church and individual experience. It provides the norm by which
both personal experience and the doctrines of the church are to
be judged. And the biblical symbols have a permanent significance for the understanding and communication of the
gospels. They cannot be simply discarded for more "modern" conceptions. Such symbols as the creation story, the story of the Fall,
and the last judgment, are not to be taken literally, as simple
historical accounts, but they must be taken seriously, for they
point to realities which can be described only in symbolic language. (Two such conceptions, original sin and the kingdom of
God, will be discussed later in this chapter.)

c. Christ the Word

One of the great gains of liberal theology was its rediscovery of the humanity of Jesus. From the point of view of more
recent Protestant thought, however, the liberal concern with the
"historical Jesus" left little room for the recognition that he is
also more than man. Thus it is felt that liberalism departed both
from the Christian tradition and from the biblical witness at a
crucial point. For if we are to be fair to the New Testament, we

[11] Paul Tillich, *Systematic Theology*, Vol. I, 35.

must see that its very center is the confession that Jesus is the Lord, that God was truly in him. Whatever is said about his life and his teaching is there only because of the faith that in him God was present to men, and that in his life and death and resurrection God was reconciling the world to himself. Jesus as man is significant for the New Testament writers just because in this man "all the fullness of God was pleased to dwell" (Col. 1:19).

This, then, is the center of the Christian faith. However much liberalism was right in insisting on the genuine humanity of Jesus, Christianity cannot be content with any view of Jesus Christ which does not make explicit his "uniqueness" among men. Uniqueness here is not a matter of degree; it means radical difference, real discontinuity. Such terms as "religious genius," teacher and prophet, are not at all adequate to express what Christian faith sees in Christ. He is more than a prophet, for a prophet is a bearer of the Word of God and has no authority in himself but only in the Word which he bears. But Jesus is himself the Word. He is the revelation of God, not because of what he says about the nature of God but because God is personally present to men in him. He is himself God come to men, seeking the response of faith. It is not enough to say that Jesus teaches and exemplifies the mercy and forgiveness of God; he *is* the mercy and forgiveness of God. He is in himself—in his coming, his life, his death, his resurrection—the divine act of forgiveness. Thus, Christian faith is not essentially a matter of believing *with* Christ, it is believing *in* Christ.

The real humanity of Christ is to be maintained rigorously. Jesus was a man among men, a Jew of the first century, and to the "disinterested" or neutral observer he may appear as no more than a moral and religious teacher who lived a good life, collected a group of followers and was put to death for his pains. But Christian faith sees in these events the presence and action of God himself, and therefore acknowledges Jesus Christ as Lord. It perceives that hidden in this historically conditioned life is none other than the Lord of history, come to men in the form of a servant, disclosing his incomprehensible love and redeeming power in the self-giving, the authoritative demand for repentance and faith, the suffering, dying and rising again, of the man Jesus of Nazareth.

Thus, recent thought shows a renewed appreciation of the relevance of the traditional doctrines about Christ as the God-man, truly God and truly man. The creeds do not explain this fact, and were not intended to do so. They were intended to express a mystery which is finally beyond human understanding, for God is ever beyond man's comprehension. But the classical affirmations of the church, even though subject to frequent misinterpretation, nonetheless gave explicit expression to the central confession that in Jesus Christ we have to do not only with man but with God, with eternity as well as time, the infinite as well as the finite—and this cannot be abandoned without falsifying the revelation itself.

Similarly, the doctrine of the Trinity has come to occupy a more vital place in Protestant thinking. For it is seen that if Christ is indeed the revelation of God, then Christian thinking about God must always start with that revelation. Belief in Christ is not something merely added to a previously held belief in God. Rather, belief in Christ involves a startlingly new apprehension of God. He is the same Lord of Old Testament faith, but now revealing himself in a new and fuller way. When the Christian speaks of "God" he means the One who has come to men in the Incarnation and the Holy Spirit, and therefore One who must be called Father, Son and Holy Spirit.

d. Man the Sinner

The most widely discussed aspect of contemporary Protestant thinking has doubtless been the conception of man as sinner. Here the revolt against liberalism has been most obvious, and has been reinforced by the course of recent historical events and by discoveries of the new psychology. The result has been a quite conclusive repudiation of the optimism of the late nineteenth century, and an explicit and thoroughgoing recognition of the tragic aspects of human existence, of the precariousness of human achievements, and of the depths to which man can and does descend.

The new emphasis has not meant a rejection of the liberal

insistence on the goodness of man as the creation of God, or the dignity or worth of man. The nineteenth century was quite correct in asserting that man is neither "innately" or "by nature" evil. He is indeed created in the "image of God," and the limits of his capacity for goodness and creativity are indefinite. So far, the new theology can go with the nineteenth century. But in two respects it insists that the classical Christian doctrine of man (especially as understood by the reformers) is more adequate than the liberal conception. First, man is a creature, he is not God— this some liberal thinkers occasionally forgot. Second, man's history is throughout characterized by a profound and tragic denial of the purpose of human existence. This is what is meant by sin, and it is defined as rebellion against God, a rebellion so deeply rooted in the human self that it can be overcome only by the redeeming activity of God. Thus, Reinhold Niebuhr, the most prominent contemporary American writer on this theme, describes the Christian view of man as involving a "high estimate of human stature" (i.e., as created in the image of God) and a "low estimate of human virtue." [12]

The contemporary analysis of sin has also revived the notion of "original sin." That doctrine had been quite consistently rejected by nineteenth-century liberalism as both a slur on human dignity and a relic of the outworn idea of the infallibility of scripture, for traditionally the basis of the doctrine had been found in the story of the "Fall" in Genesis 3. Together with liberalism, recent Protestant thought rejects the ideas of a "historical fall" and of a biological inheritance of sin and guilt. But it sees that the concept of original sin points to a reality which is independent of both these ideas, viz., the fact that all men are sinners and that every aspect of human life is involved in sin. The "Fall" is not an event which occurred in the far distant past; it is the turning away from God which is characteristic of every human life and action.

Sin is not to be identified with "wrong acts"; it is rather a distortion and perversion which exists at the center of the self. Nor is sin to be identified with the body, for the body is good and all sin has its origin in the spirit. ("Sensuality" is the self's denial

[12] *The Nature and Destiny of Man,* Vol. I, 16.

of its own freedom and responsibility by an attempt to lose itself
in physical nature.) Sin is the opposite of faith, i.e., it is the placing of ultimate trust in anything less than God. It is the opposite
of love, it is the self turned inward. Essentially, sin may be defined
as self-centered denial of responsibility to God, and it appears
most universally and subtly—and most dangerously—in the
various forms of pride, i.e., in the assertion of self by the denial
of creaturely limitation. This may be the pride of power, which
imagines itself completely master of its own existence and destiny.
It may be the frantic will-to-power which seeks final security in
itself by mastery over others. It may be the pride of intellect, or
moral or spiritual pride, which imagines its own conceptions and
values to be free from all taint of self-interest and thereby arro-
gates to itself divine authority. No aspect of life is free from such
perversion—certainly not religion, where the temptation to prideful self-assertion is peculiarly subtle and dangerous. Every claim
to infallibility or perfection is a form of self-righteousness and
self-deification which leads to the attempt at mastery over others.
Even the highest idealism is subject to transformation into an
instrument of self-will and thereby injustice. And so every pursuit
of self-interest cloaks itself in the guise of moral idealism. Moreover, egoism may be both individual and collective, i.e., it may
be expressed by societies as well as individuals. Thus, all human
achievements—moral, religious, political, economic, cultural—are
involved in the corruption of sin. And the revelation of
God in Jesus Christ is a judgment upon self-will and pretension.

Here recent thought is explicitly in the tradition of the Reformation: sin is universal, and it is total in the sense that no area
of human life is exempt from the perversion of pride and self-
centeredness and that all human actions involve at least a partial
betrayal of responsibility to God (see Ch. II). One important
qualification must be added: *the standard by which men are all
judged to be sinners is Jesus Christ.* It is not asserted that human
life is simply or wholly without goodness. Indeed, no arbitrary
limits can be placed on human capacity for good, and some
actions are vastly better than others. But when men measure

themselves by their obligation to God as revealed in Christ, they confess their continual betrayal of that responsibility.

e. History and the Kingdom of God

The chastening of the liberal faith in man has inevitably had a profound effect on the social gospel, particularly as regards its confidence in the possibility of "building the kingdom of God on earth." This has not meant a denial of the church's obligation to speak to the social orders as well as to individuals. That central concern of the social gospel has continued. But the confident assumption that the social order might be progressively transformed into the kingdom of God has been rejected. Its place has been taken by a more vivid sense of divine judgment upon all human history and by a new understanding of the hope of the kingdom of God.

God's judgment is acknowledged to apply to all social structures and programs. (And this includes the church, which is involved both in religious pretension and in the economic, social and racial injustice of society as a whole.) No social institution is free from the limitations of human finitude or the temptations of self-justification and rationalization. Therefore, all utopian hopes and schemes are naive and self-deceived—whether these be the programs of Marxist communism or evolutionary socialism or free enterprise. Every scheme for the solution of humanity's ills is subject to transformation into an instrument of power for the sake of the dominant groups, whether capital or labor or bureaucracy. This fact, and the growing complexity of social problems which requires vastly increased technical knowledge in sociology and economics, means that no social order or proposal for reform can be simply identified with the will of God. The responsibility of the church is therefore constantly to confront the existing order (including itself) with the judgment of the law of love and to seek positive ways for the establishment of relatively more just relations among men. It is to work for "proximate solutions" to problems which continually recur in new forms, for every creative achievement brings new possibilities of injustice. A full recognition of the depth and power of evil requires a more sober estimate than that of the earlier social gospel regarding the possibilities of achieving a just social order. And it requires more explicit recognition of the use of economic and political power as instruments of love and as means of restraining evil.[13]

Let us repeat, the renewed appreciation of traditional Christian insights into the depth of sin and the consequent rejection of nineteenth-century optimism about social progress, has not meant a return to a gospel for individuals only. The concern of the Christian faith with the structures of society is firmly maintained. But the hope of Christians is seen to point beyond history.

To put this in other words, the kingdom of God is not the end product of a progressive "Christianizing" of the social order. That notion of the kingdom was more the reflection of a nineteenth-century evolutionary outlook than of the New Testament hope. The kingdom of God, in the New Testament hope, is wholly *God's* kingdom, not to be established by any human effort but solely at the divine initiative. The responsibility of man is not that of "building" the kingdom but of "readiness" for its coming, by repentance and faith. Moreover, the kingdom is not a continuation of historical development. It symbolizes the end of the present age; it stands "beyond" this history.

---

[13] At this point, we must note the vigorous contemporary discussion of the extent to which the church ought to ally itself with particular social programs. It is generally agreed that the church must proclaim the judgment of the gospel upon all forms of injustice. It is also agreed that the church cannot accept any social program or institution as a pure expression of the will of God and the solution of human problems; every program remains under judgment. But there is sharp disagreement concerning the church's responsibility to give qualified support to political and economic patterns which seem to give relatively better expression to the Christian demand for love and justice.

In part, this has been a difference between Continental European and American thought. It has come to expression particularly in recent discussions within the "ecumenical" movement (see Ch. XIII), in relation to the question of the nature of the Christian hope. Does the Christian hope (as symbolized by the kingdom of God) refer exclusively to God's establishment of the kingdom "beyond" or "at the end" of history, or does it include also present manifestations of the kingdom in relatively more just social patterns which the church must explicitly support? The importance of this problem is seen in the fact that it was the central theme of the meeting of the World Council of Churches in 1954, at Evanston, Ill.

In the discussion in the text, we have sought to restrict ourselves to those general tendencies of thought which have influenced both of these points of view.

In this biblical understanding of the kingdom of God, recent Protestant thinking sees a true parable of the Christian hope and of the meaning of history. Of course, the biblical idea of the kingdom of God is a symbol, for all thinking about the end or the goal of history must be in the form of symbol or picture. But the biblical symbol (which itself includes a variety of detailed pictures of the end) is more adequate to express the Christian understanding of history than any other symbol. It refers to a divine purpose for the whole of history, to an ultimate judgment and fulfillment of individual and social life, to the full "rule" of God. This is not to be separated from the present Lordship of God. Indeed, it is just in the sovereignty of God as manifested in Christ that the hope of the kingdom is founded. Christ is the "center" of history. In him the victory of God is disclosed. In him the kingdom of God is present. So also it is always "at hand," in judgment and promise, confronting men with the claim of God's rule. It may be present in all the partial realizations of God's will in history. But all partial realizations find their meaning and fulfillment in the fullness of the kingdom, which stands always "over against" or at the "end" of history. This kingdom is the promise of the final victory over evil. The hope of the Christian reaches always beyond the accomplishments or failures of the present to an ultimate fulfillment of personal and social destiny whereby all that is good in history is preserved and completed.

XIII

The Ecumenical Movement

1. THE PROBLEM OF DIVERSITY

Nothing has caused more difficulty in the understanding of Protestantism than the problem of diversity and unity. Particularly is this true in the American scene, where more than 250 Protestant denominations may be counted, ranging in size from the nearly 10 million members of the Methodist Church to the mere handfuls of members in those denominations which are composed of only one or two congregations. To the varieties of European Protestantism which have been brought to the United States by immigration, there have been added scores of new and divergent bodies, so that often the word "Protestant" seems only a vague catch-all classification for a bewildering mosaic of religious organizations. American Christianity has of course been strongly influenced by the peculiar individualism of the American temper as well as by unique social influences. But the problem of ecclesiastical divisions has been with Protestantism from the beginning, and in order to understand the trend toward church unity (often called the "ecumenical" movement) which has come increasingly to the fore in Protestant thought and action since the beginning of the twentieth century, we need to look more closely at the nature of this Protestant diversity.

The Reformation was neither a simple nor an isolated phenomenon. It was a religious revolution which took place in the midst of several other revolutions: an economic revolution, marked by

284

the breakdown of feudalism, the stirring of the lower classes, the beginnings of modern capitalism, the rise of the middle class, and the discoveries of the fifteenth- and sixteenth-century explorers; a literary revolution wrought by the printing press; a cultural revolution, the Renaissance; a scientific revolution, centering in the discoveries of astronomy; and a political revolution, the rise of national states. All these movements were of profound influence in determining the course of Protestant development. (The growth of national states, for example, contributed both to the success of the original break with Rome and to the ordering of the churches into national units in the case of Lutheranism and Anglicanism.)

Moreover, the Reformation was itself a complex movement, comprising three relatively distinct branches: the Lutheran and Reformed traditions, which were themselves sharply divided at several points; the radical or Anabaptist wing of the Reformation, which included a wide variety of sectarian groups; and the Anglican Church, which took its theology partly from the Continent but which had its inception in a quite different complex of causes and preserved the catholic pattern of church order (see Chs. I–IV). The Reformation was thus not a uniform or homogenous movement. While there were common religious perspectives and principles for the understanding of the gospel, these were expressed with varying emphases in widely different geographical, intellectual and social contexts. Subsequent development of Protestantism has been characterized by further elaboration of this original complexity of religious elements in relation to novel social situations. This was particularly true in the appearance of the "free churches" in England in the seventeenth and eighteenth centuries and in the proliferation of denominations in the United States.

Any explanation, therefore, of the internal divisions of Protestantism must take account of several factors. Theological differences have been important, as in the early Lutheran and Reformed dispute over the sacraments, or in the conflicts regarding predestination, or the varying conceptions of proper church government, or the Baptist insistence on believers' baptism and an immersion as the only scriptural pattern. But any attempt to

understand Protestant divisions simply in terms of differing theologies or forms of worship is grossly inadequate. Numerous
Protestant denominations (e.g., the Methodists) have come out
of revival movements which did not spring from any fundamental
theological divergence, nor any intention of leaving the established churches, but which led to the formation of separate
churches because of the indifference or hostility of church leaders
to the new impulses.

Moreover, quite different kinds of social forces were at work,
and often quite intermingled with differences of religious understanding. The influence of nationalism, noted above, was paralleled by racial, economic and class interests. The issue of slavery
in the United States, for example, was one of the main factors
which led to the splitting of nearly every major Protestant denomination, the Protestant Episcopal Church being the chief
exception. And, in spite of some significant changes in recent
years, American Protestantism is still characterized by an almost
complete segregation of Negro and white churches. Economic and
social stratification among the churches has been less sharp but
equally real. The separation between the Anabaptists and the
main Reformation bodies was to a significant degree a cleavage
between the "lower" and the more favored social groups. Later
Protestantism reveals a tendency for the older communities to become identified with the middle and upper social classes (this is
true in America, for example, of the Episcopalians, Presbyterians,
Congregationalists, Methodists and Reformed, and to a lesser
extent of the Baptists and Disciples). New denominations have
most commonly appeared among the depressed and "disinherited"
social levels, and often represent emphases (e.g., emotionalism
and anti-intellectualism) which no longer appeal to the "upper"
cultural strata. This is seen today in such groups as the Jehovah
Witnesses and the "pentecostal" or "holiness" sects. Another kind
of social source of denominationalism in America was the frontier situation in which Protestantism spread. Problems of frontier
life were such as to encourage independent organizations and lay
control of the churches. Thus, even the episcopally ordered
churches were significantly influenced in the direction of more
democratic and congregational church government.

Finally, the multiplicity of Protestant denominations has to be understood in the light of what is vaguely (and not very accurately) called Protestant "individualism." At the center of the Reformation faith was the new acknowledgement of the intrinsic authority of God's self-revelation, i.e., the discovery that faith can begin only as Jesus Christ attests himself to the human soul in which his Word is made alive by the Holy Spirit. Therefore, the Protestant's religious convictions are reached only in personal responsible decision; they are *his* response to the Word of God in Christ, they are the convictions which are required *of him*. This is not the same thing as the "right of private judgment"—for that is not a peculiarly religious conception and suggests a kind of absolute sovereignty of the individual which is quite foreign to the Reformation idea. The Protestant idea of faith does not entitle a man to believe what he pleases, for every man must think in accordance with the truth. But the principle of the Reformation is that the truth of the gospel is made known to faith by the inward working of the Holy Spirit. This truth is therefore received only in decision, in personal acceptance, in an obedience to the Word of God which no man can perform for another.

It is in this sense of complete obligation to the Word of God as it compels the faith of the believer that Protestantism stands for freedom of personal judgment and belief. No finite religious authority (church, creed or even scripture) can compel conformity of conviction. Every man's faith must be *his own* faith. Such a view involves the risk that Christians might differ widely in their understanding of the gospel. This risk has seemed intolerable to Roman Catholicism (and often to many Protestants). But it is a risk which cannot be avoided without violating the Protestant understanding of faith and rejecting the religious freedom which is derived from that understanding of faith. Therefore, while it cannot be said that the Protestant understanding necessarily involves church divisions, this understanding does explicitly involve the possibility of differences in belief and practice, and these have in fact led to denominational divisions through the association of like-minded believers into distinct religious organizations. It should also be noted, however, that this process was greatly stimulated by the very different individualism of the Enlightenment, particularly by its doctrine of the complete autonomy of the individual and of the absolute "right" of private judgment. Moreover, Protestantism was slow to accept the consequences of its own implications for religious freedom. The classical Reformation churches held in practice to the notion of an "authorized" religion and denied religious freedom to the left-wing Reformation groups. Not until the eighteenth century did the ideal of religious freedom begin to be generally characteristic of Protestant thought. And, with the exception of the Church of England, Protestant churches generally assumed that there ought to be uniformity of doctrine within each communion. It is fair to say that the denominational divisions of Protestantism have resulted not so much from simple diversity of belief as from the demand for conformity within each institution, with the result that non-conforming groups were forced to organize separately.

It is easy to exaggerate the nature and extent of Protestant divisions. To say, for example, that there are 250 denominations in the United States, is seriously misleading unless it is also observed that roughly 80 percent of all American Protestants are included in the membership of thirteen of these denominations, and that 90 percent are included in no more than twenty denominations (if Protestants are grouped by "families" of denominations, i.e., all Baptist bodies counted together, all Lutherans together, etc., the concentration is even more striking). More important than this, however, is the fact that religious unity and diversity may be judged not only in terms of unity of organization, but also as regards doctrine, ethics, ritual, and outlook or intention (to say nothing of the sociological aspects of the problem). "Unity" cannot simply be equated with eccelesiastical organization. Completely separate institutions may have very similar theologies and rituals and be essentially one in spirit and intention. And a single ecclesiastical structure may include widely differing points of view. The Roman Catholic Church, for example, embraces far greater diversity than is commonly recognized. The differences between Catholicism in Spain, in Germany, in South America, and in the United States, are in fundamental respects greater than the differences between many Protestant denominations; and frequently the hostility between various monastic orders in the Roman Church exceeds that of all but the most extreme Protestant sects. The Anglican communion may also be cited as an example of a church which finds its unity in a common ritual, in the apostolic succession, and in a minimal doctrinal standard, but which prides itself on including widely differing theologies as well as independent national units. (A secular example of institutional unity with radically different points of view is the American political party.)

We shall be concerned in the next chapter in a more systematic way with the question of the unity of Protestantism, but it should be clear from our previous study that this question cannot be judged simply in terms of organizational unity and diversity. Division in Protestantism has by no means always been accompanied by a divisive spirit. In both the great awakenings and the later revivals, for example, divisions took place in the churches as new societies were established to develop and conserve the results of evangelization. And this was also true of the westward movement of Christianity in America. But these groups were conscious of participating in a common endeavor. Their social and religious divergences, while real, were recognized as subordinate to their common loyalty to Christ, and there was much cooperation between the churches. They felt themselves one "in Christ" and in the invisible catholic church. In American Protestantism particularly, this sense of unity has been more recently expressed in the practical interchangeability of denominations for an increasingly mobile population. Not only millions of church members, but also ministers, have transferred back and forth among denominations. (E.g., in 1920 Congregational churches accepted as ministers almost as many men ordained by other denominations as were ordained in Congregational churches; and between 1921 and 1926, 38 percent of the new Presbyterian ministers came from other denominations.) This kind of interchange was made possible by mutual recognition of the denominations as working together in a common cause.

At the same time, the problem of institutional disunity in

Protestantism has remained. For mutual recognition has been accompanied by powerful tendencies toward competition and divisiveness. Groups which came into existence to revitalize the life of the churches or to share in the common work of evangelization, quickly became self-conscious and concerned for institutional self-preservation. Differing heritages came to seem of more importance than the common task and loyalty to Christ. Each religious society became concerned with extending its own membership and promoting its own particular type of theology, ritual and methods of evangelization and religious education. Here, also, cultural, racial, national, and economic differences assumed increasing importance. This process occurred after the Reformation and has been repeated again and again in the subsequent history of Protestantism. Indeed, it must be said that every revival of religion, whether in Christianity or elsewhere, has tended to follow the same pattern, the work of reformers being conserved by institutions which become self-defensive and confuse themselves with the ideals they were formed to proclaim (other social institutions, of course, exhibit similar characteristics). But Protestantism has been especially subject to this sort of divisiveness and competition, for this is the peculiar temptation of the Protestant understanding of faith. The recognition of this fact has been of primary significance in the twentieth-century ecumenical movement, which rests on the convictions that, while diversity is not to be denied, the unity of Christianity must be preserved and made explicit, and that unity must be given some formal expression in belief and practice and in institutional order.

2. THE DEMAND FOR CHURCH UNITY

The term "ecumenical" (from the Greek *he oikoumene*, meaning "the inhabited earth") has in recent Christian thought come to be used as a synonym for "universal." The "ecumenical" church is the universal church, and the ecumenical movement is a movement toward unity or solidarity in Christian life and work throughout the world. This may mean simply interdenominational cooperation or it may mean working toward the merging of all Christian bodies in a single world church. Using the term in its broadest sense, however, we may say that the ecumenical movement includes all aspects of the twentieth-century trend toward the fuller realization of the unity of the Christian church. As such, this is a movement which includes not only Protestantism, but also the Eastern Orthodox churches, the Old Catholic Church, the Coptic Church—and in important ways the Roman Catholic Church.[1] It is concerned with all the breaches in the church. But the problem of division is obviously of particular relevance to Protestantism, and Protestant bodies have been especially active in this movement, both as it involves the major branches of Christianity and as it concerns the internal divisions of Protestantism.

At the root of the ecumenical movement is the sharp contrast between the actual divided state of the church and the affirmation of all Christians that the church is in some sense "one." St. Paul speaks of the church as the one body of Christ, and the Gospel of John records Christ's prayer that his followers "may all be one." Loyalty to Christ, according to the New Testament, means self-sacrificing love for one another and the transcending of those barriers which divide men. "There is neither Jew nor Greek, there is neither slave nor free, there is neither male nor female; for you are all one in Christ Jesus" (Gal. 3:28). There is "one body and one Spirit . . . one hope . . . one Lord, one faith, one baptism, one God and Father of us all" (Eph. 4:4–6). But the actual life of the churches suggests division and competition rather than unity. It is a lively recognition of the utter incongruity of this situation which has impelled recent Chris-

[1] The Roman Catholic Church has consistently held that the divisions of the church can be overcome only as other groups are willing to return to the authority of Rome. This has made it impossible for the Roman Church to participate in such organizations as the World Council of Churches. But the Roman Church has been profoundly concerned with the problem of Christian unity, and while not compromising its own fundamental claim, has not been unsympathetic toward the movement among non-Roman bodies. Especially in Europe, there has been positive mutual interchange of various kinds. For example, the Roman Catholic *Una Sancta* movement (centering in Germany) has involved for some years the carrying on of friendly discussions between Roman Catholic and Protestant leaders at various levels, with the result at least of better mutual understanding. Roman Catholic sponsored conferences on "Christian work" have included both Roman and non-Roman leaders. And official Roman Catholic observers (authorized by the local hierarchy) were present at the Conference on Faith and Order at Lund in 1952 (see below). See Karl Adam, *One and Holy,* for a liberal Catholic view of the problem of unity.

tianity in the direction of the ecumenical movement. There are
those churches, of course, which hold that they alone represent
the one true faith and community, and that the division of Christendom is the result of the infidelity and heresy of the rest of
the churches. This is the position of the Roman Catholic Church
and various other groups which insist that unity of the church
can be attained only when all Christians acknowledge the validity
of a particular church's claim to possession of the fullness of
Christian faith and life. The spirit of the ecumenical movement,
however, involves recognition that all the churches must share
in the responsibility for the disunity of Christianity and that
therefore each must learn from the others.

In addition to this aspect of the problem of Christian disunity,
there are a number of other more particular factors which have
contributed to the demand for greater Christian solidarity. One
is the new recognition of the social character of much of the
division of the churches, the awareness that many supposed differences of principle are no more than rationalizations of quite
different sorts of divisive elements. Another has come from nineteenth-century liberalism's de-emphasizing of theological controversy and its concern for the underlying (and unifying) Christian
experience. While the liberal suspicion of theology has more
recently been abandoned, it has nonetheless continued to be recognized that theological formulations, while necessary and never
to be taken lightly (as if theological differences were really of
no consequence), are still not ultimate. Moreover, theological
differences among Protestants, since the liberal influence, are
much less likely to follow denominational lines.

A third and powerful force contributing to the ecumenical
movement has been the experience of the modern missionary enterprise. As was remarked in Chapter VIII, the divisions of the
denominations were not only largely meaningless to the peoples
to whom the missionaries went, but were in the eyes of the non-
Christian majorities of these peoples a standing refutation of the
claims for the finality of the gospel. Moreover, the difficult
decisions which had to be made on social and philosophical as
well as religious and ethical questions were made even more
awkward by the lack of unity among the missionary groups.

And there was the practical problem of the relative weakness of the mission churches. Thus, the independent denominational missionary agencies were driven toward increased cooperation. Beginning in 1854, a series of seven interdenominational, international missionary conferences was held, including representatives from the major churches of the West. These were followed by the World Missionary Conference at Edinburgh in 1910, which was a primary turning point in the movement toward unity. At this conference, delegates attended for the first time from the "younger churches," i.e., from the churches established in non-Western nations as a result of the nineteenth-century missionary activity. An attempt was made at a comprehensive study of the problems of the missionary enterprise—the missionary message, the preparation of missionaries, Christian education, the condition of the church in the mission field, the home "bases" of missions, missions and government, and unity and cooperation.

The results of this conference and its over-all analysis extended in several directions. As concerns the missionary effort itself, it set into clear focus the problems of divided effort in the mission field—both the "scandal" of Christian bodies competing against each other and the sheer folly and waste of duplication of effort. This, and the growing sense of community among the missionary bodies, led, for example, to the rapid extension of "comity" arrangements, i.e., agreements whereby responsibility for missionary work in a specific area was assigned solely to one denomination, so as to avoid duplication and overlapping. Also, out of this conference came impetus for the formation of the International Missionary Council (1921) and the holding of world missionary conferences at Jerusalem (1928) and Madras, India (1938). The latter meeting was particularly significant for the large representation of the "younger churches," now accepted not as mere dependencies of the Western churches but as independent and fully participating bodies. These younger churches also made a vigorous appeal for unity among the "older churches"; as they put it, "for you unity may be a luxury. For us it is a life and death necessity."

Paralleling the move toward missionary cooperation, the Edinburgh Conference also led to recognition of the need for frank

discussion of the theological differences of the churches, with a
view to making explicit the areas of common belief and to
mutual understanding of divergent conceptions. Attempts were
made to meet this need in conferences held at Lausanne, Switzerland (1927), and Edinburgh (1937) on the theme "Faith and
Order" (i.e., belief and patterns of church organization). At
both of these meetings, representatives of Western non-Roman
churches and of Eastern Orthodoxy joined in statements of
common faith which revealed an essential unity in many aspects
of Christian belief, the chief exceptions having to do with the
nature of the sacraments and the authority of the ministry
(including church organization). This theme was developed further at the Third World Conference on Faith and Order at
Lund in 1952.

A fourth force which has accentuated the demand for Christian unity has been the church's attempt to witness to ethical and
social problems of the modern world. The acceptance of the
church's responsibility for the redemption of society as well as
the individual was the central feature of the social gospel (see
Ch. XI). But it was at once apparent that the church's function
in society could be effectively exercised only by close cooperation
of the denominations. The problems of war, of depression and
economic justice, of the rise of totalitarianism, required that the
church speak with a single voice if it was to have any influence
whatever on their resolution. As noted earlier (Ch. XI), the
Federal Council of the Churches of Christ in America was
formed partly to meet this need. The demand for unity of ethical
endeavor was also recognized at the Edinburgh Conference and,
in respect of the problem of world peace, in the formation in
1914 of the World Alliance for International Friendship through
the Churches. The joint efforts of the Federal Council and the
World Alliance were primarily responsible for the origin of what
has been called the "Life and Work Movement," an international
expression of Christian ethical concern which has developed in a
conference at Stockholm (1925), in the formation of the Universal Christian Council for Life and Work (1929), in the Conference on Church, Community and State held at Oxford (1937),
and in the first meeting of the World Council of Churches (Am-

sterdam, 1948). Each of these conferences has involved the detailed analysis of major problems of the contemporary world and has revealed a large degree of unanimity among the churches with respect to the Christian witness to these problems.

Another contributing factor from the very beginning of the ecumenical trend has been the influence of the various student movements, including especially the World's Student Christian Federation, the Student Volunteer Movement for Foreign Missions, the Christian Endeavor, the Young Men's Christian Association, and the Young Women's Christian Association. In these and similar organizations, students of differing denominations worshipped, thought and worked together as Christians, and often found there an intensity of Christian experience and a depth of community which made them impatient with denominational divisions. Moreover, in relation to the secularism of the modern universities, the divisions of the church seemed not only senseless but dangerous. It is significant that a large number of the leaders of the ecumenical movement have been participants in the Student Christian movements.

A final element in the dynamic of the present ecumenical trend has come from the experience of the churches in the Second World War. The sufferings of the Christians who resisted Nazism, particularly in occupied countries, the awakening of the churches to the necessity of opposing totalitarianism, the "orphaning" of mission churches which had been supported by European churches, the difficulty of communication between Christians across the lines of the conflict, the problems of war-prisoners, of refugees, of reconstruction—all of these served to elicit a deepened sense of world-wide community among Christians, as well as concrete joint action for the alleviation of suffering and world reconstruction. Indeed, it may fairly be said that the War revealed the Christian church to be the only actual world community.

3. PATTERNS FOR UNITY IN THE CHURCH

In the broadest meaning of the phrase, the ecumenical movement may be said to include a wide variety of institutional arrangements. It includes a large number of interdenominational and unofficial organizations having specific purposes, such as the Student Christian movements, the World Alliance for International Friendship through the Churches, etc. These groups have been examples of cooperative activity in Christian unity rather than of any formal church union. But, as we saw earlier, precisely such groups foreshadowed and demanded later concrete steps toward ecclesiastical unification.

Another sort of expression of the ecumenical movement has been the formal or "organic" consolidation of denominations. To some, this process has seemed agonizingly slow and fragmentary. At the same time, however, more than thirty formal unions have been completed in this generation, and negotiations are under way in numerous other instances. In America, actual mergers have combined twenty-eight denominations into twelve since 1900. Generally, these unions have been of churches of the same type or "family," most notably in the union of the three chief Methodist groups in 1939. The prime example in America of the consolidation of churches of significantly different denominational patterns has been the merging of Presbyterian, Congregational and Methodist Churches into the United Church of Canada (these churches, of course, all shared in the Puritan tradition). The merging of different denominations has gone on more rapidly in the "younger churches," where the need for a united front in presenting the Christian message and the relative smallness of the churches have combined to make unification a far more urgent matter than in the "older churches." The most striking union of this sort has been the United Church of South India, which has combined Anglican, English Methodist, Presbyterian and Congregational Churches, representing quite divergent forms of church government and conceptions of the ministry. (It should be noted, however, that this union was vigorously denounced by the High Church or Anglo-Catholic wing of the Church of England.)

Paralleling these various steps in organic church union has been the development of federations for joint or cooperative witness, teaching and action. This was the nature of the Federal Council of the Churches of Christ in America, now joined with parallel missionary and religious education organizations in the

National Council of the Churches of Christ in the U. S. A. This is also the nature of the World Council of Churches, formally constituted in a meeting at Amsterdam (1948), and probably the most significant of all the organizations which have come out of the ecumenical movement.

The World Council came into being as a direct result of several of the lines of development noted in the preceding section of this chapter, specifically the Faith and Order conferences, the Life and Work conferences, the international missionary conferences, and more recently the international Christian youth conferences. It is an attempt to synthesize these various aspects of inter-church cooperation and to provide at least a forum for the continued discussion of the problem of the unity of the church. The functions of the World Council are stated in its constitution as follows:

1) To carry on the work of the two world movements for "Faith and Order" and for "Life and Work."
2) To facilitate common action by the churches.
3) To promote cooperation in study.
4) To promote the growth of ecumenical consciousness in the members of all churches.
5) To establish relations with denominational federations of world-wide scope and with other ecumenical movements.
6) To call world conferences on specific subjects as occasion may require, such conferences being empowered to publish their own findings.
7) To support the churches in their task of evangelism.

The problem and the meaning of the ecumenical movement are clearly seen in the nature of the World Council. It is emphatically not a "church" and has no authority over its constituent members. It is rather a federation, including more than 160 member churches—Protestant, Eastern Orthodox and Old Catholic—joining in acknowledgment of the "basis" of the Council as "a fellowship of churches which accept our Lord Jesus Christ as God and Savior," and organizing for the discharge of stated functions. The statement of faith which is the "basis" of the Council is no more than a minimal statement, and the degree of unity indicated by this statement must not be exaggerated. Some

member churches do not recognize other member churches as
fully Christian bodies, because of creedal differences and questions of the validity of the various ministries. This mutual non-
recognition is most vividly seen in the inability of members of
some churches to participate in services of Holy Communion
with members of other groups. Thus, the Council might be
described as simply an institutional framework for discussion and
(where possible) joint action, an organization which recognizes
both the radical divisions of the churches and the "true" character of the Church as "one body," an organization, therefore,
of divided churches looking for unity.

It is particularly in the World Council that the question of
unity in the church has come most sharply into focus. On one
level, this has been a question of structural unity or uniformity.
The problem has not been simply that of differing views of the
proper ordering of the church (as to creed, sacraments, church
government, etc.), but also differing views as to whether there
is any single "correct" order of the church.[2] Some groups hold
that there are certain indispensable forms for the church, though
they disagree sharply as to what those forms are (e.g., the Baptist
insistence on believers' baptism and local church autonomy vs.
the Orthodox and Anglican insistence on episcopal succession).
Others hold that a pluralism in institutions and in forms of ritual,
ministry, and church government is quite compatible with the
underlying unity of the church—indeed, that the Reformation
principles require the allowance for such pluralism. They would
see the differences in conceptions of proper church order as
variations of emphasis capable of inclusion within a common
perspective. One element of that perspective is the recognition
that unity does not require uniformity and that there is room
(and need) in the Christian community both for the free church
emphasis on the freedom of the grace of God from all ecclesiastical bondage and for the emphasis of the Anglicans and the
Lutherans on the visible "right ordering" of the church. Ultimate
unity, which may or may not find expression in organizational
structure, is to be found in the mutual recognition of the churches

[2] These problems were most sharply posed at the Lund Conference
(1952). See esp. R. N. Flew, ed., *The Nature of the Church*.

as participants in the one body of Christ. This is not to overlook the great differences between (e.g.) the Baptist and the Quaker and the Episcopal views of the necessary constitution of the church. But this does mean that such differences exist within a genuine fellowship of Christians who recognize each other as such.

The prolonged discussion of such issues as these in the ecumenical movement has resulted in much clarification of views and mutual understanding. But it has also meant the sharpening of seemingly irreconcilable positions. Moreover, it has led to new interest in the distinctive witness of the particular denominations; thus each group becomes more conscious of its own heritage.

Yet this development has also led to a significant shift in the central focus of the ecumenical movement (beginning about the middle 1930's). In general, we may say that this has been a shift away from an "organizational" approach to the problem of unity. That approach, which characterized the movement especially in its earlier phases, assumed that unity in the church is primarily something to be achieved, by pulling together separate blocks or by bringing fragmented parts into a whole. The spirit was not unlike that of the social gospel's design of building the kingdom of God.

More recent ecumenical discussion does not begin with the idea of a fragmented organization, asking "how can we get this together?" It begins rather with the affirmation that the unity of the church is (and can only be) given by God.[3] The problem is not, therefore, the "achievement" of unity, but the manifestation of the unity of the church which by God's grace *does* exist. The question is "how can we express the unity which must be affirmed?" The World Council is certainly not itself that unity, just because it is a council of dissimilar churches which disagree in witness, faith and practice; but it is dedicated to working out the implications of an already given unity. The task of the ecumenical movement is the understanding of the unity of the church as given in Christ. Thus, one of the central decisions of

[3] The change here described is especially true of the level of discussion in the World Council of Churches and in Europe generally. It is less true of the United States.

the Conference on Faith and Order at Lund (1952) was to shift
the emphasis of subsequent discussion from the comparison of
various established doctrines of the church (there is, after all,
only so much of this that can be done) to other kinds of questions
about the church, e.g., the church in relation to the doctrine of
Christ and the Holy Spirit, the churches in relation to tradition,
and the social and cultural factors underlying disunity in the
church. So also, the Bible has increasingly been emphasized as a
source of the unity of the church, and greater stress has been
laid on biblical theology.

A further aspect of the new note in ecumenical discussion has
been the heightened concern with total renewal of the church
(or rather, repentance and renewal). The true unity of the
church can be manifested only as the life of the church is deepened in every way. Unity is not a problem which can be dealt
with alone. It is but one aspect of the larger problem of the
conversion or renewal of church life. In the light of this judgment, attention has been focused, e.g., on the problem of pro-
fessionalism in the church, i.e., the tendency so to separate clergy
and laity that the work of the church becomes identified with
the clergy, with the consequent loss of the sense of the lay
Christian life. Development here has been both toward increasing
participation of laity in ecumenical discussions and toward systematic study of the Christian doctrine of work or vocation.

The trend away from a simply organizational approach to the
unity of the church is thus also symptomatic of a much broader
and more fundamental renewal of the sense of the church as a
community which has its existence in the act of God. This sense
had been weakened in liberal Protestantism, which saw the
church as essentially a "religious institution" among other institutions, i.e., a social structure devised for the expression of certain
common religious interests and having its origin in the activities
of men. With the general rethinking of the nature of the church
in ecumenical discussions, reaction against such views has been
sharp. The church is instead to be conceived as a unique community, *given* in its existence by God, not constructed. Here the
trend of ecumenical thought has been powerfully reinforced by
the recent developments in Protestant theology (see Ch. XII),

particularly the new seriousness with respect to the Bible, revelation, the priority of God's act, and the tradition of the church. The new note in the understanding of the church has also come strongly from the Continental Protestant churches, growing out of their experiences during the Second World War.

In general, then, the ecumenical movement (as a movement concerned with the unity of the church) may be seen as one expression of a larger whole. It represents a "geographical" extension of the consciousness of the churches. But this is paralleled and deepened by an extension in time, with more profound concern for the continuity of the church with the tradition of the past. And these are both correlated with an extension in intensiveness, a cultivation of the inner life of the church.

It must be said, of course, that this whole movement is still largely a movement among the clergy, and that the new vision of the church has only begun to be meaningful to the average Protestant Christian. But in the sphere of church history, the developments toward church unity and mutual understanding may well be the most significant events of the twentieth century. So, too, in theology, the new consciousness of the church, the sense of the unity in the church which cuts across cultural, political and denominational lines, the recognition of the need for visible manifestations of that unity, and the growing interchange of thought—all these have become dominant forces in the contemporary scene and are indications of a sense of unity in faith and mission which has been characteristic of the most creative epochs in Christian history.

XIV

What Is Protestantism?

1. THE POINT OF VIEW

What is Protestantism? This is the question with which this book is centrally concerned. We have been looking at the development of Protestantism with a view to understanding both its outer history and its inner dynamics, its diversity and its unity, its success and its failure, its continuities and its varying responses to a changing world, its self-understanding in faith and its role as a social phenomenon open to analysis by the social sciences.

Our task now is to ask the question "what is Protestantism?" in a more systematic way, and to suggest a perspective from which all these elements of the Protestant development can be viewed as an intelligible whole.

Several commonly suggested answers to this question must be rejected at once as at best half-truths. These give partial expression to the essential character of Protestantism but taken alone are grossly inadequate and misleading. One such answer is the simple description of those groups willing to call themselves Protestant. Impressed by the variety and complexity of Protestant history, those who make this answer would only point to certain institutions and communities and doctrines and say "here it is." That is, Protestantism *is* simply the sum total of Lutherans, Calvinists, Methodists, Baptists, Quakers, perhaps Anglicans, etc. There is truth here, to be sure: the truth that Protestantism is a complex of histories and principles and structures. This serves to warn us against arbitrary selection and oversimplification. But this simple pointing to the variety and multiplicity of Protestantism is really a denial that there can be an answer to the question "what is Protestantism?" It is an implicit assertion that there are only Protestant*isms.*

Over against any such assertion must be placed the conviction of Protestants that they are bound together in a profound unity. Breaches within the community have been recognized as occurring *within* a real community, and sharp theological disagreement within a broad consensus. At times the bonds of community have been strained to the breaking point, but again and again appears a sense of a common loyalty and purpose. Institutional divisions have sprung largely from the motive of reform, not of separation. Individual denominational developments have been paralleled by movements cutting quite across institutional lines (e.g., pietism, the missionary movement, biblical criticism, the social gospel, and the ecumenical movement). The story of Protestantism, as we have seen it develop, can be understood only from a perspective which recognizes both diversity and unity in *this historical movement.

A second misleading way of answering the question of the nature of Protestantism interprets this movement as essentially opposition to Roman Catholicism.[1] This view is even held by many Protestants. At best, this is a partial truth. Protestantism and Roman Catholicism do exist in a continuing tension with each other. In the words of a recent interpreter, "whenever either Roman Catholicism or Protestantism interpret themselves as bearers of the Christian gospel, they must necessarily take account of each other and, by means of a mutual comparison, define their respective right to represent Christianity."[2] Thus it was the Reformation which compelled the Roman Church at the Council

[1] The common notion, found even in some dictionaries, of Protestantism as the religion of those Christians who are not Roman Catholics, is so patently erroneous as hardly to merit discussion. It overlooks not only the third major branch of Christianity—Eastern Orthodoxy—but also a variety of other "Catholic" groups which do not give allegiance to the pope, and such sects as Christian Science and Mormonism, which cannot meaningfully be called Protestant.

[2] Wilhelm Pauck, *The Heritage of the Reformation,* 157. Glencoe, Ill.: The Free Press, 1950. Chs. 11 and 12 are an excellent discussion of the relation of Roman Catholicism and Protestantism.

of Trent (1545–1563) to a further defintion of its faith, and in
particular of the basis of the church's authority and of the
sacraments. So in numerous papal encyclicals and at the Vatican
Council (1870–1871) the Roman Church has had to set its
teaching in contrast to Protestant views, and Roman Catholic
theologians have taken account of Protestant doctrines. Thus also
Protestantism has continually understood itself to be confronted
by Roman Catholicism, and has sought to define its understanding of the gospel in relation to that of the Roman Church.

But neither Protestantism nor Roman Catholicism can be understood primarily in terms of the tension which exists between
them. Attempts to do this overlook the common history and
loyalty which Protestants and Roman Catholics share. Their
loyalty is to the gospel of Jesus Christ, mediated through scripture and centuries of Christian witness. Their common history
includes not only the Bible and the ancient and medieval church,
but also the four centuries in which Roman and Protestant
groups have stood over against one another, since in the latter
period each has been continually influenced by the other. What
separates Protestantism and Catholicism is precisely the *positive*
character of the understanding of the faith which each represents.
Each claims to be a faithful interpreter of the common loyalty
and history. Just because of its understanding of the meaning
of the gospel, Protestantism has had to be critical of Roman
Catholicism. The Reformation break with Rome, the negation or
revolt, was the by-product and result of what the reformers
affirmed. There is truth in the understanding of Protestantism
as a protest against Roman Catholicism, for that protest springs
out of the heart of the Protestant witness to the nature of the
Christian faith. But it is this positive confession which must be
made central in any statement of the "nature" of Protestantism.

The duality of protest and affirmative witness can be seen in
the term *Protestant* itself. The word first had reference to the
"Protestation" of the German evangelical estates in the Diet of
Speyer (1529) (see Ch. IV). Here the meaning was partly that
of protest, but from the standpoint of affirmed faith. Few
churches ever adopted the name "Protestant." The most commonly adopted designations were rather "evangelical" and "re-

formed" (these terms continue to be used especially in the European churches and in Latin America). On the other hand, when the word *Protestant* came into currency in England (in Elizabethan times), its accepted signification was not "objection" but "avowal" or "witness" or "confession" (as the Latin *protestari* meant also "to profess"). And for a century the English "Protestant" church was the Church of England, making its profession of the faith in the Thirty-nine Articles and the Book of Common Prayer. Only later did the word "protest" come to have a primarily negative significance, and the term "Protestant" come to refer to non-Roman churches in general.

A third inadequate way of understanding the nature of Protestantism is by exclusive appeal to the Reformation. Here the norm for the interpretation of what Protestantism means and ought to mean is simply the great principles of the reformers— e.g., justification by faith, the right and duty of personal judgment in matters of faith, the sole authority of scripture, and so forth. In this view, Protestantism means "classical" Protestantism, an outlook which should determine the patterns for all subsequent Protestantism.

Certainly an indispensable truth is embodied in this appeal: Protestant Christianity cannot be understood apart from the Reformation. The heritage of the Reformation is counted as a precious thing, and the consciousness of standing in that heritage exercises a pervasive influence on all Protestant forms of worship, belief and action. Moreover, it may well be true that in the furnace of the Reformation the distinctive witness of Protestantism was so purified as to stand forth with singular clarity and concreteness. Thus, the Reformation is at least a necessary touchstone and guide for all interpretations of the nature of Protestantism.

Yet the whole course of our analysis of Protestant development shows clearly that the Reformation cannot be made the exclusive source of understanding. Protestantism has been more than the patterns of its historical origins (even these, of course, cannot all be identified with the Reformation). Nor would it be true to the intention of the reformers to fix upon their patterns as final and unchangeable norms. They rather sought forms of thought and institution which would give expression to a gospel which laid claim upon them. Their witness was not to themselves but to the God whose reality they had grasped afresh. And they were quite conscious that they stood in an historical situation which shaped the forms of their witness.

Protestantism cannot be identified with any of the particular forms which it developed, whether Calvinist or Lutheran or Anabaptist or Anglican. Nor can it be properly understood only by reference to a single historical period, not even the Reformation. There is no historical expression, no pattern or period of Protestantism which can be taken as the final norm for all its forms. Rather we must say that Protestantism, like every other historical movement, can be understood only through the whole of its development. Thus, a contemporary church historian writes:

> No historical movement can be so interpreted that the character which distinguished it as unique among other historical events is once for all fixed in the understanding. Just as the character of a person can be known only in connection with his acts in concrete situations, so the nature of a movement in human history can be comprehended only by a constantly fresh attention to the inner and outer circumstances in which it has unfolded itself. And just as the character of a person does not only impress itself upon concrete life situations but is also shaped by them, so the nature of a movement in history is conditioned by the living realities through which it proceeds. Thus Protestantism, which was born in the Reformation and then received the prophetic, dynamic character which set it in contrast to Roman Catholicism, can be fully understood only in terms of the transformations and adaptations of its nature which it effected and underwent in the course of its development.[3]

Against all interpretations of the meaning of Protestantism purely in terms of particular Protestant traditions, or of the Reformation, or of protest against Roman Catholicism, we must insist on a perspective which is more inclusive. In effect, we have to say that the answer to the question "what is Protestantism?" (or properly, "what is the essential character of Protestantism?") appears only in the entire history with which we have been con-

[3] W. Pauck, *The Heritage of the Reformation*, 131. Glencoe, Ill.: The Free Press, 1950.

cerned in the first thirteen chapters of this book. (Of course, we all come to the study of that history with a point of view which influences our interpretation, but our point of view can itself be tested and shaped by the historical materials which require to be interpreted.)

We can, however, draw together the various aspects of the understanding of Protestantism to which we have been led and set forth certain formal judgments regarding the essential nature, the dynamics or informing principles, of the Protestant movement. We cannot attribute finality to any such summary interpretation; but we can offer it as a perspective from which the Protestant development can be more adequately understood.

2. AN HISTORICAL COMMUNITY OF FAITH

Protestantism is a movement within history. Its existence is observable by all in certain events and institutions which can be located in time and space. As an historical phenomenon, Protestantism began in the early sixteenth century with certain events in the life of the Christian church in Western Europe. This was not an isolated event, but a very complex religious development which was interrelated with a variety of other movements—social, economic and political. So also the history of the Protestant movement has been intimately bound up with subsequent history in general, particularly in the West but also in the East. In this sense Protestantism means certain concrete institutions, patterns of thought and statements of faith, ways of worship, groups of persons bound together in a certain geographical contiguity and historical continuity. Such groups have shared to a greater or lesser extent not only in a common religious community but also in economic, social and political communities. This we may call the "outer history" of Protestantism. It is a history open to the inspection of everyone, subject to sociological and historical analysis as is any historical movement. It is that history which meets the eye of the non-participating observer.

But there is also what we may call the "inner history" of Protestantism. This is harder to grasp but it is more important for an understanding of the character of Protestantism. For a community is not created simply by people being "together" in time and space. Two persons living side by side may be members of radically opposed communities, e.g., political parties—though they may take part in most of the same events.

What, then, constitutes a "community"? It is sharing in a common loyalty, in common norms and goals and aspirations. It is the sharing of a perspective, a way of seeing things. Moreover, in every historical community there is the common memory of crucial events in the life of the community. If we enter into any community we identify ourselves with the history of that community, we say that this history is *our* history, that those events crucial for the life of this community are now crucial for our life. We remember and participate in those events in a way quite different from that of the external observer.

H. Richard Niebuhr has put this in a singularly vivid way, drawing a comparison between two accounts of the Declaration of Independence.[4] Lincoln's Gettysburg Address begins: "Fourscore and seven years ago our fathers brought forth upon this continent a new nation, conceived in liberty and dedicated to the proposition that all men are created equal." The *Cambridge Modern History* describes the same social event thus: "On July 4, 1776, Congress passed the resolution which made the colonies independent communities, issuing at the same time the well-known Declaration of Independence. If we regard the Declaration as the assertion of an abstract political theory, criticism and condemnation are easy. It sets out with a general proposition so vague as to be practically useless. The doctrine of the equality of men, unless it be qualified and conditioned by reference to special circumstance, is either a barren truism or a delusion."

The difference between these accounts is not a matter of true and false. It is the difference between history as lived and history as seen from the outside. One views the event as a central and determining part of a shared history which is precious and whose loyalties and aspirations are inseparable from the memory of that event. The other views the event in a neutral and detached way. In these two accounts the same event is "seen in different aspects and different contexts. . . . Lincoln spoke of what had happened in *our* history, of what had made and formed us and to

[4] H. Richard Niebuhr, *The Meaning of Revelation*, 6off.

which we remain committed so long as we continue to exist as Americans; he spoke of purposes which lie in our enduring past and are therefore the purposes of our present life."

This is what we mean by "inner history"—history in which we as persons are involved so that it has become a part of us; history in which we live, and which lives in us, in our memories, our loyalties, our hopes and our aspirations. Here the self-understanding of a community comes most clearly to light. Here, therefore, we have an indispensable clue to the nature of Protestantism. We must see this historical community not only in its external history as a social movement with certain institutional and theological configurations, but also by reference to that common memory and loyalty which makes it what it is.

1) Two aspects of this inner history of Protestantism must be recognized. First, this community sees itself as a part of that total community which is the Christian church. Its history is the history of the church. It holds in memory the story of Israel— the story of patriarchs, of bondage in Egypt and liberation, of Moses, of great prophets, of law given of God, and of the promise of a Messiah. It holds in memory the story of a "new covenant"— of Jesus of Nazareth, of preaching of the kingdom of God, of demand for repentance and faith, of teaching and healing and forgiving of sins, of crucifixion and resurrection, and of the living presence of the crucified and risen One with the community he founded. It holds in memory the story of apostles and martyrs, of the development of creeds and liturgies and church organization, of councils, of great leaders and missionaries and theologians, and of the whole company of Christians from New Testament times to the present, of the church in its glory and in its weakness.

In other words, this is a community in which it is affirmed: "All this is *our* history. The Bible is in our history. The history of the Hebrews is part of our story. Jesus Christ is an event in our past. The story of the church is our story."

At the center of this history is the gospel: the good news that in the life, death and resurrection of Jesus Christ, God was reconciling the world to himself. It is characteristic of Protestantism to hark back continually to this gospel, to recall always, as of first and decisive importance, the events of the New Testament witness and to warn against placing anything else at the center.

Thus Protestantism is marked by continual going back to the gospel, recalling the church to its central memory and loyalty. We have seen in the development of Protestantism how this concern has shown itself again and again. We found it in the Reformation. The reformers were quite clear in their intention to reaffirm the apostolic witness. Theirs was not a new gospel but the old gospel newly declared. This was why they placed the authority of the Bible above that of council or creed or pope, because in the New Testament they found the gospel of God in Christ freshly disclosed. So, too, Luther could assert that Christ was Lord even over the scriptures. And in some Reformation groups (e.g., the Anabaptists) the concern for going back to the gospel was expressed in the attempt to reinstate the earliest forms of worship and church organization.

We have seen also how this intention has shown itself in the subsequent history of Protestantism. Pietism sought to recover the warmth and fervor of the message of salvation, which had seemed to be obscured in the creedalism and theological controversy of Protestant orthodoxy. The missionary movement recalled the command of Christ to his followers to go into all the world. The theme of Ritschl was "back to the New Testament by way of the Reformation," and the goal of biblical criticism and of "liberalism" was a clearer view of him who was the gospel, Jesus of Nazareth. Thus, also, recent Protestant theology has been directed toward the recovery of the wholeness of the gospel from the partialities and distortions which had come with liberalism, and toward the restatement of that gospel to the man of the twentieth century.

If this be true, Protestantism cannot be understood as an isolated movement of reform, begun in the sixteenth century; it must be seen as continuous with reform movements of all the previous centuries. The reformers were quite conscious of their debt to those who had gone before, and we know that the way to the Reformation was prepared by numerous tendencies in the medieval church. The Reformation was not merely protest against the Roman Church; it was the ripe fruit of central tendencies within the church.

Thus the Protestant community understands its history as belonging within the history of the whole church. It remembers the story of that church as its own story. And it remembers especially the gospel of Jesus Christ, the foundation of the church, seeking always to make this gospel central in memory and to hold this One Lord at the heart of its loyalty and hope. This community thus stands in the "apostolic succession" of the gospel. Its claim to apostolicity is its maintenance of the apostolic witness. It lives in conscious continuity with all those who have sought to recall that gospel. The members of this community understand themselves as spokesmen for a succession of renewed comprehensions of the gospel.

2) In this context, we can understand a second aspect of the inner history of this community. This is the acceptance of the Reformation as an indispensable part of its history. Regardless of the differences among Protestants as to the authoritative character of various Reformation patterns and formulations, Protestants all affirm that this sixteenth-century movement bears valid and necessary witness to elements which are essential to the life of the church. Here Protestantism and Roman Catholicism diverge. The Roman Church refuses to allow the Reformation and its heritage a positive place in its inner history. It is the conviction of Protestants that thereby Roman Catholicism is weakened and perverted—because the Reformation was a genuinely creative and restorative movement, a renewed disclosure of the gospel of the living God, and therefore a movement which stood truly in the central stream of Christian faith. In the Reformation, continuity was preserved with the essential aspects of the Christian gospel, many of which were in grave danger of being lost in the medieval church.

The Reformation is remembered by Protestants, not as the beginning of a novel religious movement nor as the appearance of a new kind of Christianity, but as an expression of what from the outset has been most central to the life of the Christian community. It is remembered as an expression of a perspective, of certain themes, essential to Christian faith itself. Moreover, the

Reformation is seen as bringing this perspective and these themes into focus in a uniquely sharp and revealing way. This does not mean that the particular formulations of the reformers are irreformable, or that these are the necessary and exclusive vehicles for the communication of the gospel. It means rather that the work of the reformers must be accepted as part of the inner history of the church and that their perspective is integral to an adequate understanding of the gospel.

3. CENTRAL ELEMENTS OF THE PROTESTANT PERSPECTIVE

Can the perspective which characterizes the inner history of the Protestant community be stated in a more systematic and concrete way? What are the distinctive aspects of the way in which Protestants view the Christian movement? What are the themes or principles in the light of which Protestants seek to interpret the gospel and the history of the church?

In answering such questions, we do not try to state every item in the faith of Protestant Christians. Much of that faith is shared with Roman Catholic and Eastern Orthodox Christians, and in seeking to delineate the Protestant perspective we must always keep in mind that this is a point of view which appears *within* the common history and faith and worship of the church. Rather, we are interested only in laying bare the distinctive elements of the way in which Protestant Christians receive and understand the gospel. These are the qualifications in the light of which Protestants view the whole of the faith.

Protestants claim no historic monopoly on this view of Christian faith. On the contrary it is the Protestant conviction that this understanding has been characteristic of the church wherever it has been at its best. It is the concern of Protestants only that this understanding should be recognized by the whole church as integral to the true reception and proclamation of the gospel, and therefore should mold the common loyalty and worship and memory of Christians. This is not just a "Protestant" perspective, but more importantly a Christian perspective, which has repeatedly been lost and recovered in the church.

The elements of this understanding are not uniformly present

in all Protestant groups at all times. The process of loss and recovery, of continual renewal of memory and understanding, is
characteristic of Protestantism as it is of the whole of the Christian community. Indeed, it is of the essence of the Protestant
perspective that this should be so. The characteristic themes of
Protestantism are dynamic elements which appear in varying
forms and with varying emphasis, sometimes dropping out of
sight, but continually coming again to the fore in the Protestant
witness.

1) The first element of the Protestant understanding has
sometimes been called the "Protestant Principle." It is the spirit
of prophetic criticism, or creative protest, which springs from
the acknowledgment of the sovereignty of God and of the living
character of his revelation of himself in Jesus Christ. This is certainly not the sole Protestant principle, but it is truly a viewpoint
which influences the whole of this community's witness. However
often this spirit has been lost, it must be made central in any
interpretation of Protestantism. The understanding of the
dynamic character of revelation, the notion of the sole authority
of the Word of God, the understanding of sin and forgiveness,
the idea of the church, the principle of continuing reformation
and the actual pattern of recovery and reform which has characterized the development of Protestantism—all these are bound
up with this creative and critical principle.

This principle is a dual one. On the one side, it is a principle
of criticism and protest. In the name of the sovereign God who
transcends all the limitations and distortions of finite existence,
this principle requires the rejection of every human claim to
finality and absoluteness. This is the truth in the interpretation of
Protestantism as protest against Roman Catholicism. For the
Roman Church precisely claims that it is infallible and irreformable and has absolute authority in matters of faith and morals
(i.e., by virtue of the guidance and protection of the Holy Spirit).
Against every such claim to absoluteness (whether religious or
social and political) Protestantism must protest. Every religious
institution, every creed, every pattern of worship, shares in the
limitations and distortions (i.e., sin) of human existence. No religious pattern or form can be exempt from criticism in the light

of fresh apprehension of the truth. Though our apprehension of God in Jesus Christ may be an apprehension of ultimate truth, it is still *our* apprehension and subject to the limitations of our perspectives as historically conditioned and as sinful human beings.

The principle of criticism in Protestantism is not simply directed against Roman Catholicism. It must also be directed against Protestantism. Where Protestantism is true to the principle it is open to God's judgment and therefore *self-critical*. Protestantism protests against itself. Though the development of Protestantism shows repeated claims of finality, that development also shows the presence of continual protest against such claims and thus of continuing reformation and rebirth. Because Protestantism is ultimately committed to the principle of criticism in the light of the Word of God, there is always the possibility of inner renewal. Protestantism is able to see itself as standing under the judgment of God, and needing to be reformed. This is both the strength and the peril of Protestantism—strength because of the possibility of rebirth (the hope of resurrection), peril because of possible uncertainty and confusion.

But this principle is not primarily negative, or simple protest. The demand for criticism is prophetic and creative. The protest springs from the positive Protestant understanding of the gospel, of the sovereignty of the God who was in Christ and of the dynamic character of that revelation and gospel. It is the acknowledgment that God in Christ continually meets man in new historical situations. Therefore the knowledge of faith must ever be expressed in relation to new situations. The witness of the Christian community to the gospel springs from a *dialogue* between God and man who responds in faith out of his particular place in history. The gospel is directed to man where he is. The gospel itself judges and demands continual reinterpretation in terms of the world in which it is to be proclaimed. The gospel remains the same, but the forms in which it is expressed are diverse and continually changing.

This is the reason why no single form of Protestantism can be simply identified with the essential nature of the Protestant movement. Protestantism is a movement calling attention to a reality which transcends itself. The central elements in the Protestant witness do not appear in fixed forms which can be taken as normative and final. No system or ecclesiastical organization can rightly claim to embody the Protestant witness fully, though many Protestant groups have claimed to do so. Protestantism is a spiritual attitude which recognizes that faith in the living God expresses itself in new ways of life and thought in response to the new situations.

Thus the breaking down of old patterns and claims to finality which characterizes the development of Protestantism is not simply a protest against partialities and distortions. It is precisely the appearance of new and creative forms which demands the rejection of forms which have become irrelevant and therefore false and misleading. It is the renewed apprehension of the gospel which calls forth criticism and self-criticism. The gospel of God in Christ is a dynamic reality which makes impossible the enclosure of the Christian witness in any finally fixed and unchangeable form.

2) This first aspect of the Protestant perspective is intimately related to several others. Indeed, we can really see the meaning of the creative protest only as we see it in the context of the other Protestant motifs. The _sovereignty of God_ has already been mentioned. The protest against claims to infallibility and absoluteness in religious or cultural forms is launched in the name of the lordship of God. It is a protest against the deification of the finite and the historical. The recognition of new and creative forms stems from the acknowledgment of the freedom of God to work outside the established patterns and institutions; it is a confession that God can and does make his truth known in new ways.

The sovereignty of God is given most vivid expression in the writings of the reformers, especially in their theme of _sola gratia_. The doctrine of salvation by grace alone is in part a confession of the inadequacy and perverseness of all human claims to righteousness before God. But this doctrine is also and primarily a testimony to the utter priority of God's action. Wherever man turns in relation to God, he finds that God has preceded him. All human seeking after God, all faith, all obedience, is perceived to be a response to God's gracious dealing with man. Thus, the doctrine of predestination has occupied such a large place in Protestant theology. Thus, a recent interpreter of Luther could summarize the reformer's thought in the demand "Let God be God!" [5] Thus the liberalism of the nineteenth century was quick to understand evolution as the means by which God worked to achieve his sovereign purpose of bringing into existence responsible selves in community with each other and with him. Thus a social gospel could appear to apply the word of judgment and redemption to social processes and structures as well as to individuals.

The renewed acknowledgment of the sovereignty of God has been a source of the variety of Protestantism. To be sure, there have been many other causes of Protestant differences: social stratification, economic and political conflict and controversy, human perversity, arrogance and conceit, individualism, rigid insistence on uniformity of belief and practice within the religious community, etc. But these differences are also the result of the consciousness that God alone is wholly sovereign and free. This has brought into Protestantism a persistent note of dissent and non-conformity which can call into question every apprehension of God and every attempt to restrict his Spirit to unchangeable forms. The cry "no popery!" is but one instance of renewal in Protestantism of the spirit of the Old Testament prophets' perennial warning against idolatry. It is a spirit expressed not only in the Protestant critique of Roman Catholicism but also in the recurrent reformations within Protestantism. It is a spirit which acknowledges that God is Lord even over religion, over the church, over scripture, over creeds.

3) *The living Word, Jesus Christ.* Much that was said about the sovereignty of God could be said in another way in terms of Protestant insistence on the *living* Word of God, Jesus Christ. We have remarked on the persistent concern in Protestantism to return to the gospel, to make unmistakably central in the memory and loyalty of this community the act of God in Christ and to let this gospel speak freely and directly to men in their own concrete situations.

This was the motive of the reformers in appealing from church

[5] Philip Watson, *Let God be God.*

and council to the authority of the Bible. The forms in which the gospel had been cast by much of the development of the Middle Ages seemed to stand in the way of the living presence of Christ and the word of forgiveness. But in direct confrontation by the witness of the Bible, men could again come to know for themselves the full power of the gospel of God's act in Christ. Thus, the churches of the Reformation sought to make the Bible accessible to everyone and rejected the hierarchical and sacramental forms of the medieval church.

So also, the biblicism of Protestantism, as the symbol and means of the concern to recover and be faithful to the gospel, continued to nourish the understanding of the living lordship of Christ. In Protestant scholasticism, rigid doctrines of verbal inspiration tended to circumscribe the living Christ within the pages of the Book. But devotion to every word and line of the Bible could result not only in intellectualism and pride in "right belief," but also in the recovery of the sense of the immediate personal presence of Christ in pietism and the Wesleyan Movement and in the resurgent vitality of the awakenings and the missionary movement. In the liberalism of the nineteenth and twentieth centuries, criticism tended to reduce Christ to a figure of the historical past. But that very criticism was informed by the desire to recover again the Jesus of the gospels, whose real humanity had often seemed obscured in Christological doctrine. And that same concentrated and diligent historical interpretation of the Bible led in turn to the discovery that this "Jesus of history" could not be separated from the apostolic witness—and thus to a renewed awareness of the Christ who is not only a figure of the past but the living Lord who encounters man in every present.

Though in quite diverse ways, these movements within Protestantism revolve around the acknowledgment of the living presence and sufficiency of Christ, who as revealer, reconciler and judge is the expression of the sovereignty of God. He alone is Head of the church.

This understanding of Christ has implications also for the meaning of forgiveness. Christ is a Word of grace, of reconciliation, of forgiveness. For Protestantism, this means that forgiveness is a personal act of God in relation to man, and the restoration of personal relationship between man and God. It cannot mean the infusion of a character or virtue, of a substantive grace channeled to men by sacramental means. Grace and forgiveness are rather terms descriptive of the new situation in which a man stands and to which he responds in faith.

4) *The response in faith.* In discussing both the sovereignty of God and the living authority of Christ, we have seen how the Protestant understanding undercuts attempts to regularize religious experience or to limit the means of grace—whether in moralistic or institutional or sacramental or dogmatic or bibliolatrous ways. The development of Protestantism shows frequent lapses into all of these ways; but there has also been present the recognition of God's freedom to create or use any means whatsoever to bring men to the knowledge of his love in Christ.[6] God is not coerced or bound to doctrinal form or good deed or rite. "The Spirit bloweth where it listeth." In Christ, God's revelation and reconciliation comes to men through finite forms, but at the same time directly and freely.

The immediacy and freedom of this relationship is expressed from the human side in the response of faith. The classical Protestant insistence on "justification by faith" is not only a warning against the inadequacy and perversity of human attempts to win the favor of God. It is even more a recognition of the priority of God's gracious act of forgiveness and an indication that his reconciliation is actualized in human life by the intensely personal response of faith. Faith is the act in which the sovereignty of God and the living lordship of Christ are truly acknowledged. In faith God becomes God "for me." This is a response which can be made only by me. As Luther put it: "Every one must do his own believing as he will have to do his own dying."

This conception has been the subject of perennial misunderstanding, both outside and within Protestantism. Faith has sometimes been reduced to so-called "right belief" or "sound doc-

---

[6] The great temptation in Protestantism has not been the idolatry of particular forms, but the opposite, viz., the lack of concern for all religious forms and the consequent weakening of the sense of the sacred. A religious perspective which rejects all finite claims to ultimacy runs the risk of failing to see that the ultimate is known only through finite vehicles. This risk is taken, however, in order to maintain the freedom and spontaneity of the human encounter with God.

trine." Or, as in pietism and some forms of liberalism, the emphasis has been turned away from God who is the object of faith and toward the subjective attitudes and emotional state of the believer. Or, and this is an almost universal stereotype of the Protestant perspective, the demand for faith has been misinterpreted as individualistic and as meaning simply "the right of private judgment."

But the central theme of the Protestant view of faith is none of these. It is the confession of the intrinsic and immediate authority of the Word of God, which can come fully alive in the human spirit only as by the Holy Spirit this Word is received in the responsible decision of faith. This is not the suggestion that every man has a right to believe what he likes, for a man has the obligation to believe what is true. But Protestantism views this truth as given only in the believer's personal acknowledgment that this is what God leaves *him* no alternative but to affirm. Christian convictions can truly be held only by one who personally judges them to be true. There is here the peril of freedom and of difference in belief, which has been fully exhibited in the development of Protestantism. But this is a risk which Protestantism accepts, in the assurance that only so can the gospel truly be received. Each man, though he stand in the midst of the community of believers and bound to them by the demand of the gospel, must acknowledge for himself the truth of that gospel.

Here lies a deep root of religious freedom, an implication of the reformers' witness which they themselves were loathe to recognize. It appeared in some groups of the Reformation and later came to be almost universally affirmed by Protestants as an inevitable corollary of their understanding of the gospel. So, too, this view militates against every effort to reduce persons to mere items in the collective whole, against all tendencies to the "mass man," whether religious or economic or political.

The understanding of man's response in faith is expressed also in the classical Protestant doctrine of the "priesthood of all believers." As we saw in our study of the Reformation, this phrase did not mean that every man is his own priest, but was a recognition of the *community* of faith and of the opportunity and responsibility of the believer toward his neighbor. The command-

ment is not only to "love God" but to "love your neighbor as
yourself." The universal priesthood means that each man is a
priest to every other; he can, in Luther's words, be a Christ to
his neighbor. No believer can exist merely unto himself; he always stands in the church, which is a "mutual ministry of
believers."

Perhaps no principle of Protestantism is more thoroughly exhibited in its institutional development than this one. The Protestant "minister," "preacher," pastor," or "rector" is set apart for
the performance of certain functions in the church, but he is only
one among equals in the community of faith. For the sake of
discipline, and perhaps of tradition, there may be a hierarchy of
authority in the church, but the distinction is wholly functional.
"Clergy" and "laity" are on one level in their responsibility to the
gospel and to each other. Each is bound to wrestle with the gospel
for himself and to be servant of the other. Emphasis on the role
of the ministry can be made only with full consciousness of the
equal status of all Christians before God. (Even the Anglican
view of the "priesthood," except perhaps for some Anglo-
Catholics, differs radically from the Roman view of the distinction of clergy and laity and of the role of the hierarchy.)

The Protestant perspective as it comes to focus in the understanding of faith and the mutual responsibility of believers, has
led in several further directions. In services of worship, it has
meant the use of the language of the people, and the creation of
hymns and liturgies, so that all might share fully in the common
worship. It has meant the revival of preaching, the proclamation
of the Word assuming a central place in Protestant worship. It
has meant a continuous emphasis on the translation of the Bible,
that all might be confronted directly with the biblical witness,
and the production of a vast religious literature. It has led also
to a profound concern for public education, as the means of
creating a literate and informed constituency.

5) *The common life.* Equally important has been the Protestant revaluation of the common life and of Christian "vocation."
For Protestantism there can be no sharp separation of vocations
into "religious" and "secular," as if the former had a higher
"dignity" than the latter. God is the Lord of the whole of life

and he is to be served just as truly in the "earthly" calling as in the so-called "religious" life. The daily round of work can be fully a means of glorification of God and the expression of love for the neighbor. Any honest and useful work, acknowledged as the place in which one is called to responsibility to God and pursued with concern for the common good, has a religious meaning and significance quite on a par with the functions of the ministry or with formal acts of devotion. The service of God in the calling is no substitute for public and private worship, but the common life is given a new dignity and status.

The widening of the concept of vocation means responsibility as well as opportunity. The Christian is obliged so to perform his daily work as to make it an expression of his faith and love. We have seen how this awareness developed in the ideals of honest and faithful labor, of discipline and simplicity of life, of thrift and sobriety, and of earnest stewardship (especially in Calvinism). We saw how this moral and religious purpose served as a stimulus to a youthful capitalism, yet at the same time sought to apply checks to acquisitiveness and injustice—rejecting wealth as an end in itself and insisting that all must be used for the glory of God and with a view to the common good. And when the inadequacy of this method of Christianizing the economic order became obvious, the social gospel appeared as a new expression of the Christian claim upon the whole of life. It brought new understanding of the complexity of social responsibility and of the need for judgment and redemption of social structures as well as individual persons.

6) *The Church.* Many of the aspects of the Protestant perspective which we have delineated could be summed up as elements of the understanding of the church. The principle of creative protest in response to the reappropriation of the gospel, the sovereignty of God and the sole headship of Christ, the understanding of faith and of the mutual ministry of believers, the estimate of the common life—these inform the Protestant view of the Christian community. Indeed, it could be said that what is uniquely Protestant is its view of the church.

Protestants vary widely in the precise ways in which they define the church. But implicit throughout the Protestant development, and continually becoming explicit, is the dialectic between loyalty to the historic community with its traditions and persistent protest against absolutizing the forms and institutions of that tradition.

The tradition in which we stand cannot be abolished or rejected so long as we remain in the church. It is the history of which we are a part, which shapes us, and to which our witness and worship contribute. The Christian engages in continual conversation with the past as well as with other present members of the community, and he seeks to be loyal to the One who is Lord of the community. In general this has meant for Protestantism a continuation of the central patterns of the church's belief and ritual (though Quakers, for example, feel no need of external sacraments). But these are affirmed in the conviction that loyalty to the gospel not only permits but often requires reformation in the church. The tradition is shaped both by the living activity of God in Christ and by the response of men in particular historical situations; the tradition is not irreformable.

Thus, Protestant Christians understand the church broadly as an historical community of faith. It has its existence from God. It is a community which has its reason for being in the act of God in Jesus Christ. Christ is central in its memory, loyalty and hope, in its worship, belief and work. It seeks always to bear witness to the gospel. When it is affirmed that the church is the congregation of believers in which the Word is truly preached and the sacraments rightly administered, the reference is centrally to God's gracious act in Christ. The preached word and the sacraments set forth that act.

The church is not only a community of the proclamation of the Word; it is a community of grace. It is a community which is being redeemed and is at the same time a means of redemption. It is a fellowship of those who confess their faith, forgiven sinners who have been led to a new life of growth in grace. It is a mutual ministry of believers, who are means of grace to each other and to all men. Yet sin remains, and the church is forbidden to claim infallibility or absolute authority. It must always point away from itself to the One who is the source of its life. It finds its unity in common loyalty to him, a loyalty which may be expressed in a rich variety of ways. It finds its continuity in maintenance of witness to the gospel. Its life is in God, and its historical existence is preserved as it remains open to God's judgment and redemptive activity. It looks to a transcendent gospel which judges all human claims to finality and calls for reaffirmation and new response.

4. A GOSPEL FOR EVERY PRESENT

We have sought to indicate the nature of Protestantism as an historical community which stands in the history of the whole Christian community and seeks always the recovery of the gospel, a community which is also informed by certain themes for interpretation of that gospel. To these two aspects of Protestantism must now be added a third, which has its rationale in the Protestant perspective. This is the peculiar relation of Protestantism to culture.

Frequently in our study of the Protestant movement, we have seen how developments in Protestantism, particularly in Protestant thought, had to be interpreted in intimate relation to the changing social, intellectual and economic patterns of Western society. Protestantism cannot be understood simply as a self-contained unit, or by reference to a purely internal principle of authority, of theological tenet or spirit. To be sure, there is in Protestantism, as we suggested earlier in this chapter, an inner memory, loyalty and hope which binds these Christians together in genuine religious community. And every description of institutional and theological developments tends to exaggerate differences and discontinuities, and thus to obscure the basic unity and continuity of the faith and piety of the body of believers. But the varieties of the Protestant development are truly symbolic and expressive of something which is essential to the life of this community.

Protestantism by its nature exists in a give and take with the cultural whole. So long as Protestantism continues to exist, its history *must* be marked by constant re-relation and readjustment to varying human situations. This is required by the Protestant understanding of the historical limitation and distortion in every religious expression. Equally important—and this we saw to be but the other, positive side of the principle of protest—is the Protestant impulse to maintain the vitality of the connection between the witness of faith and a changing culture. This is an understanding of the ways of God with man, which sees a relevance of the gospel to every human situation. The response of Protestantism to cultural change can never be simply negative; it must always bear witness to the presence of God's redemptive activity as well as of his judgment.

Thus, in spite of obvious failures to maintain its own perspective, Protestantism has been able to be open to the flux of the world in which it exists. Though Melanchthon opposed Copernicus, it was only in the Lutheran schools that the new astronomy early found a welcome place. Though its proponents may seem now to have gravely weakened the substance of Christian faith, the natural religion of the nineteenth and eighteenth centuries was an attempt to communicate the gospel in the new philosophy and science of the Enlightenment. Thus, also, Schleiermacher saw in romanticism a means for the expression of depths of the religious life not realized by rationalism or orthodoxy. The same pattern appears in the nineteenth century acceptance of biblical criticism and of the findings of the sciences, especially of the theory of evolution. And contemporary Protestant thought is marked again both by the recovery of classical Christian perspectives and by concern with the analysis of modern culture. This may be seen particularly in the contemporary criticism of liberalism and of the social gospel, which involves a revival of traditional concepts of sin but with the new appreciation of its social dimension; in the almost universal concern with the new psychology; and in the various statements of the faith in terms of existentialism and process philosophy (see Ch. XII).[7] The whole of our survey of the Protestant development shows the presence of this pattern.

The same point can be expressed in another way in the assertion that Protestantism has no culture of its own. Though it is always expressed in cultural forms and influences culture, it can-

[7] Compare the attitude of the papal encyclical *Humani Generis* (August, 1950) which seeks to restrain Roman Catholic thinkers from substituting "novel" philosophies, especially existentialism, for the traditional "sound philosophy" of Thomism.

not be found bound to any one form—not even to Western civilization as a whole. Though the history of Protestantism has been intimately related to the Western world of the last four centuries, it is the essence of the Protestant movement to be finally free from this or any other cultural form. Protestantism cannot be content with the perpetuation of the cultural patterns of any given epoch, nor can it absolutely reject such patterns in the development of its own ritual, theological and institutional life. Rather, the inner dynamics of Protestantism are in constant interrelation with the dynamics of the social whole—and this is not accidental but a matter of principle, as Protestantism seeks to give expression to God's redemptive activity in every present world. The continual return to the past which characterizes the Protestant perspective is paralleled by a continual openness to the present.

Let no one suppose that this understanding has been uniformly expressed in Protestantism. We have seen departures from this perspective in two directions. The openness to a present world has again and again led to a dissolving of the substance of the faith into the thought forms of a contemporary culture, e.g., in the individualism and natural religion of the Enlightenment and in the scientism of some "liberalism." On the other side, the impulse to maintain the truth of the gospel has led recurrently to false absolutisms: thus Protestant orthodoxy in its creedalism and rigorous biblicism, and in our own time the extreme fundamentalist effort to perpetuate not only an outworn view of biblical inerrancy but the social and economic patterns of a past era.

But this very duality compels us to recognize the continuing operation of the dual motif of protest and creative renewal in the Protestant movement. The weaknesses of Protestantism are the weakness of its virtues. Protestantism recognizes within its own history the Christian theme of resurrection. That history is marked by recurrent dissatisfaction with dead ends, with "orthodoxies" and conventionalism—whether of medieval sacramentalism and moralism, of Protestant forms of scholasticism, of rationalism, or of reductionist liberalism. And protest against these is for the sake of renewal, as in the Reformation, in the evangelical revivals, in romanticism, in the missionary movement, in evangelical liberalism, in the social gospel, in recent Protestant thought, and in the ecumenical movement. Yet each movement of revival may in turn become a static form which must be broken down for the sake of renewed apprehension of the gospel. It is the Protestant conviction that this process can be given no simple historical or sociological explanation, however much such factors may be operative, but that ultimate explanation can be found only in the continuous and living activity of God in Christ, which works in the forms of life and thought of the church but always transcends them. In Protestantism, the church itself is seen as the object of Christ's injunction, "whoever would save his life will lose it, and whoever loses his life for my sake will find it."

At the end, then, we must return to the assertion made earlier in this chapter, that no form or epoch in the life of Protestantism can be taken as definitive for the nature of Protestantism. What Protestantism is can be seen only in the light of its development. The dynamics of Protestantism have been operative both in biblical literalism and in the criticism of that view in the name of historical analysis, both in the Calvinistic reinforcing of the spirit of capitalism and in the sharp critique by the social gospel. Protestantism is a life in community which expresses itself in a variety of forms and yet points to a gospel which both creates and transcends those forms. It is a continual reappropriation of Christian faith by a community which lives always in interaction with the whole human community. Thus, it is a community which can understand itself and its past, and the whole history of the church, only in a critically appreciative way. It has faith in the God and Father of Jesus Christ who is ever creating, judging and redeeming.

SUGGESTIONS FOR FURTHER READING

I. A NEW ERA BEGINS
II. A NEW THEOLOGY DEVELOPS

Bainton, Roland H., *Here I Stand,* Nashville: Abingdon-Cokesbury, 1950
  The Reformation of the Sixteenth Century, Boston: Beacon, 1952. Chs. I–IV
Calvin, John, *Institutes of the Christian Religion*
  Instruction in Faith, Philadelphia: Westminster, 1949
Dowey, Edward A., Jr., *The Knowledge of God in Calvin's Theology,* New York: Columbia Univ. Press, 1952
Farner, Oskar, *Zwingli the Reformer,* New York: Philosophical Library, 1952
Fosdick, Harry Emerson, *Great Voices of the Reformation, An Anthology,* New York: Random House, 1952. (See the selections from Wyclif, Huss, Luther, Melanchthon, Zwingli, Calvin.)
Kerr, H. T., Jr., (ed.), *A Compend of Luther's Theology,* Philadelphia: Westminster, 1943
The Loci Communes of Philip Melanchthon, tr. by C. L. Hill, Boston: Meador, 1944
Luther, Martin, *The Babylonian Captivity of the Church; An Open Letter to the Christian Nobility; A Treatise on Christian Liberty.* (These can be found in numerous editions.)
  The Bondage of the Will, Grand Rapids: Eerdmans, 1931. (Tr. 1823)
  Commentary on St. Paul's Epistle to the Galatians
Pauck, Wilhelm, *The Heritage of the Reformation,* Glencoe, Ill.: Free Press, 1950, Chs. I–VI
Sykes, Norman, *The Crisis of the Reformation,* London: Centenary Press, 1946, Ch. I

III. OTHER REFORMATION PATTERNS

Bainton, Roland H., *The Reformation of the Sixteenth Century,* Boston: Beacon, 1952, Chs. V and X
Bosher, Robert S., *The Making of the Restoration Settlement,* New York: Oxford Univ. Press, 1951
Fosdick, Harry Emerson, *Great Voices of the Reformation,* New York: Random House, 1952. (See the selections from writings of the Anabaptists and Richard Hooker.)

327

Littell, Franklin H., *The Anabaptist View of the Church,* Hartford: American Society of Church History, 1952

McNeill, John T., *The History and Character of Calvinism,* New York: Oxford Univ. Press, 1954, Chs. VI–VIII

Mennonite Quarterly Review (especially valuable for articles on the Anabaptist tradition)

More, P. E. and Cross, F. L., *Anglicanism,* New York: Morehouse, 1935

Rupp, E. G., *The English Protestant Tradition,* New York: Cambridge Univ. Press, 1949

Sykes, Norman, *The Crisis of the Reformation,* London: Centenary Press, 1946, Ch. IV

Watson, Edward W., *The Church of England,* New York: Oxford Univ. Press, 1950

IV. THE REFORMATION CHURCHES

Bainton, Roland H., *The Reformation of the Sixteenth Century,* Boston: Beacon, 1952, Chs. VI, VIII–IX

Heppe, Heinrich, *Reformed Dogmatics,* London: George Allen, 1950

McNeill, John T., *The History and Character of Calvinism,* New York: Oxford Univ. Press, 1954, Chs. I–V, IX–XVIII

Schaff, Philip, *The Creeds of Christendom,* New York: Harper, 1877, Vol. I, Chs. V–VII; Vol. III, Parts First and Second

Schmid, Heinrich, *The Doctrinal Theology of the Evangelical Lutheran Church,* Philadelphia: Lutheran Publication Society, 1876

Sykes, Norman, *The Crisis of the Reformation,* London: Centenary Press, 1946, Chs. II–III

V. PURITANISM AND RELATED MOVEMENTS

Brauer, Jerold C., *Protestantism in America,* Philadelphia: Westminster, 1953, Chs. I–II

Brinton, Howard H., *Friends for 300 Years,* New York: Harper, 1952

Davies, Horton, *The English Free Churches,* New York: Oxford Univ. Press, 1952, Chs. I–V

Fox, George, *Journal,* New York: Dutton, Everyman Edition of 1948

Haller, William, *The Rise of Puritanism,* New York: Columbia Univ. Press, 1938

McNeill, John T., *The History and Character of Calvinism,* New York: Oxford Univ. Press, 1954, Chs. XIX–XX

Nichols, James Hastings, *Democracy and the Churches,* Philadelphia: Westminster, 1951, Ch. I.

Sweet, William W., *Religion in Colonial America,* New York: Scribner, 1951, Ch. I

Miller, Perry, *The New England Mind: The Seventeenth Century,* New
    York: Macmillan, 1939
    The New England Mind: From Colony to Province, Cambridge:
    Harvard Univ. Press, 1951
    Roger Williams, Indianapolis: Bobbs-Merrill, 1953
    Orthodoxy in Massachusetts, Cambridge Univ. Press, 1933
Sykes, Norman, *The English Religious Tradition,* London: SCM Press,
    1953, Chs. VI–VII, X–XI
Trinterud, Leonard J., *The Forming of an American Tradition,* Phila-
    delphia: Westminster 1949, Ch. I

VI. REVIVAL OF THE EVANGELICAL SPIRIT

Brauer, Jerold C., *Protestantism in America,* Philadelphia: Westminster,
    1953, Ch. III
Burtner, Robert W. and Chiles, Robert E., *A Compend of Wesley's
    Theology,* Nashville: Abingdon Press, 1954
Cameron, Robert M., *The Rise of Methodism,* New York: Philosophi-
    cal Library, 1954
Faust, C. H. and Johnson, T. H., (ed.), *Jonathan Edwards,* New York:
    American Book Company, 1935
Fosdick, Harry Emerson, *Great Voices of the Reformation,* New York:
    Random House, 1952. (See selections from Jorn Wesley.)
Lindström, Harald, *Wesley and Sanctification,* Stockholm: Nya Bok-
    förlags Aktiebolaget, 1946
McGiffert, A. C., *Protestant Thought Before Kant,* New York: Scrib-
    ner, 1936, Ch. IX
Sykes, Norman, *The English Religious Tradition,* London: SCM Press,
    1953, Chs. XV–XVII
Trinterud, Leonard J., *The Forming of an American Tradition,* Phila-
    delphia: Westminster, 1949, Chs. III–VII

VII. TRENDS IN AMERICA AND ON THE
    CONTINENT

Brauer, Jerold C., *Protestantism in America,* Philadelphia: Westminster,
    1949, Chs. IV–VII
Cassirer, Ernst, *The Philosophy of the Enlightenment,* Princeton:
    Princeton Univ. Press, 1951, Ch. IV
Hudson, Winthrop S., *The Great Tradition of the American Churches,*
    New York: Harper, 1953, Chs. I–IV
McGiffert, A. C., *Protestant Thought Before Kant,* New York: Scribner,
    1936, Ch. X
Nichols, James Hastings, *Democracy and the Churches,* Philadelphia:
    Westminster, 1951, Ch. III

Trinterud, Leonard J., *The Forming of an American Tradition*, Philadelphia: Westminster, 1949, Chs. X–XVI

VIII.   A CENTURY OF PROTESTANT EXPANSION

Brauer, Jerold C., *Protestantism in America*, Philadelphia: Westminster,
1953, Chs. VIII–XV
Hudson, Winthrop S., *The Great Tradition of the American Churches*,
New York: Harper, 1953, Chs. V–VI
Latourette, Kenneth S., *A History of the Expansion of Christianity:
The Great Century* (Vols. IV–VII), New York: Harper, 1941,
1943, 1944, 1945
Sweet, William W., *The Story of Religion in America*, New York:
Harper, 1939, Chs. XVI–XX

IX.   THE FORMATION OF LIBERAL THEOLOGY
X.   PATTERNS OF LIBERAL THEOLOGY

Channing, W. E., *The Works of William E. Channing*, Boston: Amer-
ican Unitarian Association, 1895
Grant, Robert M., *The Bible in the Church*, New York: Macmillan,
1948, Chs. XI–XII, XIV
Harnack, Adolf, *What is Christianity?*, New York: Putnam, 1901
Machen, J. G., *Christianity and Liberalism*, New York: Macmillan,
1923
McGiffert, A. C., *The Rise of Modern Religious Ideas*, New York:
Macmillan, 1915, Chs. V–XIV
Ritschl, Albrecht, *The Christian Doctrine of Justification and Recon-
ciliation*, Edinburgh: T. & T., Clark, 1902
Schleiermacher, Friedrich, *Speeches on Religion*, London: K. Paul,
Trench, Trübner & Co., Ltd., 1893
The Christian Faith, New York: Scribner, 1948
Van Dusen, H. P. and Roberts, D. E., (ed.), *Liberal Theology*, New
York: Scribner, 1942

XI.   THE CHRISTIAN CRITICISM OF SOCIETY

Bennett, John C., *Christian Ethics and Social Policy*, New York:
Scribner, 1946
Hopkins, C. H., *The Rise of the Social Gospel in American Protes-
tantism*, New Haven: Yale Univ. Press, 1940

SUGGESTIONS FOR FURTHER READING

Hudson, Winthrop S., *The Great Tradition of the American Churches*, New York: Harper, 1953, Ch. X

Niebuhr, H. Richard, *The Kingdom of God in America*, Chicago: Willett, Clark, 1937

Rauschenbusch, W., *A Theology for the Social Gospel*, New York: Macmillan, 1919

Tawney, R. H., *Religion and the Rise of Capitalism*, Baltimore: Penguin Books, Inc., Edition of 1947

XII. DIRECTIONS IN RECENT PROTESTANT THOUGHT

Anderson, B., *Rediscovering the Bible*, New York: Association Press, 1951

Barth, Karl, *The Knowledge of God and the Service of God*, New York: Scribner, 1939

Brunner, Emil, *The Divine-Human Encounter*, Philadelphia: Westminster, 1943

Niebuhr, Reinhold, *The Nature and Destiny of Man*, New York: Scribner, one vol. edition of 1949

Tillich, Paul, *Systematic Theology*, Vol. I, Chicago: University of Chicago Press, 1951

Weber, Otto, *Karl Barth's Church Dogmatics*, Philadelphia: Westminster, 1953

XIII. THE ECUMENICAL MOVEMENT

Flew, R. N. (ed.), *The Nature of the Church*, London: SCM Press, 1952

Hodgson, Leonard, *The Ecumenical Movement*, Sewanee, Tenn.: University Press, 1951

Horton, Walter Marshall, *Toward a Reborn Church*, New York: Harper, 1953

Jenkins, Daniel, *Europe and America, Their Contributions to the World Church*, Philadelphia: Westminster, 1951

Man's Disorder and God's Design (Amsterdam Assembly Series), New York: Harper, 1949

Morrison, Charles Clayton, *The Unfinished Reformation*, New York: Harper, 1953

Pauck, Wilhelm, *The Heritage of the Reformation*, Glencoe, Ill.: Free Press, 1950, Ch. XIX

Van Dusen, Henry P., *World Christianity*, Nashville: Abingdon-Cokesbury, 1947

XIV. WHAT IS PROTESTANTISM?

Ferm, Vergilius (ed.), *The American Church of the Protestant Heritage,* New York: Philosophical Library, 1953

Jenkins, Daniel, *Tradition, Freedom and the Spirit,* Philadelphia: Westminster, 1951

Kerr, Hugh Thomson, Jr., *Positive Protestantism,* Philadelphia: Westminster, 1950

Nichols, J. H., *Primer for Protestants,* New York: Association Press, 1947

Niebuhr, H. Richard, *The Meaning of Revelation,* New York: Macmillan, 1941

"Protestantism" in *Encyclopedia of Social Sciences*

Pauck, Wilhelm, *The Heritage of the Reformation,* Glencoe, Ill.: Free Press, 1950, Chs. VIII–XVI

Tillich, Paul, *The Protestant Era,* Chicago: University of Chicago Press, 1948

INDEX

Act of Supremacy, 72
Act of Toleration (1689), 115
Act of Uniformity, 72, 115
Adam, Karl, 291n.
Agricola, Johann, 83
Albert of Brandenburg, 15
Amsterdam Conference, 253, 295
Anabaptists, 27, 50f., 58–67, 88, 95, 110, 111, 285, 286, 306, 310
Andrewes, Lancelot, 74
Anglicans and Anglicanism, 24, 58, 67–77, 100, 106f., 111ff., 127f., 129f., 135, 143f., 165, 242, 285, 286, 288, 289, 296, 298, 299, 305, 306, 320
Anti-clericalism, 161, 177
Antinomianism, 83
Apostles' Creed, 8, 71
Aquinas. See Thomas Aquinas.
Aristotle, 4
Arminianism, 90ff., 123, 137
Arminius, 90
Asbury, Francis, 135f.
Augsburg Confession, 79, 81, 84
Augustine, St., 29, 31, 52, 101, 257, 269
Avignon, 12
Awakenings, Great, 123, 135, 136–140, 142, 145, 146, 148, 150, 171, 180, 289, 317

Bainton, Roland H., 15n., 20n.
Baptism, 23, 50f., 61, 64, 66, 110f., 175, 298
Baptists, 62, 99, 109ff., 114, 139f., 141f., 145, 147, 148, 163, 165, 172, 173, 252, 285, 286, 298, 299
Barclay, G., 119
Barlow, William, 74
Barth, Karl, 255ff., 273
Baumgarten, 153
Beecher, Edward, 243
Beecher, Lyman, 148
Belgic Confession, 89
Bender, Harold S., 66n.
Bergson, Henri, 267
Bernard of Clairvaux, 5
Beveridge, William, 74
Bible, authority of, 22, 24f., 28, 45ff., 60, 62f., 67, 73, 75, 85,
95f., 99f., 106f., 116, 120, 129, 147, 152, 155, 167, 171, 188, 195ff., 204, 215, 223, 227f., 275f., 301, 317, 320; historical criticism of, 129, 155, 160, 182n., 189–198, 203, 212, 213, 220, 227f., 259ff., 274f., 303, 310, 317, 324, 326; translation of, 8f., 174, 190
Bible Presbyterians, 151
Bible societies, 151, 164, 174
Bisschop, 90
Boethius, 32
Boleyn, Anne, 70
Book of Common Prayer, 69, 71f., 76, 107, 113, 115, 128f., 133, 143, 305
Book of Concord, 84, 85
Box, Clifford, 246
Bramhall, John, 71, 74
Brethren of the Common Life, 6
Brotherhood of the Kingdom, 248
Brown, W. A., 215, 216
Browne, Robert, 108
Browning, E. B., 219
Bucanus, 94
Bucer, Martin, 69, 79
Buddeus, 153
Bullinger, 89
Bultmann, Rudolf, 266n.
Bunyan, John, 233
Burnet, Gilbert, 74
Bushnell, Horace, 244, 248
Butler, Bishop, 128

Cajetan, Cardinal, 21
Calhoun, R. L., 254
Calling, Doctrine of. See Vocation.
Calvin, John, Ch. II *passim*, 58, 63, 64, 74, 78, 81, 85–98, 132, 146, 187, 234f., 269, 273
Calvinism, 26n., 27, 43, 58, 61, 63, 67, 74, 76, 78, 85–98, 99ff., 110f., 114, 116, 136, 137, 143, 148, 188, 233ff., 285, 306, 321, 326. See also Puritanism.
Cambridge Platform, 117
Capitalism, 87, 105f., 234ff., 239, 245, 285
Carey, W., 166, 170, 172, 174
Carlstadt, Andreas, 59

333

338

Williams, D. D., 267n.
Williams, Roger, 111f., 117, 119
Winstanley, G., 241n.
Witherspoon, John, 143, 146
Wittenberg prophets, 59
Wolff, Christian, 152f., 155
Wolleb, 95
Wolsey, Cardinal, 12, 68
Woolman, John, 237, 238n.
Woolton, John, 74
Word of God. See Bible; Revelation
Works, 34, 35, 38–41, 64, 70, 83, 134, 154. See also Christian Life.

World Alliance for International Friendship through the Churches, 294, 296
World Council of Churches, 253, 282n., 297ff.
World War I, 165, 254, 259
World War II, 259, 295
Wyclife, 12, 16, 22, 25, 67

Xavier, F., 168

Zinzendorf, Count, 126
Zwingli, Ulrich, 51f., 57, 61, 62, 63, 72, 78, 81, 85